INTERNATIONAL INTERVENTION AND THE PROBLEM OF LEGITIMACY

INTERNATIONAL INTERVENTION AND THE PROBLEM OF LEGITIMACY

Encounters in Postwar Bosnia-Herzegovina

Andrew C. Gilbert

CORNELL UNIVERSITY PRESS ITHACA AND LONDON

First published 2020 by Cornell University Press

Library of Congress Cataloging-in-Publication Data

Names: Gilbert, Andrew, author.
Title: International intervention and the problem of legitimacy : encounters in postwar Bosnia-Herzegovina / Andrew C. Gilbert.
Description: Ithaca [New York] : Cornell University Press, 2020. | Includes bibliographical references and index.
Identifiers: LCCN 2019046922 (print) | LCCN 2019046923 (ebook) | ISBN 9781501750267 (hardcover) | ISBN 9781501750274 (epub) | ISBN 9781501750281 (pdf)
Subjects: LCSH: Intervention (International law)—Political aspects. | Legitimacy of governments—Bosnia and Herzegovina. | Postwar reconstruction—Bosnia and Herzegovina. | Ethnicity—Political aspects—Bosnia and Herzegovina. | Bosnia and Herzegovina—Politics and government—1992–
Classification: LCC DR1752 .G55 2020 (print) | LCC DR1752 (ebook) | DDC 949.74203—dc23
LC record available at https://lccn.loc.gov/2019046922
LC ebook record available at https://lccn.loc.gov/2019046923

Contents

Illustrations

Acknowledgments

This book has been a long time in the making, and my list of debts both scholarly and personal is long and stretches back well over a decade. It must begin in Bosnia and Herzegovina, which is rightly famous for the generosity and warmth of its people, and this must be infectious, because I experienced it equally among Bosnians and foreigners alike. In Sarajevo, for their generous hospitality and willingness to share their time and particularly their space with me, I thank Tobi and Milena, Massimo, Peter, Bodo and Azra, Rhodri, and Erika.

Intellectual solidarity is not always easy to come by in Bosnia, making the friendship and collegiality of Nerzuk, Dino, and Asim all the more important. Miodrag Živanović deserves special recognition for the oasis of sanity and good humor he provided for me in his office at the Filozofski fakultet at the University of Banja Luka.

My research would not have even gotten off the ground if the staff of a wide variety of international organizations had not taken time out of their days to answer my questions. The staff of the Reconstruction and Return Task Force at various offices of the Office of the High Representative (OHR) in northwestern Bosnia were quite helpful, in particular Lawrence, Michelle, and John. The same goes for the staff at the UNHCR field office in Prijedor. Conversations and field trips with the staff of the numerous nongovernmental organizations active in northwestern Bosnia were invaluable in revealing the scale and depth of the refugee return process, and their good will and openness to my constant queries were much appreciated. These include those working for World Vision, Catholic Relief Services, United Methodist Committee on Relief, Technisches Hilfswerk, Dorcas Aid, International Orthodox Christian Charities, Swiss Caritas, and Lutheran World Federation. The staff at the Prijedor and Sanski Most field offices of the Organization for Security and Co-operation in Europe (OSCE) deserve special recognition for allowing me to be present at numerous meetings, for their openness and their friendship. The many insights gained in this book would have been impossible without them.

For my understanding of the basic dilemmas and politics of refugee return in Prijedor, I must thank the patient staff of the *Fondacija za obnovu i povratak "Prijedor 98"*: Gorana, Sead, Anel, Emira, Mirjana, Čela, Sanela, and Mirsad. Among other returnees to Prijedor, my conversations with Muharem, Nusreta, and

Nijaz were particularly useful. In Sanki Most, Vukica, Đuro, Slobodan, and Gojko stood out as valuable interlocutors, and helped facilitate my understanding of returnee issues there.

In Prijedor, it would be almost impossible to overestimate my personal debt to the Grahovac family: Mladen, Amira, Vedran, Dijana (and Sandi!). They provided a home away from home for me in Bosnia, and I cannot put into words what their friendship, warmth, and humanity meant to me.

The nature of fieldwork means that most anthropologists in one fashion or another come to rely heavily on others, as participants, cultural brokers, gateways to important social networks, and as guides in navigating the wilds of foreign bureaucracies. Often one or two people emerge as vital in this regard, and for me this was person was Zoran Ergarac. His friendship, his intelligence, his openness, and his willingness to help me with almost everything were indispensable during my field research.

I owe much to Susan Gal, as well as to John Comaroff, John Kelly, and Victor Friedman for their mentorship while I was at the University of Chicago. In important ways my first real engagement with Bosnia and Yugoslavia began with Nada Petković, language instructor and friend, and I thank her for the lengths she went to make my research possible, from classroom time to facilitating some of my first contacts in Sarajevo and Banja Luka. Other valuable interlocutors in Chicago include Anya Bernstein, Larisa Jašarević, Andy Graan, Mike Cepek, and the many members of the Anthropology of Europe Workshop. Jessica Greenberg has been a treasured friend, colleague, and intellectual companion for the better part of the last two decades.

Early in my experience at the University of Toronto I was introduced to Edith Klein at the Centre for European, Russian and Eurasian Studies, and I thank her for the support and opportunities she opened up for me as a newcomer to Canadian academia. I am also grateful for the writing time and support afforded me by my colleagues in the Department of Anthropology at McMaster University.

Various ideas in this book were first tried out at conferences and in conversations too numerous to list here, but at one time or another the comments and engagement of Katherine Verdery, Elizabeth Dunn, Susan Woodward, Keith Brown, Chip Gagnon, Kim Coles, Bob Hayden, Elissa Helms, Stef Jansen, Bodo Weber, and Tobi Vogel stand out as particularly valuable. I treasure the conversations with participants in the 2013 workshop "Towards an Anthropology of International Intervention": Greg Beckett, Bianca Dahl, Anila Daulatzai, Antonio de Lauri, Andrew Graan, Jesse Grayman, Pierre Minn, and Vivian Solana.

Principal funding for my research on international intervention in Bosnia came in the form of fellowships and scholarships from the International Research &

Exchanges Board (IREX) and American Councils ACTR/ACCELS. Fellowships from the American Council of Learned Societies and Harry Frank Guggenheim Foundation provided valuable time to write up that research, and small grants from the Woodrow Wilson International Center for Scholars and the Russian, East European, and Eurasian Center at the University of Illinois, Urbana-Champaign provided important opportunities to share my research findings. Most of this list of diverse funding sources—including a scholarship that supported an intensive summer introduction to the Serbo-Croatian language (as it was still called then)—was supported by US state resources aimed at developing and enhancing area studies knowledge and expertise, much of it focusing on Eastern Europe and the Balkans. Despite its complicated origin in the Cold War, area studies funding has been indispensable in producing a large repository of valuable knowledge and critical scholarship, and in supporting the careers of generations of scholars. For well over a decade now, such funding has been repeatedly slashed in a succession of federal government budgets. Witnessing this has made me even more grateful for the support I received, even as I lament the short-sighted, even dangerous, lack of investment in future generations.

For their role in bringing this book into its final form, I am grateful for the unflagging support of Jim Lance and careful stewardship of Ellen Murphy at Cornell University Press. The generous feedback of anonymous reviewers also helped improve the manuscript, at times significantly.

Judy and Rob Gilbert have supported my choice to follow an academic path for a long time now, and I am so very thankful for their curiosity, their patience, and their loving encouragement. I am also grateful to Olive and Liliana, who always recharge and reinvigorate no matter how exhausted and depleted I might feel. Finally, Andrea Muehlebach has been with me on this journey from the very beginning, as friend, wife, colleague, and counselor. Our countless conversations about this book in its many iterations always helped make the most inchoate and opaque matters clearer, and sharing with her the process and passion of writing, thinking, and teaching continues to make the practice of anthropology a meaningful part of my life. It seems woefully inadequate to the role she has played in my life to say simply that without her support, commitment, understanding, and love, this book would never have been written. But that does not make it any less true.

Some of the analysis in the Introduction and in chapter 1 first appeared in an article entitled "Legitimacy Matters: Managing the Democratization Paradox of Foreign State-Building in Bosnia-Herzegovina," in *Südosteuropa* 60, no. 4 (2012):

483–496. Most of chapter 1 first appeared as "The Limits of Foreign Authority: Publicity and the Political Logic of Ambivalence in Postwar Bosnia and Herzegovina," in *Comparative Studies in Society and History* 59, no. 2 (2017): 415–445. Most of chapter 4 first appeared as "From Humanitarianism to Humanitarianization: Intimacy, Estrangement and International Aid in Postwar Bosnia and Herzegovina," in *American Ethnologist* 43, no. 4 (2016): 717–729.

INTERNATIONAL INTERVENTION AND THE PROBLEM OF LEGITIMACY

Introduction

INTERVENTION ENCOUNTERS IN A NEW WORLD ORDER

Encounters

On November 2, 2000, just over a week before countrywide elections were to be held in Bosnia and Herzegovina (BiH),[1] the Circle 99 Association of Intellectuals in Sarajevo hosted a speech by Austrian diplomat Wolfgang Petritsch. Petritsch was the international community's High Representative in Bosnia and Herzegovina, and his speech seemed animated by two sets of concerns. The first was to inspire citizen participation in the upcoming election, part of the international community's goal of promoting democracy and securing legitimacy for the Bosnian government; the second was to justify the continued presence of foreigners in Bosnia, as well as to defend how they exercised the extensive powers at their disposal.

Years of international intervention had already significantly shaped postwar politics in Bosnia and Herzegovina. Comprising an uneasy encounter between and among the political classes claiming to represent one of Bosnia's three main ethnic groups (Croats, Serbs, and Bosniaks)[2] and a wide array of foreign agencies like the one headed by Petritsch, these interventions ranged from indirect relations of supervision to the direct participation of foreign agents in Bosnian government. Indeed, Petritsch and his predecessors in the Office of the High Representative (OHR) had often exercised the powers at their disposal in ways usually associated with state government, such as creating a common currency and promulgating property legislation. They had also exercised it in extraordinary ways, such as removing the duly elected president of Bosnia's Republika Srpska from office.

Moreover, political dysfunction in postwar Bosnia and Herzegovina was widely recognized as rooted in its multiple, contradictory, and incomplete state-building projects, which were based on differing definitions of the self-determining polity—monoethnic, multiethnic, or nonethnic. These projects were all products of the 1990s war which the internationally brokered Dayton Agreement had partially legitimized and institutionalized, and all Bosnian politicians staked their legitimacy on being proponents of one or another state project. This situation subordinated all domestic political and legislative questions to a calculus of which vision of the state they would support or undermine, creating one parliamentary impasse after another. For this reason, Petritsch was regularly called upon by Bosnian and international voices alike to exercise his powers more extensively and break through such paralysis. Some Bosnian intellectuals even argued, somewhat paradoxically, that the best solution to the country's stalled democratization would be to suspend Bosnia's representative government and make Bosnia and Herzegovina a full protectorate of the international community—something which Petritsch had publicly rejected on more than one occasion.

In his speech, made available by the OHR's industrious press office in English and Bosnian/Croatian/Serbian[3] (OHR 2000g), Petritsch was clearly concerned with justifying his continuing refusal to make Bosnia and Herzegovina a full protectorate and thus supersede its current condition as a country under international supervision. At the same time, he put forth an argument that justified those occasions when he *did* assert his powers, as he had recently done by imposing the Law on Travel Documents that governed the issuance of passports. His speech thus amounted to a delicate balancing act: he sought to justify the presence of the international community in Bosnia and Herzegovina, while arguing that such a presence was temporary and was in fact promoting "local ownership" over Bosnian government. And with upcoming elections, which like all elections after the war were being organized and run by the international staff of the Organization for Security and Co-operation in Europe (OSCE), he needed to make a case for why the people of Bosnia and Herzegovina should bother voting at all when so much decision making was being carried out by unelected foreigners.

He did this by pointing to the obstruction and fearmongering of the country's Serb, Croat, and Bosniak politicians as the reason why continued international presence was necessary. At the same time, he argued that postwar fears were waning. As evidence, he pointing to the successful return of refugees to areas of the country from which they had been "ethnically cleansed," an accomplishment he credited to the efforts of the international community. Petritsch then constructed two visions of the future. One was of continued ethnic divisions, stagnation, and frustrated desires. The other was one without hate or fear, in which the people of Bosnia and Herzegovina, united in their desire for a "normal life," would choose to proceed down the path toward their European future in the European Union (EU). Likening the current moment in Bosnia and Herzegovina to the post–Second World War period when former enemies in western Europe seized the benefits of functionally integrating into an economic community (that eventually became the EU), he argued that similar economic benefits awaited the citizens of Bosnia and Herzegovina if they would elect politicians which would put aside the wartime past and cooperate more closely.

Throughout the speech he returned to the issue of the legitimacy of the international community, asking at one point "Do the powers of the High Representative make a mockery of the whole elections process in the first place? When laws such as the one of travel documents can be imposed whenever he or she wishes it?" (OHR 2000g). In this regard, he noted that a recent article in a Sarajevo-based magazine had criticized how he exercised his powers by claiming they unfairly targeted Bosniaks. While Petritsch disagreed with this criticism, he did note that the perception that the OHR had "Olympian powers" and was "unaccountable to Bosnian citizens" was a serious concern. Here he clearly stated that he was first and foremost "answerable to the 55 countries and international organisations that make up the Peace Implementation Council and ultimately their taxpayers,"[4] but noted that this was "cold comfort for a Bosnian citizen." He repeated that the situation was a transitory moment particular to Bosnia's postwar circumstances—"extraordinary powers for an extraordinary time"—which would come to an end as soon as the country had responsible politicians who would govern in a way such that Bosnia no longer needed foreign supervision. Thus for him, a protectorate was not the right answer. Rather, what Bosnia and Herzegovina required was "energetic leaders with vision to take this country back to Europe." The international community's role was to help Bosnia's citizens and its leadership to get there, not to do it for them. Still, he said, "The OHR, I myself, the International Community will continue to do all it can to help bring light to this beautiful and potentially prosperous country."

If the return of refugees to their prewar homes was to create the foundation for the High Representative's vision of a peaceful, postwar multiethnic Bosnia, those tasked with overseeing refugee return on the ground often found themselves overwhelmed. For example, a little over two years after Petritsch's speech, on a February evening in 2003, I met Markus,[5] a human rights officer with the Organization for Security and Co-operation in Europe (OSCE), for drinks. He worked in a local office in Sanski Most, a small town in northwestern Bosnia. His office existed to support the refugee return process by serving the large numbers of Serb returnees in Sanski Most and other neighboring Muslim-majority municipalities. Markus confessed to being worried. He had been trying for months to structure a good working relationship with the Serb returnee community, but things had recently taken a turn for the worse. One self-styled returnee representative, Miroslav Pantić, had just threatened to organize a blockade of the main transit road if conditions for Serbs in Sanski Most did not improve. Things had been particularly tense, Markus said, ever since it had been decided that courts in Bosnia, and not just the international court in The Hague, could try cases for war crimes. He had heard there were twenty-nine ongoing investigations of crimes committed in Sanski Most between 1992 and 1995, and it was likely that they would all be crimes committed by Bosnian Serbs against Bosnian Muslims. Although he had nothing to do with the decision on court jurisdiction, he had to deal with the local political consequences of that decision.

As a member of the international community in Bosnia and Herzegovina, Markus was regularly approached by Serb returnees as an authority responsible for realizing the vision of a multiethnic Bosnian state, primarily by securing refugee return. In a political and discursive environment in which the assertion of international impartiality and neutrality was constantly challenged—with claims made about a lopsided prosecution of Serbs in The Hague, about the disproportionate number of Bosnian Serb politicians removed from their positions by the High Representative, about a purported imbalance of international resources dedicated to Muslim refugee return over Serb refugee return—foreigners like Markus were vulnerable to accusations of being "anti-Serb." In this case, Markus worried that the Bosnian news media would not cover war crimes trials fairly and that the process would thus not be seen as just. He also worried that this would negatively influence his relationship with the Serb returnees by being taken as evidence of the international community's bias against Serbs. It added urgency to the already strong demand upon him to show he was not biased by responding to the nearly constant complaints of Serb returnees about the discrimination they faced in the Sanski Most municipality.

Markus told me about an incident that day that had touched off Pantić's threat and that confirmed his fears about the local repercussions of the decision to try war crimes in Bosnia and Herzegovina. Pantić had complained that Muslim authorities in the municipality had brought up war crimes investigations in a threatening manner in interactions with Serb returnees, and connected this with a book that was circulating in the area entitled *Zločin je zaboraviti zločin!* (It Is Criminal to Forget Evil!) (Figure 0.1), in which Pantić had been labeled a war criminal. Markus said he first heard about the book at a recent public meeting of Serbs in Sanski Most, where they demanded that it be denounced by the local Bosnian authorities and international community because it named 293 "intellectuals" as criminals without a trial.

Markus confessed that he had not seen the book and did not know how serious it was. But his impression was that the returnees he spoke with—through his

FIGURE 0.1. Cover of Zihad Ključanin and Hazim Akmadžić, *Zločin je zaboraviti zločin! Sanski Most u ratu, 1992–1995. Svjedočenja/Documenti*. (It Is Criminal to Forget Evil! Sanski Most in the war, 1992–1995. Witness statements/documents) (Sanski Most: Sanki Most Municipality).

Bosnian assistant, who acted as interpreter—saw this book as part of a general campaign to hold all Serbs, and only Serbs, guilty of war crimes, and to use a thesis of collective guilt as a moral pretext to deny Serbs their rights in Sanski Most. As the sole identifiable representative of the "international community" in Sanski Most, and as the officer charged with monitoring the state of human rights in the area, he felt that he should do *something* about the situation, to perhaps denounce the book and underscore that everyone is innocent until proven guilty, to try to maintain at least an *appearance* of fairness. And yet he felt constrained by the fact that it would take a lot of energy to confirm what had thus far appeared as accusation, rumor, or hearsay. Besides, getting involved in these kinds of disputes was not really in his job description or part of his mandate. Moreover, the fact that Pantić's name had appeared in a book of this nature raised the possibility for Markus that any action he took would be—or could be construed as—aiding a war criminal. Without seeing the book and having it translated, without more reliable information about who was threatening whom with war crimes investigation, and without satisfying himself of Pantić's relative guilt or innocence, he did not feel confident to act. And yet he felt the burden of inaction just as heavily.

It might at first appear puzzling to put these two vignettes side by side. What unites them is the presence of foreign officials clearly concerned over their legitimacy in interactions with Bosnians. But that does not resolve still other questions: Given the extraordinary powers and purview of the High Representative, why engage in an act of accounting for his power and presence before such a small audience? And given that both issues fell outside of his mandate or power to resolve, why should Markus be bothered by the fight over a self-published book or court processes taking place far from his area of operation?

Such scenes—a minor speech to a relatively inconsequential group of intellectuals and expressions of doubt and anxiety by a foreign official far from any center of political power—are absent from standard studies or critiques of international intervention in Bosnia or elsewhere. Standard studies usually concern themselves with questions of success and failure, and how to improve current and future interventions. Speeches and expressions of uncertainty are thus not part of such evaluations. Critiques of intervention are often aimed at demonstrating how foreign officials are not improving conditions in target societies, or they go further to argue that intervention is a form of neo-imperial domination. Against that backdrop, the anxieties expressed by Markus or the careful balancing act in Petritsch's speech—claiming a desire not to exercise his powers while offering a rationale for when he regularly did—would seem disingenuous, maybe worth a footnote at best. This book takes the opposite view. I argue that students and scholars of international intervention should center their analysis on such engagements between and among foreign officials and members of target populations, for they point to powerful dynamics and instabilities that decisively shape the politics of such interventions as they unfold, one interaction at a time.

This book is a study of international intervention and the problems of legitimacy that emerge in and through what I call "intervention encounters."[6] I analyze international intervention as a series of encounters to reveal the creative processes of cultural production and social transformation that happen in everyday interactions by members of unequally positioned groups (Faier and Rofel 2014). What makes an interaction part of an "intervention" encounter as opposed to some other kind of encounter? For the purposes of this book, I define "intervention encounters" as those engagements across difference and inequality that are

FIGURE 0.2. Some intervention encounters are one on one, while others are collective, such as this interaction between returning refugees and the US ambassador to Bosnia and Herzegovina Clifford Bond in the Stari Grad neighborhood in the town of Prijedor, a site of significant refugee return.

Photo by author.

set in motion by policies, projects, and programs that aim to accomplish some goal of postwar transformation. As the opening vignettes indicate, these goals might be democratization, state-building, conflict resolution, or "remixing" the population through the return of refugees to their prewar homes. Intervention encounters need not solely be between or among those usually categorized as "foreign" and those categorized as "domestic," although this is often the case, both in this book and more generally. For example, an intervention encounter could feature a Bosniak working for a foreign aid organization interacting with Bosniak refugees around the terms of housing reconstruction (as in chapter 4), but the forms and relations of difference and inequality would certainly be distinct from those at play in interactions between a foreign human rights officer working for the OSCE and a Bosnian Serb returnee. Intervention encounters also need not be face-to-face: they may take place in the public sphere through mass news media (as in chapters 1 and 2) or between people in less mediated, more direct interactions (chapters 3, 4, and 5) (Figure 0.2).

One of the tasks of analyzing intervention encounters is to sort out and account for those forms and relations of difference and inequality as they are produced in relation to intervention objectives. As I will discuss below and demonstrate throughout this book, considerable effort is spent by Bosnians and non-Bosnians alike in (1) trying to structure relationships by defining the categories of difference among various actors involved in intervention projects, and then (2) using those categorical distinctions and relationships to justify particular actions and compel others to act towards particular goals. This book argues that these efforts and their often unanticipated effects only become visible if we focus on the encounters in which they occur.

In developing this approach to international intervention, I draw inspiration from historical studies of colonialism or what many have called the "colonial encounter" (Cohn 1996; Comaroff and Comaroff 1991; Dirks 2001; Stoler 2002). As Faier and Rofel note, these studies were among the first to take seriously questions of encounter across social and cultural difference, and they offer a complex vision of how power works, showing it not as top-down or as unidirectional, but rather as unpredictable, "involving processes of negotiation, resistance, awkward resonance, misunderstanding, and unexpected convergence" (2014, 365). More importantly, these studies demonstrate that the meanings, practices, identities and inequalities that came to constitute colonialism were "produced *through* these processes rather than as uniform impositions" (365–366, emphasis added).

Two key points follow from this. The first is that an encounters approach to understanding the politics of international intervention involves some basic semiotic, ontological, and epistemological claims: that the *meaning*, if not the very *existence*, of something like "humanitarian aid" or "democracy" in any site of international intervention is produced, charged, and animated in and through practical encounters across difference and inequality, and that we come to *know* that meaning best by documenting and analyzing those encounters. The second point is that although the relations of power in intervention encounters may be unequal—think here of Petritsch speaking before the Bosnian intellectuals in Sarajevo, or Markus grappling with how or whether to respond to the complaints and demands of fractious returnees—they are also unstable. Indeed, one of the hallmarks of my encounters approach is that I pay central attention to the volatile and ad hoc ways in which such engagements unfold, how they prompt "creative friction" (Tsing 2005, 1) or "unexpected responses and improvised actions, as well as long-term negotiations with unforeseen outcomes" (Faier and Rofel 2014, 364). By focusing upon a diverse set of encounters in postwar Bosnia and Herzegovina, this book foregrounds and analyzes the open-ended, innovative, and unpredictable nature of international intervention that is usually omitted from the ordered representations of the technocratic vision and the confident assertions of many critiques.

But the focus on intervention encounters promises to do more than just demonstrate unpredictability and contingency in engagements between and among foreign officials and the targets of their intervention. It also identifies key instabilities that emerge out of such engagements, and demonstrates how the politics and effects of international intervention are produced at the very moment that different actors seek to manage those instabilities in their favor. Such processes are often animated by questions of legitimacy, a key source of social power.

Legitimacy and Its Instabilities

For many years the designers and practitioners of international intervention did not concern themselves with the issue of legitimacy, and neither did most of those studying those interventions. There were many reasons for this, from the technocratic way in which interventions were imagined and the belief that success and failure depended upon the resolve and resources of foreign actors, to the sense that broaching the question of legitimacy might create an obstacle to the successful implementation of intervention goals. Moreover, most intervention agents (and those studying them) were not equipped with the cultural, linguistic, or historical knowledge necessary to assess the issue of legitimacy even if they were interested. This usually meant that if the issue was raised at all, it was not by scholars trying to understand how intervention projects worked in practice, but by critics trying to discredit those projects.

This began to change as both intervention practitioners and scholars realized that the issue of legitimacy was indeed an obstacle to the success of intervention projects and goals. Moreover, ignoring this issue threatened to be an expensive mistake because without legitimacy a large international presence might be required indefinitely for state-building, peacebuilding, or democratization efforts to work. This led to a new interest by practitioners in generating "local participation" in and "local ownership" over intervention initiatives for the legitimacy—and shorter time horizon—this could bestow.

At the same time, some scholars began to focus on the issue of legitimacy in international state-building and global governance (Charlesworth and Coicaud 2010; Clark 2005; Lake 2016; Sending 2015; Zaum 2013). These analyses have produced important insights, but are often limited to thinking about the legitimacy of and within institutions—either those coordinating or doing the intervening (such as the UN or international nongovernmental organizations, or NGOs) or of the institutions of government that are being "built" by intervention agents. Such a focus also keeps analytic attention on members of the international community. Other scholars, particularly those focused on international peacebuilding, have used the issue of legitimacy to recenter the emphasis of intervention scholarship away from the actions and perspectives of its practitioners and onto those of its targets. This is often portrayed as a shift from the "international" or "global" to the "local" and "everyday," where "authentic legitimacy" or "contextual legitimacy" is located. This shift is championed as a way to render visible and consequential the ideas and agency of the supposed beneficiaries of international intervention which earlier models had ignored. These scholars carry out this work by pointing to the gap between "international" frameworks and "local" perspectives and experiences, or by exploring the "local" social and political life of intervention projects and discourses, and then showing the disinterest in and resistance to intervention goals in addition to other unintended consequences (Björkdahl et al. 2016; Heathershaw 2009; Kappler 2014; Mac Ginty and Richmond 2013; O'Reilly 2018; Sabaratnam 2017).

This book shifts the lens from institutional legitimacy and "local" agency to focus on the instabilities that the question of legitimacy introduces into intervention encounters between and among foreign officials and their Bosnian interlocutors. I argue that it is in this crucible of confronting and managing instabilities that important effects and outcomes of international intervention are forged. I view the issue of legitimacy ethnographically—that is, in a fine-grained empirical way—seeing it as a part of the everyday life of international intervention. Such an approach to legitimacy, as always produced by and emergent from within everyday practice, makes sense if we just look at common definitions of legitimacy as that which is considered to be right, justified, or valid—the state or quality of being in accord with established rules, principles, or standards. These are general concerns in a wide variety of social interactions, regardless of the broader context. Thus we should not be surprised to find that the legitimacy or validity of any claim in intervention encounters could be (and probably was) contested, and that this constituted a concern that foreign officials had to regularly grapple with, as my opening vignettes showed.

For example, how could the High Representative legitimately claim to be building an independent, democratic state when the very means at his disposal violated principles of democracy and state sovereignty? How could foreigners largely ignorant of Bosnian language, history, and culture come to feel that their actions to secure and transform Bosnian politics and society were legitimate and valid when their Bosnian interlocutors repeatedly criticized those actions? How could an aid worker claim to be apolitical and thus legitimately humanitarian under highly politicized circumstances? And on what grounds and through what practices were these claims to legitimacy contested or accepted by a range of Bosnians, from returnees to party politicians? The instabilities introduced by such questions of legitimacy result from their everyday nature as well as out of the contradictions of intervention. But they also emerge out of the fact that responding to and managing them are almost always performative acts.

In the past decade or so, scholars have begun to explore the performative character of international politics.[7] Some draw upon speech act theory to point to the ways in which repetitive, iterative, and citational discursive practices have a performative capacity to constitute the objects of which they speak, whether those objects are global actors like "America," targets of intervention like "Afghanistan" (Gregory 2004, 17–19), or sources of authority like "the international community." Others have written about how, in contexts of international intervention, abstractions like "development" (Mosse and Lewis 2006) or "security" (Bialasiewicz et al. 2007; Higate and Henry 2009; McLeod 2016) are best understood through the embodied performances and enactments that constitute them. Jeffrey (2013) has further shown that internationally instigated performances can stabilize particular state ideas in the contentious environment of postwar Bosnia and Herzegovina.

Yet there is one problem that most of the performative approaches to international politics leave unexplored: the question of recognition. That is, they tend not to ask or analyze whether, how, and why such enactments of identities or performances of politics succeed or fail, or whether they are seen as legitimate or not. In this book, I demonstrate that the mere claim to be "building democracy," or "representing the popular will," or "acting as a humanitarian," or "occupying a neutral position," is not enough to be recognized as such. Instead, such claims require evidence which must be submitted to a range of others for evaluation and scrutiny. I thus show how making such basic claims as "occupying a neutral position" can bestow ongoing performative requirements for foreign officials like Markus to constantly demonstrate this neutrality to fellow officials and returnees, and how his ability to do so was a condition of possibility for fulfilling his role as a human rights officer and realizing a range of intervention goals. This was a source of instability in intervention encounters because his ability to convincingly and thus legitimately enact "neutrality" depended upon things he could not always anticipate, such as the cultural norms which Bosnians used to evaluate his enactments or actions taken elsewhere and beyond his control—the decision to try war crimes in courts based in Bosnia and Herzegovina, the local publication of a book he could not read, or how local news media covered these events.

This need for recognition is related to the broader fact that intervention projects require participants and thus must recruit them, as well as construct and negotiate the parameters for and meaning of participation. For example, the overall goal of democratizing Bosnia and Herzegovina required that citizens participate in (foreign-run) elections; the project of building up a common independent state that needed no foreign supervision required local politicians to extend "ownership" over and govern through that state; attempts to remix the population required refugees to return to their prewar homes; efforts to reform municipal administration and make it more efficient and transparent needed the participation of diverse "stakeholders," ranging from elected politicians to returning refugees. Yet the possibility remained that citizens would not vote in numbers large enough to bestow legitimacy on future governments, or that they would elect politicians who had no intention of taking ownership over an internationally brokered common state, or that refugees would not return, or that "local stakeholders" would be uninterested in foreign-instigated municipal reform. If unable to secure and maintain such participation on favorable terms, democratization and state-building efforts could founder.

Thus what we find through a focus on intervention encounters is that a significant part of international intervention is made up of highly performative practices of persuasion, often in response to concerns about the legitimacy of international actions, roles, and claims. Markus needed to persuade returnees in Sanski Most of the legitimacy of his claim that he was not an anti-Serb foreigner. Petritsch needed to persuade a broad audience that participation in elections was important, despite disappointment with Bosnian political elites and the fact that foreigners made so many decisions. He was also compelled to legitimize his actions and dispute his critics—both those who complained about how he exercised his state-like powers, as well as those who complained that he did not exercise them more fully.

My focus on intervention encounters thus opens up whole arenas of practice otherwise overlooked. For example, in Bosnia the mass-media practices of the OHR are barely discussed or analyzed, despite the fact that we can see a massive increase in the productivity of the OHR press office alongside an increase in the exercise of the High Representative's powers. Indeed, the two are clearly linked: Petritsch handed down 250 decisions in his two and a half years as High Representative, and during that same period the OHR press office was annually issuing, publishing, or documenting around 275 press releases, sixty press conferences, upward of seventy-five interviews or articles, and fifty speeches—always simultaneously addressing a Bosnian and an international audience. As I show in depth in chapter 1, the mass media was a significant site of intervention encounters, and it was through OHR media practices that Petritsch developed strategies to legitimize his perspectives and actions in the face of a range of critics, both Bosnian and international. He also used mass media to recruit or compel Bosnian politicians to act in ways supportive of his priorities and projects, even as they were doing the same with him and other foreign officials. And this is just one of many examples of how the emergence and management of instabilities related to the question of legitimacy acted as an engine of intervention politics, propelling, shaping, and limiting what was possible in engagements between and among foreign officials, aid workers, and Bosnians.

Studying Intervention Encounters

Intervention encounters are sites of social and cultural production where social roles and relations are defined and demarcated, where obligations are cultivated and responsibilities are distributed, where political logics are innovated and the nature of authority is contested. Most scholarship misses this because it overlooks the encounters in which they happen, and thus does not anticipate their complexity and cannot imagine their creativity—or the ways these dynamics bind, limit, enable, or otherwise shape intervention. There are many reasons for this oversight. Most of them stem from the fact that scholars of intervention share the conceptual and temporal coordinates of intervention practitioners, as well as their categories of practice, objects of analysis, and concern with success and failure. This is the case for both those that follow a more positivist, problem-solving paradigm and those that take a more critical stance.[8]

For example, many scholars focus almost exclusively on foreign actors and ideas and thus give the impression that power and change are unidirectional, that is, that any transformation—positive or negative—is solely the result of foreign action or inaction. These studies and critiques also tend to share the limited temporal focus of intervention practitioners and their projects, attending more to the short-term timetables of occupation, supervision, or aid projects than to the *longue durée* in which these projects unfold.[9] This orientation both discounts the influence of history and thus the need to know it,[10] and also constructs the sites of intervention as a kind of tabula rasa upon which intervention agents can construct their social and political visions.

Another dominant feature of intervention and its scholarship is the reliance upon an epistemology of intervention underwritten by norms of nation-state-based sovereignty, which frame intervention in binaries of "inside/outside" (foreign/domestic, external/internal, international/local, universal/particular) built up around the common sense of the national order of things (Malkki 1995). These norms divide the practice of politics into two realms, the international (that which happens between states) and the domestic (that which happens within states), and they act as a warrant to focus on people, ideas, and processes classified as "international" and to ignore those classified as "local." This is the same for many critics of intervention, who rely upon the same norms of nation-state sovereignty in their critiques of "foreign" domination over "domestic" populations.

This normative division of the world means that there is no need for practitioners of intervention to develop the kinds of knowledge of language, history, or culture necessary to understand the perspective or actions of the targets of intervention. Indeed, the cadres that "intervened" in Bosnia (and elsewhere) were not chosen for their area knowledge but for their expertise in those things Bosnia was presumed to lack (democracy, rule of law, gender equality, etc.), which are presented as having transcultural, transhistorical, and thus universal validity. Reinforcing this tendency is the fact that the problem-solving paradigm often imagines intervention as a technical issue, "doable if we get the formula right and it is properly resourced," as British general David Richards put it in Afghanistan (quoted in Stewart 2011, 33). Perception or persuasion—the very currency of legitimacy—should not matter for the successful implementation of a technical formula. This creates a propensity to locate project failures in the "local," which makes a virtue out of practitioners' ignorance of "local" knowledge. And finally, ignorance of "local" knowledge, combined with the requirement that intervention agents stand as neutral in postconflict zones, can lead to an avoidance of social relations with Bosnian or other target populations because such relations could create the appearance of bias and thus compromise the position of international neutrality (see Coles 2007, 61–67). The result is that if the practitioners feel that they can ignore the complexities of history, culture, language, or historically embedded social relations, then those who study them can as well.

I have already indicated some of why this is a flawed assumption, noting how the participation of intervention's target population can certainly have a significant effect on the outcomes of any intervention project, so to ignore their actions and perspectives would produce an incomplete, distorted, or simply wrong account of how and why intervention projects unfold as they do. And as I will show later in this book, one of the major contradictions of international intervention is that while foreign officials are encouraged to believe that they don't need culturally specific knowledge to fulfill their mandates, they regularly face situations in which they do. As a result, my focus on encounters combines a knowledge of Bosnian history, culture, and language with a set of ethnographic research methods that allow me to capture and make sense of the complex engagements across difference and inequality that make up intervention.

My approach to intervention encounters is not the same as the remedies offered by other critics of the major oversights outlined above. As suggested earlier, such critiques usually include a call to focus away from the "international" and onto the "local"—often portrayed as a realm of particular kinds of people, practices, or agencies and made visible through ethnographic research methods (Autesserre 2014; Kappler 2014; Mac Ginty and Richmond 2013; O'Reilly 2018). The problem with that, as I demonstrate in this book, is that "international" and "local" are categories of practice whose meaning and politics we cannot take for granted. For example, is an Austrian diplomat like Petritsch best understood as "international" or somehow "external" to Bosnian politics if he exercises the power to impose laws? To what degree does a critique of such impositions make sense if "local" or "domestic" populations have in fact explicitly asked him to exercise those powers in the name of greater freedom and democracy—a request he usually refused? Who is "local" if Bosnians have been recruited to work for international agencies? Indeed, the boundary between "international" and "local" is particularly unstable. Thus rather than approach intervention assuming that I am analyzing "the local" or "the international," I investigate how people deploy these terms in the course of purposive action. Indeed, the categorical distinction between "international" and "local" is precisely the kind of difference that gets defined, temporarily stabilized, undone, or otherwise produced through encounters, and this is how it ought to be studied.[11]

This practice-oriented approach does not ignore agency, but makes it an empirical question to be explored and clarified. My analysis assumes that various agentive capacities will be differentially available to and exercised by a range of actors involved in an intervention encounter, depending upon the circumstances. As I will show in the chapters that follow, the task is thus to account for those circumstances and so contextualize the exercise of agentive capacities (or the wielding of means toward ends). When we do so, we find that those with significant powers (like the High Representative) or significant resources (like international aid organizations) are sometimes dependent upon those less powerful (like refugees) in unexpected ways, opening up pathways for the latter to influence and shape the process and outcomes of intervention projects.

The kind of boundary work described above also indicates why hybridity (Mac Ginty 2010, 2011; Richmond 2012) is not a useful concept for analyzing the process or product of intervention encounters. The notion of hybridity might work to unsettle top-down models of intervention and give us a sense that intervention projects are made up of engagements across difference. But despite the claims by its proponents that hybridity is not about the mixture of essentially separate things or ideas (such as the "international" and the "local"), it still carries this connotation and can limit our analysis of intervention encounters by diverting attention to sort out which part of the encounters' hybrid product belongs to the "international" and which to the "local." Indeed, with its focus on mixture and combination, hybridity is not well suited to document and analyze the production of difference and distinction that so regularly occurs in intervention encounters.

Closer to my conceptualization of intervention encounters is Anna Tsing's notion of "friction" (2005), which has been adopted by some scholars of peacebuilding interventions (Björkdahl et al. 2016) to understand the unpredictable, "nonlinear," and creative nature of "global-local interactions" in such interventions, and to account for the "hybrid or mixed agencies" that emerge from them (Björkdahl et al. 2016, 5). Most of these scholars, however, stop at simply documenting the complex, unpredictable, and unexpected nature of encounters, without identifying or accounting for the creativity involved. My focus on intervention encounters allows me to identify and conceptualize a broader range of processes, practices, entanglements, and interdependencies than those who propose "friction" or "hybridization." For example, Björkdahl and colleagues point to "localization" (Acharya 2004) and "vernacularization" (Levitt and Merry 2009) as illustrations of "frictionalized" processes, the former to show the adaption and local adoption of "foreign ideas by local actors" (Acharya 2004, 245), and the latter to indicate how when globally circulating ideas "connect with a locality, they take on some of the ideological and social attributes of the place, but also retain some of their original formulation" (Levitt and Merry 2009, 446). Both of these are useful ways of thinking about what takes place in certain kinds of intervention encounters, but they do not allow us to account for a similar phenomenon that operates in the opposite direction—not how "locals" engage with "global" ideas, but how the foreign agents of intervention must pursue their intervention projects (like democratization) using ideas, institutions, or other cultural materials specific to the site of intervention. I propose the term *recontextualization* to analyze how intervention agents take an idea or concept out of one historical or institutional context and repurpose it to serve the goals of intervention; such materials, however, bear the traces of their former contexts, and thus resist any attempts to redefine them more narrowly for specific purposes. This process can serve to alter the social and political landscape in places like Bosnia, just not always in the ways hoped for. Recontextualization allows us to track this unpredictable process of cultural production without privileging directionality, and to identify an important limit to the exercise of power, both by "internationals" and "locals."

My arguments for the value of my approach to international intervention also help explain my distinct perspective on the question of success and failure, seeing it not as a motivation for research but as a part of the everyday life of international intervention. In other words, success/failure issues are reflected in my analysis because most of the people I spoke to or observed in the course of my research were very much concerned with them, in the broad sense that the question of success or failure is part of all purposeful human action. But that broadness indicates the problem with starting an analysis around such questions: where a foreign state donor might define the success or failure of a housing reconstruction project around the question of whether refugees have moved back to their prewar homes, the aid organization implementing that project might define success or failure around the question of whether it led to contracts for future aid projects. Bosnian officials might define the success or failure of that same project around the question of whether they can restrict the return of an unwanted ethnic population or limit the addition of new demands on aging and overextended municipal infrastructure. And returnees may define the success or failure of that project around the question of whether they can find durable solutions to housing needs while also preventing the sudden influx of aid resources from damaging the bonds of neighborly reciprocity upon which they depend for survival. To analyze the encounters that occur around such a project by privileging the success/failure concerns of any single actor would not only produce an incomplete account, but would also miss how the outcomes of such projects are made in the clash of such multiple concerns.

This empirical approach to success/failure questions, or to questions of agency for that matter, does not preclude a critique of international intervention. But the critical impulse to render judgment is all too often animated by a set of concerns or ethnocentric perspectives that are not shared by those involved in interventions. I argue that any critique must take into account the perspectives and concerns of the people involved in intervention, and this requires that we proceed with a healthy sense of scholarly and political humility before the complexity and open-ended nature of engagements across social and cultural difference. My aim is thus to first seek an adequate account of international intervention, and then explore the critical possibilities that such an account makes possible.

As an anthropologist, I am pleased to see ethnographic, field-based methods of research being used to study international intervention.[12] However, I see ethnography as more than a set of research methods. It is also a mode of representing that research. Most studies of intervention that employ fieldwork-based methods offer readers very little sense of the unfolding, real-time interactions that constitute international intervention. This may be due to a more positivist impulse to generalize beyond the particularities of one case, or a desire not to spend too much time contextualizing these interactions for readers impatient at the prospect of having to learn specific details of history, culture, or language. Yet those details and particularities matter; they are, in fact, what explain the unpredictability, volatility, and productivity of international intervention. My book certainly offers insights and concepts that are relevant to cases of intervention beyond that of Bosnia and Herzegovina, from Afghanistan, Democratic Republic of Congo, and Gaza to Timor-Leste, Haiti, and Syria. But it comes to and communicates those insights through detailed descriptions and deeply contextualized accounts of the interactions that made up intervention encounters in Bosnia, from those mediated by mass publicity to those directly observed by me.

This last observation points to an important way in which my ethnographic approach to intervention encounters is distinct from nonanthropological studies that employ ethnographic and field-based methods. It comes from recognizing that my study of intervention encounters is the product of an ethnographic encounter, that is, the encounter of the researcher with people during research.

It is a truism in sociocultural anthropology that the conditions of the research context matter to what is learned; researchers do not stand outside of that context, but rather are a part of it. Thus instead of writing myself out of this book as most researchers of intervention do, my study of encounters accounts for my presence. As is made plain in the later chapters of the book, my presence in postwar Bosnia was underwritten by international intervention and played a role—sometimes directly, sometimes indirectly—in the interactions from which I learned about the politics of intervention encounters. Where relevant and possible, I have tried to include this fact in the analyses that follow.

Book Organization and Chapters

This book is split into two sections. The first begins by laying out the contours of international authority created in the response to the Bosnian war of the 1990s, and it introduces readers to postwar Bosnia's political settlement and explains why refugee return became such an important site of intervention encounters. I then move on to two chapters which analyze intervention encounters in the mass news media, an understudied site and instrument of international intervention. In chapter 1 I show how foreign officials like the High Representative and a range of Bosnian political elites used mass publicity to legitimize and authorize their state-building actions and delegitimize those of their opponents. I also investigate how Wolfgang Petritsch used the media to engage domestic politicians in attempts to guide their behavior toward foreign state-building goals, even as they sought to shape his actions to serve their own goals. In doing so, this chapter identifies political innovations as well as important limits to internationally instigated political transformation.

Chapter 2 analyzes encounters with and within history, showing how foreigners often had to pursue their goals by using cultural forms and historical materials not of their choosing. I show how such materials bore the traces of their former contexts, and thus resisted attempts to redefine them more narrowly for specific purposes. Specifically, I analyze mass media artifacts to show how High Representative Petritsch, by taking a key Bosnian political concept out of one historical, interactional, or institutional context and repurposing it to legitimize foreign state-building in another (a process called *recontextualization*), did manage to alter the Bosnian social and political landscape, just not in the ways he had hoped for.

The second section comprises three chapters which analyze intervention encounters in the refugee return process, and opens with a brief discussion of the sites, methods, and social settings of my fieldwork in northwestern Bosnia. Chapter 3 describes how ideas about ethnic identity functioned as an important heuristic, helping foreigners to navigate a social and political field most knew nothing about. Such ideas also served to legitimize a role for the international community in postwar Bosnia as a neutral mediator between antagonistic ethnic groups. I detail how these ideas and roles informed returnee behavior when they engaged foreigners and tried to enlist them to serve their goals. In addition to describing an interactional field underwritten by ideologies about ethnicity, I also reveal the instabilities created by reliance on them.

One of the most significant undertakings in postwar Bosnia and Herzegovina was the massive housing reconstruction projects run by international aid organizations as part of a highly politicized effort to move refugees back to their prewar homes. Alongside the usual technical tasks of such projects, aid workers spent considerable time and effort in their encounters with refugees creating the social and cultural conditions conducive to humanitarian action–a process I call *humanitarianization*. Chapter 4 analyzes these efforts and demonstrates that the humanitarian status of such aid projects was never more than provisionally settled. I argue that this unstable, provisional nature of humanitarian action forms an underexplored dynamic shaping and limiting aid interventions in Bosnia and beyond.

Chapter 5 explores the role played by an understudied but widespread practice of international intervention: *entextualization*, or the production and circulation of English-language text artifacts. I show how entextualization practices helped foreigners manage the uncertainty created by the expectation that they did not need to know much about Bosnia in order to transform it, and their experience that their ability to fulfill their roles was limited precisely by their lack of this knowledge. Entextualization processes stabilized foreign knowledge of Bosnian politics and society by rendering it in terms that foreigners could understand, and this knowledge became the basis for intervention projects of various kinds. But the reliance on entextualization also created problems in intervention encounters between OSCE officials and returning refugees. I show how the very practices designed to decrease uncertainty for foreign officials actually increased uncertainty for returnees, and this limited the ability of OSCE officials to fulfill their mandate to combat human rights violations and promote refugee return.

In the concluding chapter, I recap some of the major arguments and observations of the book and demonstrate the comparative opportunities and broader relevance of a focus on encounters for the study of international intervention.

INTERLUDE

International Authority and Bosnia after Dayton

A New World Order and the International Community

At a workshop held in Toronto in 2009, I was part of a discussion focused on state-building and international authority in post-Yugoslav states and societies. At one point an older gentleman, silent until that point, asked to speak. He identified himself as a retired Canadian diplomat and told the following story. Some decades earlier, he had arranged a tour of cities in Yugoslavia by a group of mayors and municipal officials from Canadian cities. Among them was Hazel McCallion, who would go on to become the long-serving mayor of Mississauga, Ontario. As part of the tour she met the mayor of the Bosnian city of Banja Luka who had overseen the government response to a devastating earthquake in 1969 that destroyed nearly 60 percent of the city's buildings. Apparently, after the earthquake subsided there had been some confusion among various organizations—fire, police, local territorial defense units, health services—as to how to direct the response to the disaster, and the mayor of Banja Luka had told of a pivotal moment when he took charge and played a critical coordinating role. Ten years later, in 1979, a 106-car Canadian Pacific freight train carrying chemicals derailed in Mississauga, Ontario, and an explosion and subsequent fire released a cloud of chlorine gas into the air which threatened to poison the densely populated area around the tracks. According to the retired diplomat, in the early chaotic hours following the derailment, as the regional police and fire services, provincial ministry of the environment, a host of transportation ministries and departments, and municipal officials were alerted and figuring out how to respond, then Mayor McCallion seized a leadership role, stating "I learned this from the mayor of Banja Luka!"

The point of the diplomat's story was to identify a rupture in international politics and the birth of new global hierarchies. He did this first by recalling a historical moment in which Bosnia and Herzegovina, as part of Yugoslavia, was seen as a place where Canadians might learn something valuable about government administration or how to respond to a natural disaster, something that could serve as a model for problems and challenges they might face at home. He then contrasted that historical moment with our own, noting how it would be almost unthinkable that Canadians or members of any other modern industrialized country would today be encouraged to think that they had anything to learn from the people of Bosnia and Herzegovina. He recalled with bewilderment the moment in the early 1990s when this shift happened—when hostilities and armed conflict broke out in Yugoslavia and its peoples went from being seen as more or less equals and peers on the world stage to being seen as inferior. Given his experience in the region, he recalled finding the abruptness of this change disconcerting, and lamented that this new view of the region encouraged, at best, indifference toward the people of Bosnia—their history, culture, and experience—and at worst, discriminatory relations of rule.

I mention this story because it points to a key transformation that underwrote the complex interactions, relations of authority, and arguments about legitimacy that structured the international response to the conflict in Bosnia and Herzegovina and its aftermath. It may be difficult to recall that in 1990, before armed conflict broke out in Yugoslavia, NATO had never had a military engagement, let alone led a peacekeeping mission; it had never bombed another European country, unprovoked, for "humanitarian" reasons, as would occur in Yugoslavia in 1999. The Organization for Security and Co-operation in Europe (OSCE) was still the *Conference* for Security and Co-operation in Europe (CSCE), and had no organizational basis, let alone the capacity to supervise elections or independently monitor human rights conditions in member states. Rather, Europe in 1990 was still in the grips of the euphoria that came with the fall of the Berlin wall and the end of the Cold War. This was a time when those very institutions that had secured Europe's Cold War order, like NATO and the CSCE, were exploring what role, if any, they had to play in a post–Cold War Europe. Even at the United Nations there was a sense that its moment had finally arrived with the end of superpower rivalry. David Rieff supplies a fitting characterization of the mood at the time:

> In 1989 and 1990, another war in Europe seemed an impossibility. There was a building consensus that, after so many wars and calamities, Europeans at last might be freed not just from war (there had been no war on the continent since 1945), but even from the threat of war. And it no longer seemed utopian to extrapolate from a Europe at peace and undivided to a peaceful order for the world as a whole. This was the era of UN Secretary-General Boutros Boutros-Ghali's "Agenda for Peace," and George Bush senior's New World Order. Liberal internationalism, with its commitments to human rights, humanitarianism, democratic . . . societies, and the rule of law, seemed to have swept all before it. (2002, 123)

As it turned out, such optimism was premature, and the conflict that tore apart Yugoslavia—particularly the war in Bosnia and Herzegovina—gave these and other international institutions like the UNHCR a new *raison d'être* (Kaufman 2002; OSCE 1992; OSCE MBiH 2006; Rieff 2002).[1]

The remaking of these institutions in response to Bosnia's war and its postwar peace heralded the coming-into-being of the "international community" as the dominant protagonist of a post–Cold War order structured around the values of peace, democracy, the rule of law, humanitarian solidarity, and the inviolability of human rights. This order was presented as more or less universally valid—the "end of history" (Fukuyama 1992). According to Feher, the first sign of this new world order's presumed universality was its rhetorical reframing of local conflicts as cultural (and thus particularist and personal) rather than as political (and thus as potentially rivaling other political ideologies, including that of the new internationalism): North American and European governments "no longer envisioned local conflicts in terms of ideological persuasion and political allegiance" (2000, 39). Instead, their official enemies were now called "rogue states" and "treated as international outlaws rather than exponents of a rival political agenda" (39). Thus the war in Bosnia and Herzegovina was conceptualized as essentially cultural to its core—a matter of ancient ethnic hatreds in a region known for its blood-soaked history and fractured unruliness.[2] The conflict was seen in nonideological terms, and this is why international intervention had to be, or had to appear to be, neutral and nonpartisan. It is also why the first response to the war by members of the "international community" like the United States and United Kingdom was a humanitarian one that blamed all "sides" as more or less equal belligerents, and sided with all civilian victims. The moral high ground was to care for civilians first, while acting as transcendent agents of peace and reconciliation.

Another key sign that the "international community" was promoting an order with claims to universal validity was that its intervention was designed to promote what Feher calls a "cultural leap" (2000, 50). While most Bosnians were seen as innocent victims of violence, they were also portrayed as illiberal and thus in need of education out of the primitive sectarianism and "rule of blood" that was the true cause of their suffering. The long-term resolution of such conflicts thus lay in conciliation, education, and cultural transformation. This was another argument for the neutrality and impartiality of the "international community" regarding post–Cold War conflict:

> Because the transition from civil war to democracy was meant to express a cultural evolution rather than political verdict, the representatives of the international community argued that they needed to be neutral about the past and privilege stability in the present. That is, they had to put an indiscriminate blame on all the formerly warring factions for having resorted to violence, but also praise and reward them equally for embracing peace and embarking on the road to democracy. (Feher 2000, 50)

As indicated in the introduction, the self-image of the promoters of this new world order as impartial and neutral vis-à-vis the particulars of a given conflict also meant that they did not have to concern themselves with the messy and challenging matters of history or actual politics. Politics was seen more often than not as simply the expression of an individualized will-to-power, an undifferentiated warlordism, clientelism, or self-enrichment. The international community, as the bearers of the new order, was best when it remained transcendent of any particulars, especially since those very particulars were often identified as factors which might hinder democratic and peaceful transformation.

One final claim to universal validity was found in the assumption, noted earlier, that transformation was largely an issue of technical transfer, a matter of the right mix of legal, electoral, and institutional reforms and the political will to see them through. In Bosnia as elsewhere, such transformation was best promoted through training in the various techniques, procedures, and organizational forms that would help participants learn about the basic building blocks of democracy: free and open media; regular, free, and fair elections; a robust and independent civil society; transparent and accountable government; and respect for human rights secured by the rule of law. The universal validity of this model of transformation was a restatement of modern teleology, which would secure basic human freedom by liberating its subjects from the cultural constraints and fetishes of tradition and collectivist hypnosis. The emphasis on education and the confidence in the universal validity of this model of political order was expressed in a reluctance by foreign agents to impose transformation or coerce Bosnian authorities in a heavy-handed way. Rather, with the right education, they expected Bosnians to recognize the right way and act to follow it willingly and on their own.

The universal validity of this post–Cold War model thus bestowed two main roles and sets of hierarchical relations on the agents of intervention: that of *mediator* above and between conflicting parties, and that of *civilizing missionary* or *educator* of not fully modern people(s). Successfully occupying either role required a constant demonstration of neutrality. However, as will become clear, working out what it meant to be "neutral" in the everyday encounters of international intervention across relations of difference was often a vexing and unpredictable endeavor.

Grounds of International Authority: Recognition and Relations of Hierarchy

The claim of the international community to bear a universally valid model of political order and human flourishing was based upon a political imaginary that grounded how international interventions were legitimized and authorized. This claim relied upon the same scalar imagery through which nation-state officials project *their* authority and legitimacy. For example, Ferguson and Gupta (2002) have described how state power relies upon and reproduces metaphors of "verticality" (the state lies "above" federal units, provinces, entities, cantons, municipalities, etc.) as well as "encompassment" (with state agencies located within a series of ever-widening circles that begin with the family and local community and end with the global system of nation-states). This imagined topography of stacked, vertical levels also structures many representations of political and social action, which are portrayed as coming "from below," as "grounded" in rooted lives and communities. According to this metaphoric imagery, the state can thus be conceived as reaching "down" into communities, intervening in a "top-down" manner, to manipulate or plan social transformation (2002, 982–984).

Moreover, Ferguson and Gupta argue that these metaphors of scale are not merely spatial, but are also *hierarchical*: the higher one sits on the scale, the greater the claim to universal value and significance, and the more general one's knowledge and interest. Just as the state is conceived of as "higher" than the civil society its sits "above" and encompasses, so too did the representatives of the "international community" implicitly rely upon the notion that they embodied greater superiority and universality—more universally valid forms, norms and practices—than other actors, whether of individual states or any other "level" of institutional power that lies "lower" on the vertical scale and is encompassed by the "international." Such images of vertical encompassment are powerful, however, mainly because they are embedded in and extended through the routinized practices of state bureaucracies, supranational or transnational intergovernmental agencies and NGOs, and the strategies of activists and others trying to promote social and political transformation. Not surprisingly, we find this imagery used to conceptualize relations in intervention encounters.

This scalar imagery feeds back into and underwrites the notion of foreign neutrality in Bosnia, in that those occupying the "international" position could claim to inhabit a position outside of, "above," or external to the social and cultural field into which they were "intervening." Thus, while foreign actors were not at all external to or disinterested in the politics of a place like Bosnia, their authority to intervene and mediate in a context defined by antagonistic ethnic difference came in part from claiming to be so. As I wrote above, this self-conceptualization relied upon and organized interventions around the core binary distinction differentiating the foreigner or "international" from the domestic or "local." Research shows that this distinction has been used by foreign officials across intervention contexts to define the "international" as external, cosmopolitan, apolitical, neutral, and nonpositioned, while the "local" is always rooted in place, monoethnic, political, biased, and always positioned. Such terms are always relational, and presume and reproduce a power-laden field of distinction and difference: the use of "international" implied the "national" or "local" or "Bosnian," and the invocation of "international" also positioned its object in a hierarchical relationship to those people or things who were classified as belonging to these other "levels."

This reinforces a point made in the introduction, namely that imagining the world in this way acts as a warrant both for ignoring or disregarding the value of "local" knowledge as well as for believing in the universal applicability and desirability of "international" models of political and social organization. One indication of this valuation were the changes put in place in 2001 by the UK Foreign Office when it came to career advancement—according to Stewart, it "deliberately reduced the weight previously given to knowledge of languages and geographical areas . . . in favour of administrative skills. Linguistic or deep country knowledge became irrelevant for promotion" (2011, 16).

One clear product of these hierarchical relations of distinction was the power of international recognition. Of course, recognition is a common theme in this book because it plays a central role in performative claims to legitimacy and the exercise of authority. What I want to emphasize here, however, are the ways in which people, institutions, laws, or discourse identified as representing or embodying the "international" could bestow a unique and powerful legitimacy and authority on people, institutions, laws, or discourse within Bosnia. Perhaps the most fundamental example is the way in which the existence and legitimacy of state forms in the Balkans has long depended upon the recognition by powerful European states and thus upon the ability of domestic officials to fulfill the requirements for such recognition.[3] But this power extended far beyond the question of state form; the legitimacy and authority of Bosnian politicians also relied in part upon their ability to gain and maintain international recognition. This served, of course, to restate relations of authority that benefitted the "international community," for to seek international recognition was to acknowledge the power of the international community to bestow it. This is another example of how relations of authority based upon often unstable categorical distinctions were coconstituted in interactions between and among both Bosnians and "internationals" alike.

This instability meant that occupying the "international" position of difference in everyday interventions encounters was not always easy—or desirable. For example, according to nation-state forms of democratic representation and legitimacy, law making by "foreign" officials is illegitimate if it is opposed by elected officials who can better claim to represent "local" interests or the "will of the people." Like the need to demonstrate neutrality, "being an international" or "representing local interests" bestowed a set of performative requirements that constituted an instability in the authoritative claims of both foreign officials and Bosnians, because such claims were dependent upon the evaluation of others who might have different ideas about what or who was "international" or "local" and what those designations implied. In other words, because these categories were deeply implicated in how relations of inequality were produced in intervention encounters, the ability to define, ascribe, and occupy them was often fiercely contested.

To deepen a point made earlier, then, the simple application of such categorical distinctions (international/local, foreign/domestic, *strani/domaće*) is inadequate to capture the complexities of intervention encounters because those encounters include struggles over the very meaning and use of such categories. Yet precisely because they are so powerful and all-pervasive, they are hard to avoid when writing about international intervention. It is my hope that readers will keep in mind the performative and potentially unstable nature of these and other key categories of practice (like "humanitarian") when coming across them in this book. And in order to understand the stakes of such categorical politics and international recognition in postwar Bosnia and Herzegovina, we must lay out the basic contours of the 1990s war.

The Bosnian War and the Dayton Order

The post–Cold War euphoria in Europe that ended with the war in Bosnia saw a brief resurgence with the Dayton Peace Agreement. In Western foreign policy circles, the Dayton Agreement was seen to provide for the kind of deep sociopolitical intervention and significant latitude needed for international institutions to implement the defining features of the post–Cold War order: free and fair elections, the growth of civil society, the development of an open media space, respect for and compliance with international human rights standards, the marketization of the economy, the privatization of socially owned property and businesses, and the eventual integration of Bosnia into common European institutions. Postwar reconstruction would have to do double-time as postsocialist transition, carried out by an army of NGOs and aid organizations, financed by Western states and countries with large Muslim populations, and overseen by international institutions like the OSCE, NATO, and UN who had already begun to see in Bosnia a new *raison d'être*.

However, it would be a mistake to begin with the Dayton Agreement and overlook how the various institutions within the newly coalescing "international community" played a decisive role in the region prior to the break-up of Yugoslavia. For example, by recognizing the independence of Bosnia and Herzegovina from Yugoslavia, the Badinter Arbitration Commission of the European Community (EC) played a significant part in the political crisis that led to the war. Through its response to the war—an arms embargo, the delivery of humanitarian aid, the deployment of UN peacekeepers to protect civilians in designated "safe areas"—the "international community" influenced its conduct.

Perhaps most importantly, the international acceptance of the logic of independent statehood was crucial to how war in Bosnia unfolded. During the 1980s, regular disagreements between federal and republican governments in Yugoslavia over the economic and political reforms of an IMF debt-repayment package became a constitutional conflict over whether to recentralize the Yugoslav Federation around the federal government in Belgrade or to continue the process of decentralization begun in the early 1970s and give more powers to the individual republics (Bosnia and Herzegovina, Croatia, Macedonia, Montenegro, Serbia, Slovenia) and autonomous regions (Vojvodina and Kosovo). This eventually became a crisis of the state itself among republican Communist Party elites unwilling or unable to reach a compromise (Hayden 1999; Woodward 1995). In this atmosphere, the Communist Party leaderships in Slovenia and Croatia asserted that sovereignty and self-determination lay with the individual republics, on the basis of a national polity, ethnically defined (i.e., Slovenia for the Slovenes, Croatia for the Croats). Both eventually declared their independence from Yugoslavia in 1991 on this basis. The logic of their claims to independent statehood was legitimized and rewarded when they received recognition by the European Community.

The logic behind Slovenia and Croatia's declaration of independence could not hold for the Republic of Bosnia and Herzegovina, however, because it contained no majority ethnonational group and its territory and its large towns and cities were ethnically mixed. Indeed, Bosnia was home to a relatively diverse population of religions and ethnonational identifications[4] with a long history of dense coexistence (Bringa 1995; Fine 1983, 1987; Jelavich 1983; Malcolm 1996). This condition was encouraged and evolved by a state commitment to "brotherhood and unity" among Bosnia's (and Yugoslavia's) peoples, exemplified in a definition of sovereignty as coconstituted between and among its ethnic peoples and working peoples. In a context of fear about the future of Yugoslavia, the first multiparty elections in Bosnia resulted in a governing coalition of three nationalist parties, each claiming an ethnic constituency of either Croats, Muslims, or Serbs. When invited by the EC to consider the question of independence, a referendum was organized by Bosnian Croat and Muslim parties (who generally favored independence) over the fierce protest of Bosnian Serb politicians (who did not). It passed without the participation of most of Bosnia's Serbs (nearly a third of the population), and Bosnia was recognized as an independent state on April 6, 1992. War broke out the next day.

It was thus from the start a war over state form, in which some factions sought to violently "un-mix" Bosnia and Herzegovina's population to create and territorialize monoethnic populations and thus form the basis of two separatist projects, a Serb republic and a Croat republic (which could then be attached to the neighboring republics of Serbia and Croatia). The Muslim-majority leadership of the existing Republic of Bosnia and Herzegovina was left to defend a multiethnic state within existing borders. Between 1992 and 1995, over half the population was displaced and at least 100,000 were killed.

It is thus consequential that western European negotiators accepted that the best political and military solution to the war in Bosnia was some sort of territorial partition, ethnically drawn, but within existing territorial boundaries of the socialist republic. Throughout the war, then, the state-building tactics and military engagements between the three main forces (the Army of Bosnia and Herzegovina, the Croat Defense Council, and the Republika Srpska Army) were directly influenced by the international acceptance that an eventual peace settlement would include some sort of ethnoterritorial partition. This doomed various peace plans as each side had an interest in postponing settlement while it tried to make new territorial gains.

The current state of Bosnia and Herzegovina was created as part of the Dayton Peace Agreement, which was primarily a political agreement to end the war rather than to institute a new social contract or state order. This context likely accounts for the ways in which it cobbled together and gave partial legitimacy to the multiple, contradictory state-building projects of the war. It recognized the "ethnically cleansed" territories of the Republika Srpska and Muslim-Croat Federation as Bosnia's constituent political units, or "entities." At the same time, however, the Dayton Agreement provided for mechanisms and processes meant to undo precisely that ethnically divided status quo. These included most prominently the return of refugees to their prewar homes, but also an institutional and legal architecture meant to secure the human rights and political participation of individual citizens regardless of their ethnonational background. It is telling that most of that architecture was put under the jurisdiction of international institutions rather than local bodies, for it was precisely these aspects that Bosnia was understood to be lacking and therefore had to be brought from outside. It was probably this decision more than any other that set the stage for so many intervention encounters.

Formally, then, Bosnia and Herzegovina is an internationally recognized state with a multiplicity of jurisdictions and institutional competencies divided along state, entity, canton, and municipal lines.[5] The Dayton Agreement laid the groundwork for an abundance of intervention encounters by creating extensive roles for international institutions, most prominently the OSCE, the UN, and the Office of the High Representative (OHR), an institution unique to Bosnia. When the Dayton Agreement took effect in 1996, the federal or state level was weak and its institutions were organized around a basic ethnic calculus requiring an equal division of posts or seats to be occupied by Serbs, Croats, and Muslims. In 1996, it was the "Serb" and "Muslim-Croat" entities (*entiteti*) that wielded the real power, with parliaments, separate militaries, police forces, courts, border and customs administration, and responsibility for setting and implementing everything from education policy to the tax code.

The Republika Srpska entity is a monoethnic state project founded on the European model of national self-determination and is made up of a territory that at the end of the war had been largely "cleansed" of its substantial non-Serb population. Bosnian Serb political elites from the Republika Srpska tend to be hostile to the state level of government and to pursue maximal independence for the entity.

The Federation entity is the result of the 1994 Washington Agreement, an internationally mediated settlement for peace between Bosnian Croat forces and the army of the Republic of Bosnia and Herzegovina that recognized an ethnic division of territory into cantons, most of which were either Bosniak-majority or Croat-majority. Bosniak political elites tend to advocate a single multiethnic state and thus pursue a strong state level, while Croat political elites tend to pursue a strong entity and cantonal system, or to advocate for a third, Croat-only entity modeled on the Republika Srpska. All politicians sacralize their state projects by pointing to the blood spilled in the 1990s war.

The Dayton Agreement thus kept multiple state-building projects in play, and political developments over the last two and a half decades have thus been dominated by efforts to sustain one of these visions at the expense of the others, in a kind of war of attrition. International authorities have tended to work toward realizing a multiethnic unified state, and sought to strengthen the central state government by arguing that this state form was necessary for membership in pan-European institutions like NATO and the EU. Other political actors have pushed back and obstructed such attempts, particularly by pointing out that the Dayton Agreement guarantees the existence of the entities and the notion of ethnonational territoriality and collective rights that undergirds them. The unstable nature of Bosnia and Herzegovina's state form has made the cultivation of good relations with powerful states and international institutions, or at least their recognition of one's authority, a continuing priority.

International involvement in postwar Bosnia and Herzegovina has varied in intensity. The first few postwar years witnessed significant activity fulfilling military provisions of the Dayton Agreement (separation and demobilization of military forces, disarmament) with very little movement regarding its political provisions, particularly in the institutions of the joint state. At the end of 1997, the OHR was granted extensive powers in an effort to prevent the ongoing obstruction by Bosnian parties of the political and other provisions of the Dayton Agreement. This ushered in a high-interventionist phase of liberal state-building under Wolfgang Petritsch which came to an end when his successor, British politician Paddy Ashdown, finished his tenure at the OHR at the beginning of 2006.

By that time, international resources and attention had passed to other sites of intervention: Kosovo, Afghanistan, Iraq, and East Timor, to name just a few. Most international NGOs followed the aid money and decamped for more recent war zones and disaster sites. Many areas under international jurisdiction were either transferred to local institutions or to joint European institutions as part of a Europeanization process, with the understanding that Bosnia's future lay within the EU. Although the OHR continues to exist at the time of this writing, there have been only a few attempts to exercise its extensive powers since 2006.

This periodization matters because the intervention encounters that I document and analyze in this book occurred during the high-interventionist phase under Petritsch and Ashdown. International strategies to build a multiethnic unified state during this period can be divided into two, mutually reinforcing approaches: one which worked to create a multiethnic constitutional order by focusing on Bosnia's legal and government institutions, and another which promoted refugee return—especially those returning to areas in which they would be an ethnic minority—in order to create the social and demographic conditions necessary to realize that legal and institutional order.

Refugee Return

From the beginning of the war through its postwar peace, the question of refugees (creating them, placing them, caring for them, returning them) has linked the international community to Bosnia. For instance, the internationally sanctioned logic and grounds for partition directly affected the placement of ethnically marked refugees during the war, such that they were used to settle areas under one or another authority in order to strengthen the control of the Bosnian Serb or Bosnian Croat forces, or the Bosniak-dominated government of Bosnia and Herzegovina (Kumar 1997). The Bosnian refugee population outside of Bosnia neared one million within one year of the war's start, and early insistence by Bosniaks and Bosnian Croats that the right to return be maintained for refugees dovetailed nicely with the goals of EC countries burdened by so many displaced persons. Refugee questions were central to the various peace negotiations (Holbrooke 1998), ranging from the right of return to where refugees should be allowed to vote.

Once the war was concluded, it was the interstitial, liminal position of the hundreds of thousands of refugees in Bosnia and abroad—by definition unsettled and out of place in the "national order of things" (Liisa Malkki's felicitous term for the ideology which naturalizes the division of the world into nation-states)—that most clearly kept the question of the state unsettled. Thus more than any other provision of the Dayton Agreement, it was the right of refugees to return to their prewar homes (Annex 7) that provided the potential to unmake what the war had wrought. Although initially wary about the security problems posed by the prospect of so-called minority return (the return of refugees to areas in which they would be an ethnic minority), the rhetorical commitment by Western officials to refugee return offered a position from which to make good on what was already being posited in 1996 as Europe's greatest moral failure since the Second World War: inaction in the face of genocidal violence, represented most prominently by the Srebrenica massacre in which over 8,000 unarmed Muslim men and boys were taken from a UN "safe area" and killed by Serb military and paramilitary forces. Once refugee return began in earnest around the turn of the century, "reversing the effects of ethnic cleansing" called into being relations of obligation that gave intervention in Bosnia a moral force that it had previously lacked. Eventually, promoting minority return came to be seen as a way to break the hold of uncooperative nationalist forces on municipal and cantonal government[6] and to substantiate their commitment to "multiethnic" communities, routinely touted as a supreme "European" and "democratic" value.[7]

The experience of the international authorities up to that point led many of them to believe that domestic authorities were likely to obstruct refugee return, so the process was promoted largely outside of already existing institutions of Bosnian government. UNHCR delivered tents and food to returnees living on the rubble of their destroyed homes. Stabilization Force military units moved their bases to provide security. The UN International Police Task Force monitored the Bosnian police in sites of return and provided funds to train and hire new officers from the "returnee community." The OHR dealt with the "political" problems, and the OSCE monitored the human rights situations of returnees and other vulnerable populations and helped them advocate for their rights when those rights were being ignored.

This is important context, because I did not set out to study refugee return; rather, my aim was to study the politics of international intervention. As an anthropologist focusing on how such politics emerged from the interactions that made up intervention encounters, I sought out sites where such interactions were happening most regularly. In the early 2000s, the most regular site of face-to-face interactions between Bosnians, foreign officials, and aid staff was the refugee return process, and this process was most intensive and sustained in northwestern Bosnia. Thus while refugee return shaped the encounters from which I develop my analyses in the second half of this book, it is not my object of analysis. Rather, I am interested in refugee return first and foremost as a problem space of international intervention, of encounters between the agents of the international community and their Bosnian interlocutors, and also for the ways in which the refugee return process figured in attempts to constitute the "international community" while at the same time remaking postwar Bosnia. Therefore, although this book offers much to those interested in refuge return, this is not a book that asks or answers many of the questions posed by those who serve or study refugees and displaced persons.[8]

Before turning to the refugee return process, however, I explore those intervention encounters that took place through the news media, for the decisions taken here proliferated so many of the interactions I analyze in the second half of the book.

1

THE LIMITS OF FOREIGN AUTHORITY

Publicity and the Political Logic of Ambivalence

> **Removing officials is, of course, hardly a shining example of democracy at work. It jars with the philosophy underlying all my work in Bosnia and Herzegovina, that of "ownership."**
>
> —Wolfgang Petritsch

In January of 2000, a group of four Sarajevo-based intellectuals put forth a bold and controversial proposition in the weekly magazine *Dani* (Pećanin et al. 2000) (Figure 1.1). Citing the active obstruction of the functioning of the state by the political classes of Bosnia and Herzegovina, and seeing no way out of this situation within the political framework created by the Dayton Peace Agreement, they called for Bosnia and Herzegovina to be established as a full protectorate of the international community for one year. They directed their appeal at Wolfgang Petritsch, then seven months into his tenure as the international community's High Representative in Bosnia and Herzegovina. They called upon him to exercise the considerable powers at his disposal to suspend all parliamentary bodies at all government levels as well as the presidency of the state, and to assume their powers himself; to make all official institutional and administrative bodies in Bosnia and Herzegovina part of the administration of the Office of the High Representative (OHR); to postpone the elections planned for later that year; to reorganize domestic military forces in Bosnia and Herzegovina; and to reconstitute domestic governmental administration to fit the requirements for membership in the European Union (EU).

Their proposition was not as far-fetched as it might first appear. Recall that years of international intervention had already significantly shaped postwar politics in Bosnia and Herzegovina, and Petritsch and his predecessors in the OHR had often exercised the power at their disposal, such as creating laws, in ways ordinarily associated with state government. They had also exercised it in extraordinary ways, such as removing elected officials from office.

Moreover, most analysts and commentators recognized political dysfunction in postwar Bosnia and Herzegovina as rooted in its multiple, contradictory, incomplete state-building projects. Indeed, because all politicians staked their legitimacy on being proponents of one or another of these state projects, all domestic political and legislative questions were subordinated to a calculus of which vision of the state they would support or undermine. For many observers, the unfinished nature of the state regularly brought politics to an impasse and acted to block most new legislation or reforms.

The provocation of the four intellectuals took the existing powers of Petritsch's office and the paralysis of the war and postwar intervention to a logical conclusion: They sought to compel Petritsch to dispense with all pretense of democracy by abandoning what, for them, was the halfway and halting exercise of his powers. They demanded that he instead act decisively to create the framework for democratic government, settle the question of the state, and thereby sideline the forces of obstruction.

Petritsch publicly responded to their provocation with an argument that reflected the very ambivalence and hesitation which the proposition's authors repudiated. In his reply (OHR 2000a), also published in *Dani*, Petritsch rejected international responsibility for Bosnia and Herzegovina's political paralysis (Figure 1.2). He argued for patience in building democracy, while acknowledging deficiencies among Bosnia and Herzegovina's politicians, who "lacked responsibility," as well as its citizens, who "lack political maturity." It was precisely in the interests of the twin goals of building democracy and an independent state that he ruled out a protectorate: "People will only learn how to run their country when they are given a chance to do it by themselves. In Bosnia and Herzegovina, even the limited powers of the High Representative have led to a certain culture of dependency. A protectorate would . . . subjugate Bosnia and Herzegovina's society and structures and make it impossible for them to ever become independent and self-sustaining. For the International Community, a protectorate would be a commitment with no end in sight."[1]

Framed within a discourse of "local ownership," Petritsch argued that the state had the task to "become stronger and legitimize itself by offering its citizens real values," and that its citizens were obliged "to accept the state as their home country and work on making it comfortable." It was the political classes and the citizenry of Bosnia and Herzegovina that had the primary responsibility for solving the problems of the country. At the same time, he expressed sympathy with the frustration of the authors and noted that there were occasions when circumstances required him to abandon his passive, supervisory position. Thus while "the process must be led and conducted by the people of Bosnia and Herzegovina," he

DESET TEZA ZA BOSNU I HERCEGOVINU

Piše:
Senad Pećanin
Ivan Lovrenović
Nerzuk Ćurak
Mile Stojić

U situaciji kada je evidentno da postojeća rješenja iz Općeg okvirnog mirovnog sporazuma za Bosnu i Hercegovinu predstavljaju limitirajući faktor u konstituiranju stabilne, demokratske i prosperitetne državne zajednice; u situaciji kada je očito da postojeći odnos političkih snaga onemogućava i elementarno funkcioniranje državnih institucija i organa vlasti; kada nema naznaka da bi se u dogledno vrijeme mogao značajnije promijeniti postojeći odnos političkih snaga; kada se svaki pokušaj dogradnje Općeg okvirnog mirovnog sporazuma od strane lokalnih političkih aktera proglašava unitarističkim ili separatističkim težnjama;

polazeći od činjenice da ni četiri godine od završetka rata postojeće političke strukture nisu smanjile ovisnost Bosne i Hercegovine od angažmana i pomoći međunarodne zajednice; suočavajući se sa realnošću smanjivanja dosadašnjeg angažmana i pomoći međunarodne zajednice; polazeći od činjenice sasvim izvjesnog sučeljavanja sa bezizlaznom situacijom opće stagnacije, propadanja i sigurne socijalne katastrofe za sve građane Bosne i Hercegovine; suočeni sa pogubnim osjećajem potpune bespomoćnosti i besperspektivnosti koji uzrokuje svakodnevni odlazak ogromnog broja pripadnika mladih generacija iz svih krajeva zemlje; uvjereni da je način funkcioniranja postojećih struktura vlasti jedino u interesu samih tih struktura; mi, dolje potpisani, predlažemo:

1. Potrebno je suspendirati sve skupštine na svim nivoima vlasti u Bosni i Hercegovini – državnom, entitetskim, kantonalnim i općinskim.

2. Potrebno je da Visoki predstavnik međunarodne zajednice u Bosni i Hercegovini preuzme sve ingerencije suspendiranih skupština.

3. Potrebno je da Visoki predstavnik međunarodne zajednice u Bosni i Hercegovini suspendira Predsjedništvo Bosne i Hercegovine.

4. Potrebno je da Visoki predstavnik međunarodne zajednice u Bosni i Hercegovini preuzme sve ingerencije Predsjedništva Bosne i Hercegovine.

5. Potrebno je da postojeći izvršni organi vlasti na svim nivoima – državnom, entitetskim, kantonalnim i općinskim – postanu dio administracije Visokog predstavnika međunarodne zajednice u Bosni i Hercegovini, koji preuzima sve ovlasti koje su imale suspendirane skupštine na svim nivoima vlasti prema izvršnim organima.

6. Potrebno je da Visoki predstavnik međunarodne zajednice u Bosni i Hercegovini odloži zakazane općinske i opće izbore u Bosni i Hercegovini planirane za 2000. godinu.

7. Potrebno je da Visoki predstavnik međunarodne zajednice u Bosni i Hercegovini zakaže opće i općinske izbore za 2001. godinu koji će biti održani u skladu sa Izbornim zakonom baziranim na odlukama Ustavnog suda Bosne i Hercegovine i najvišim standardima zaštite građanskih prava.

8. Potrebno je da Visoki predstavnik međunarodne zajednice u Bosni i Hercegovini postojeću strukturu oružanih snaga u Bosni i Hercegovini uskladi sa standardima NATO saveza.

9. Potrebno je da Visoki predstavnik međunarodne zajednice u Bosni i Hercegovini tokom prelaznog perioda konstituciju Bosne i Hercegovine prilagodi zahtjevima evropskih integracija i principima efikasnog i ekonomičnog ustroja državnih organa.

10. Potrebno je da Visoki predstavnik međunarodne zajednice u Bosni i Hercegovini svoje ovlasti ograniči na period od jedne godine, to jest do održavanja općih i općinskih izbora u 2001. godini.

FIGURE 1.1. Senad Pećanin, Ivan Lovrenović, Nerzuk Ćurak, and Mile Stojić, "Deset teza za Bosnu i Hercegovinu" (Ten theses for Bosnia and Herzegovina), *Dani.* 139 (January 28, 2000), 16–17. Article addressed to High Representative Wolfgang Petritsch.

Reprinted with permission.

was not above exercising his powers to create a framework that would help that process along:

> There are laws that each state simply needs, and I am willing to impose them if a majority of parliament members are not capable of doing it themselves. I have zero tolerance for obstructionists and nationalists and consider them poison for this country; I will continue to use my powers against them. There are issues of such importance that I will do whatever I can to further them—such as economic reform, growth and job creation, such as refugee return and the Rule of Law.

> My goal is to establish a framework that will give the officials and citizens a chance to act responsibly and take their fate into their own hands. It is up to them to seize this opportunity.

It might be tempting to brush aside the provocation of these four intellectuals as unrepresentative or unserious, or to see Petritsch's attempt to disavow his role in shaping the state of Bosnia and Herzegovina politics as disingenuous. It is hard to overlook the inconsistency between the claim to promote "local ownership" by Bosnian politicians and citizens while at the same time regularly imposing laws outside of the legislative process. Yet I open this chapter with this public demand and ambivalent disavowal because they perfectly exemplify two means/ends contradictions common to post–Cold War international intervention (Heathershaw 2012; Paris and Sisk 2007; Toal and Dahlman 2011; Zaum 2012): a democratization paradox of "imposing democracy," that is, promoting democratic ends through undemocratic means, and the state-building paradox of building an independent

OVO NIJE NAŠA ZEMLJA

Krajem januara, urednički kvartet *Dana* zatražio je, kroz tekst *Deset teza za Bosnu i Hercegovinu*, od Visokog predstavnika Wolfgonga Petritscha da u BiH praktično uvede jednogodišnji međunarodni protektorat. Austrijski diplomata zavidnog iskustva odgovara *Danima* sa svojih 10 teza, insistirajući na bosanskoj "odgovornosti", iznoseći istovremeno tačnu i zabrinjavajuću teoriju: građani BiH ne osjećaju Bosnu i Hercegovinu kao svoju državu

Piše: Dr. Wolfgang Petritsch

1. Puno se postiglo u implementaciji Dejtonskog sporazuma:

FIGURE 1.2. First page of article by High Representative Wolfgang Petritsch, "Ovo nije naša zemlja" (This is not our country), *Dani.* 144 (March 3, 2000), 23.

Reprinted with permission.

state by violating the principle of popular sovereignty that underwrites the UN model of national self-determination. The exchange between Petritsch and the intellectuals also illustrates a crucial strategy through which Petritsch sought to pursue his goals despite these contradictions, and it exemplifies a common but underexplored site of encounter and form of political communication that is shaping and limiting the effects of nation-building intervention in the twenty-first century: mass-mediated public culture.

In this chapter I draw upon the Press and Public Information archive of the OHR, together with Bosnian news media documents, to investigate and describe the OHR's *practices of publicity* or being-in-public, where engagement took place in press releases and press conferences, broadcast interviews, and published letters. While for many readers the term "publicity" may conjure up images of the kinds of promotional material and media campaigns intended to grab attention for the release of a new film, television program, or other product, I use it in an expanded sense to refer to the use of mass media to address an indefinite, open-ended, public audience and thereby accomplish a variety of ends. In this way, publicity is imagined as an arena—sometimes called the public sphere—that is structured by the mass circulation and consumption of text, speech, and images, but also as the practices that animate that circulation (issuing press releases, holding press conferences, making speeches, and so on).

The interactions that took place through practices of publicity bear many of the hallmarks of encounters described in the introduction: they are made up of attempts by unequally positioned participants to define and delimit the roles, relations, obligations, responsibilities, goals, and legitimacy of intervention. Mass-mediated interactions were engagements across difference and inequality, and defining and contesting the nature of that difference and inequality was itself part of the encounter. Analysis of foreign publicity reveals the dialogic nature of international intervention, the ways in which powerful figures like Petritsch and a range of both domestic and foreign actors were forced to contend with one another's speech and action as they pursued their various goals. It demonstrates how Petritsch's contradictory positions forced him to improvise and innovate, as did the fact that he had to pursue his aims according to a timeline, events, and cultural materials not of his choosing. It also locates important limits to foreign-instigated transformation in the performative requirements, entanglements, and interdependencies produced as locals and foreign agents tried to put one another into the service of their political projects.

First and foremost, an analysis of OHR publicity reveals ambivalence as a political logic of intervention. This is ambivalence not in the sense of uncertainty or indecisiveness, but in the sense of occupying a position that must simultaneously accommodate demands that pull in opposite directions, or reconcile rationales for action that appear contrary. Rather than ignore or seek to overcome the two normative contradictions of his position, I show how Petritsch sought to legitimize his perspective and actions in ways that both sustained the norms of democracy and sovereign statehood which he advocated and suspended the contradictions behind how he promoted them.[2] This allowed him to argue that the use or nonuse of the quasi-sovereign powers at his disposal were something other than arbitrary decisions. It also allowed him to retain a broad range of pragmatic responses to the vagaries of Bosnia and Herzegovina politics as he pursued the goal of political transformation. In discursively stabilizing the ambivalence of his position, Petritsch relied upon and reproduced an image of postwar Bosnia and Herzegovina as caught in a transitory temporality, a temporary state of exception to the normal nation-state order of things.[3]

Operating according to a logic of ambivalence afforded Petritsch a calculated flexibility to tack back and forth between various positions of legitimacy and authority. This became clearest in the way he shifted between different voicings and positions in the circuit of communication described in democratic theory of the public sphere (Fraser 2007; Habermas 1989). That theory posited the public sphere as a realm of public communication where members of the citizenry generate public opinion which is supposed to reflect the general interest concerning how the state should govern, and address that opinion and interest to the state. This is understood to be a mechanism of democratic accountability, for if the state responds positively to the communicatively generated public interest it gains democratic legitimacy (for it is governing according to the "will of the people"); if the state does not respond to public opinion, then that legitimacy is withheld. This theory thus posits various positions of communication, most basically an addressee (the party to whom public opinion is being aimed, most often the state) and an addressor, the articulator of that opinion.

At times, such as in the exchange in the pages of *Dani*, the High Representative occupied the position of the addressee of local public opinion, a representative of state-like power responding to being called upon to act. By occupying the position of addressee, he could take up a position as an articulator of some element of Bosnian public opinion, voicing demands on Bosnia and Herzegovina politicians for particular legislation or official accountability. However, Petritsch also created additional circuits of communication when he occupied the position of the addressee of *international* opinion, responding to being called upon by the international community to act. At other times, when making demands of Bosnia and Herzegovina politicians he positioned himself as an articulator of international opinion.[4]

In other words, he used publicity to generate multiple positions of legitimacy by defining and delineating the sources that he claimed authorized his speech and action ("the people," "the international community"), as well as to demonstrate his relationship to these sources. This reflects a broader point found in other studies of the mass media's role in the practice of international politics, namely, that repetitive, iterative, and citational discursive practices have a performative capacity to constitute the objects of which they speak (see Dodds and Carter 2014 on film; Dodds 1996 on political cartoons; and Robison 2004 on print media).[5] Such discursive practices do not exist in a vacuum, however, but in dialogue with and against similar practices carried out by a range of other participants in the public sphere. In fact, the majority of OHR publicity was animated by the instabilities created by operating according to a logic of ambivalence. In this chapter, I trace four such instabilities.

The first instability was illustrated by the opening exchange: Exercising state-like powers and claiming to do so in the interests of a Bosnia and Herzegovina public made Petritsch an addressee for demands like those made by the intellectuals. This compelled him to define and delimit the relations of representation which he had generated by acting in the name of others, and thus limit the obligations that they entailed. A second instability was created by the movement between multiple positions of authority: his ability to occupy them *all* was contested; the claim that he was motivated by or aligned with some representation of "the people" in Bosnia competed with many others doing the same thing, most prominently politicians. He operated with an obvious legitimacy deficit as an unelected foreigner whose position stood outside of Bosnia and Herzegovina's constitutional order. Petritsch responded by using publicity to summon and perform relations of accountability outside of those institutionalized in processes like elections. He also utilized the OHR press office to circulate and monopolize the authorizing discourses of democracy and Europe in ways that deflected the democratization paradox.

A third instability came from having to communicate with, persuade, and respond to multiple and distinct audiences, often simultaneously. Most prominently, these were audiences in Bosnia, with whom communication was in Bosnian/Croatian/Serbian (B/C/S), and international audiences, with whom communication was in English. One example of this tension was that the major state sponsors and guarantors of the Dayton Agreement were constantly exerting pressure to reduce the international presence and exercise of power; the High Representative regularly worked to convince them to support a longer timeline for both, such as in speeches at the UN and editorials in the *New York Times*. Yet, as we saw in the opening exchange with the four intellectuals, such arguments for a longer timeline could be taken as evidence that Bosnian politics were facing the kind of obstruction that demanded more forceful intervention on Petritsch's part—hence the need to persuade domestic audiences that his refusal to do so was justified and legitimate. The political logic of ambivalence was born of this tension.

A final instability was related to the transitory temporality that underwrote the logic of ambivalence, the claim that the disorder of postwar politics made the powers of the OHR necessary but exceptional. By itself, such an argument was a claim seeking evidence and bestowed upon Petritsch the obligation to demonstrate that he was working to overcome this disorder and end the state of exception, thereby ushering in political relations that followed the norms of the nation-state order and making his position obsolete. Publicity was thus also part of an effort to call forth "responsible government" with the will to carry out necessary reforms. Toward this end, Petritsch orchestrated enactments of "democracy at work" or "local ownership," which in order to be persuasive needed the active participation of elected officials as the privileged representatives of the popular will. And that participation could not be taken for granted.

A focus on these instabilities opens up new insights about the performative dimension of international intervention, particularly in the creation of proof to support the High Representative's contested claims. I show how performances of "democracy at work" or "local ownership" were initiated to create persuasive evidence for OHR claims to legitimacy and authority. In doing so, I reveal that publicity was a site not only where such performances were orchestrated, but also where various actors sought to define, circulate, and contest the criteria for evaluating their success or failure. It was a matter of considerable international interest whether the enactments of democracy and local ownership were persuasive enough to collapse the temporal state of exception.

Attempts by Petritsch to end the state of exception by inciting Bosnian elite participation in acts of "local ownership" show that mass communication can work as a technology of governmentality, an instrument to shape "the conduct of conduct" and "to control the possible field of action of others" (Foucault 2002: 341; see also Graan 2016). Indeed, OHR publicity was replete with "tactics of education, persuasion, inducement, management, incitements, motivation, and encouragement" (Rose and Miller 1992, 273; see also Inda 2005) that sought to shape the will, desire, and calculations of Bosnian political elites. And yet, such attempts can be quite difficult to pull off.[6] Indeed, events of "democracy at work" or "local ownership" became occasions for Bosnia and Herzegovina politicians to stage enactments of their own authority and legitimacy, enactments which also reveal a set of ambivalent tensions. On one hand, these politicians sought to demonstrate that they could gain and maintain international recognition, an important currency in domestic politics. On the other, the requirements for international recognition could undermine core self-authorizing discourses for Bosnian politicians, such as that of "national self-determination." Bosnian politicians thus also operated according to a logic of ambivalence, and developed their own discursive and pragmatic strategies to manage the political risks and rewards of these intervention encounters.

After examining the four instabilities which illustrate the promise and risk that come with operating according to a logic of ambivalence, I conclude with a reflection on how a focus on publicity opens up unique insights regarding the political dynamics and limits of international democratization and nation-building intervention. The last few decades have shown that the UN nation-state model remains the normative form for delimiting political communities and containing conflict (Kelly and Kaplan 2009), and that the language and rituals of representative democracy hold strong attraction for interveners and local political actors alike. And yet, as Borneman has observed, despite what may appear to be the nearly global use of the language of democracy and self-determination, this is not matched by any "cross-cultural agreement" on the particulars, "on what might constitute an adequate system of 'representation,' or what power is actually being yielded in a 'delegation of authority,' much less to speak of principles of 'popular will' or 'majority rule'" (2003, 37). He concludes that "democratic arrangements will always be historically contingent, varying greatly by region and place, by local forms of power and authority" (ibid.). By focusing upon publicity as a site of encounter and instrument of intervention, this chapter provides an example of just such a "democratic arrangement" in the making. I build on an anthropological, nonnormative, and practice-based approach which argues that in order to understand what "democracy" is or what it means you need to look at how it is used in the context of specific actions and interactions; this study, then, has something to tell us about democracy per se, rather than as some distorted, underdeveloped, or "Balkan" version of democracy. I also expose critical and empirical blind spots that come with framing international intervention as a form of transnational hegemony or (neo)imperial domination, and offer an example of how the effects of what is projected to be a temporary state of exception can accumulate and gain a durability that ultimately makes that exception unsustainable.

The OHR and State-Building in Post-Dayton Bosnia and Herzegovina

The question of Bosnia's status as an international protectorate was not envisioned when the position of High Representative was created by the Dayton Agreement. As the international agent mandated to oversee the implementation of the "civilian aspects" of that agreement, it was originally conceived to play a temporary mediating role. Still, Dayton did make the High Representative's position "the final authority in theatre regarding interpretation" of those civilian aspects. The boundaries of what that interpretive authority entailed were further determined and elaborated by the Peace Implementation Council (PIC), an international body that was established after the completion of the Dayton Agreement.[7]

It was initially foreseen that the High Representative would need to play its coordinating role between the parties to the Dayton Agreement for only about a year. That was revised when it became clear that many of those parties had no intention of abiding by its terms. The first High Representative, former Swedish prime minister Carl Bildt, found himself powerless when Bosnian politicians, hostile to the Dayton state form and its multiethnic principle of government, deliberately blocked the functioning of state institutions and ignored key provisions of the Dayton Agreement. A critical moment in the expansion of the High Representative's powers came at a December 1997 PIC meeting in Bonn, in which the council welcomed "the High Representative's intention to use his final authority in theatre regarding interpretation of the Agreement . . . in order to facilitate the resolution of difficulties by making binding decisions, as he judges necessary" (OHR 1997). The exercise of this authority became known as the "Bonn powers" and with them the High Representative could now: remove officials, including democratically elected politicians, from public office and ban them from future government roles; impose legislation; and take other measures including executive decisions and financial sanctions. Behind the Bonn powers stood a NATO-led military force and a UN police force ready to back up any decree made by the High Representative.

The first use of the Bonn powers by the then High Representative, Spanish diplomat Carlos Westendorp, was to impose the basic building blocks of a common state: a citizenship law, flag, national anthem, currency, and license-plate system. Having thus established a precedent linking Bosnian statehood to the presence and power of the international community, Westendorp turned to the other area that was critical to realizing the goal of common statehood: the return of refugees to their prewar homes, a process that had the potential to reverse the effects of ethnic cleansing. For the remaining eighteen months of his two-year tenure, Westendorp exercised the Bonn powers through a total of seventy-two decisions, nearly all of them related to refugee return. This exemplified and cemented the international community's commitment to a political and moral order in Bosnia and Herzegovina premised on the reality of ethnic groups and their coexistence on Bosnia and Herzegovina territory. In order to further stabilize this new/old order, the High Representative's decisions included the imposition of property laws and other return-related arbitration as well as the removal of elected officials who obstructed refugee return—indeed, anything that was considered against the "spirit and letter" of the Dayton Agreement. Over time, while a large number of OHR decisions continued to be return-related, increasing pressure to make Bosnia self-governing saw the exercise of the Bonn powers expand to include institution building (and an expansion and strengthening of state institutions) and economic reform.

As mentioned in the first Interlude, this was the beginning of the high-interventionist phase of liberal state-building in postwar Bosnia and Herzegovina. Westendorp's successor as High Representative, Wolfgang Petritsch, handed down 250 decisions over the course of two and a half years. He was to be outdone by his successor, British politician Paddy Ashdown, who handed down an astounding 430 decisions during his three-and-a-half-year tenure as High Representative. This period was thus characterized by a veritable avalanche of intervention that laid bare the paradox inherent in "imposing democracy."

The expanded use of the Bonn powers was paralleled by expanded use of publicity[8] and expanded intervention into the broadcast and print media sphere,[9] in part because of the need to legitimize the use of those powers. This was not only true of the OHR, but also other international actors in Bosnia; indeed, the presence of foreigners and foreign-sponsored media campaigns[10] in Bosnia's public sphere was ubiquitous. And because of this, international institutions like the OSCE and OHR began to more closely monitor local media: each day B/C/S-language articles and TV broadcasts that featured the OHR and other international institutions were tracked and translated into English so that foreign staff could monitor responses to their actions and media campaigns. For a while in the early to mid-2000s, a daily Media Roundup report was available on the OHR website, offering English speakers access to a critical source of domestic public opinion about international intervention. For many foreign staff, such reports may have been their only source.[11]

In his analysis of international oversight and foreign publicity in postconflict Macedonia, Graan (2010) describes the ways in which foreign speech in the Macedonian public sphere was dominated by registers of expertise and evaluation. This is an apt characterization of the international presence in Bosnia and Herzegovina news media: no matter what the immediate issue being reported upon, foreigners routinely used these occasions to offer evaluations of Bosnia and Herzegovina politics and society, of its past, present, and future. Bosnia and Herzegovina politicians were also routinely asked for their reaction and commentary on such foreign evaluations, which animated further replies by foreign officials. All of this was fodder for Bosnia and Herzegovina's commentariat and everyday conversation. The ubiquity of such assessments helped account for the widely held notion, shared by international and domestic populations alike, that Bosnia and

Herzegovina politics hinged to a greater or lesser degree on the power of outside forces and the recognition they could bestow or withhold.

Foreign Publicity and the Power of the High Representative

The High Representative's use of publicity followed a logic of ambivalence as Petritsch worked to legitimize his actions in ways that sustained the norms of democracy and sovereign statehood which he advocated, while suspending the contradictions behind how he promoted them. In what follows, I illustrate this politics of ambivalence by delineating the multiple participant roles that Petritsch invoked and through which he developed a calculated flexibility to tack back and forth between various authorizing positions. As suggested above, occupying these various positions created opportunities that he sought to take advantage of, and instabilities that he sought to manage, by calling upon different authorizing discourses. I thus also briefly touch upon the OHR's use of each of these discourses, all the while keeping in mind the ways in which the public sphere was a political field of struggle and competition.

One authoritative position was as a representative of the "international community." Here the OHR's use of publicity accomplished what Bourdieu (1991) described as the power of spokespersons, individuals whose authority is delegated by those they represent. Bourdieu points out that spokespersons effectively create the group that they claim to speak for—they evoke such groups as they invoke them as a source of authority. In important respects, the power of the High Representative was linked to the "international community," an amorphous yet powerful abstraction which Petritsch brought into being precisely by constantly invoking it, and his relationship to it, in public, through his speech and actions. These actions could include orchestrated meetings with ambassadors and visiting foreign ministers, speeches at the UN General Assembly, or regular reports to the PIC, all duly reported by the OHR press office and circulated by Bosnia and Herzegovina's mass news media in B/C/S as well as on its website in English.

As a representative of the international community, he could take one of two authorizing positions. The first was that he could articulate international opinion when making demands of Bosnia and Herzegovina officials, offering the benefits of international recognition or the sanction of international disapproval: "My Office and the international organisations operating in Bosnia and Herzegovina will continue to insist on progress and an improvement in the lives of the country's citizens. . . . The international community is on the brink of losing interest in Bosnia and Herzegovina. The honeymoon is over for good. If we do not achieve a decisive breakthrough in 2001, Bosnia and Herzegovina will find itself on the outskirts, but not part of European wealth and prosperity" (OHR 2000d).

Alternately, he could position himself as an addressee of international opinion, legitimizing his actions as a response to demands made upon him: "I did not dismiss 22 officials because I wanted to punish anyone. . . . I did it because it is becoming increasingly difficult to explain to the representatives of the outside world, who pay for the peace process in Bosnia and Herzegovina, why people who blatantly violate laws and the Dayton Peace Agreement, who stamp on citizens' rights, hold positions here" (OHR 1999b).

However, various High Representatives conceived of their power as also linked to their ability to speak and act according to the interests of the people(s) of Bosnia and Herzegovina. This is the second set of relations of authority and accountability that Petritsch sought to conjure and demonstrate through his use of publicity. The claim to act according to the interests of the population of Bosnia and Herzegovina was often demonstrated when he responded as an addressee of their desires and demands, such as in an open letter to pensioners: "Dear Pensioners, As the winter is knocking at Bosnia and Herzegovina's door, my office is flooded with letters from you, worried that you will not have enough money for food, medicines or heat. I understand your concerns" (OHR 2000e).

Or take the speech delivered by Petritsch to the Circle 99 Association of Intellectuals and described in the introduction to this book, (OHR 2000g), in which he argued that citizens should vote in an upcoming election. It shows that he cultivated a sense of accountability with an undifferentiated Bosnian public by directly articulating the contradiction behind such a call to vote coming from him: "Do the powers of the High Representative make a mockery of the whole elections process . . . [when laws] can be imposed whenever he or she wishes it?" In his response to this question, he repeated that his powers were necessary because of the transitory temporality which Bosnia and Herzegovina inhabited—"extraordinary powers for an extraordinary time"—while professing his goal to see Bosnia and Herzegovina return to an ordinary time when his presence would no longer be needed. Until that happened, he would be ready to exercise his powers, but he foregrounded this as part of his responsibility to the international community; at the same time, he also noted that that was "cold comfort to the Bosnian citizen." He furthermore made his points dialogically by commenting upon a series of comics by the cartoonist for *Dnevni Avaz*, a prominent Sarajevo-based daily newspaper, some of which were critical of the OHR. Not only did this perform a kind of accountability as the addressee of a Bosnian public opinion, but it also gave his response to such critiques a kind of cultural authenticity as a coparticipant in the Bosnia and Herzegovina public sphere.

As an addressee of Bosnian desires and opinion, he could switch to take the position of an articulator of the population's interests, such as when he addressed non-Bosnian audiences in speeches outside of the country. More importantly, however, taking the position as an articulator of the interests of an undifferentiated Bosnia and Herzegovina public, or one or another of Bosnia and Herzegovina's ethnically defined peoples, allowed him to dispute Bosnia and Herzegovina officials doing the same thing. This was particularly important when he acted against them, such as when he removed Ante Jelavić from his position as a member of the Bosnian Presidency: "Mr Jelavic is not concerned about the well-being and position of the Croats, the people he allegedly represents, but the well-being and position of extreme nationalists and perhaps even criminal elements in his party. . . . This is of course . . . not what I want. I want the Croats of Bosnia and Herzegovina to participate in and profit from the improvement of conditions here—economic, social and cultural conditions. I will not allow only a few . . . to get richer and richer . . . while ordinary people are left behind" (OHR 2001i).

Discourses of Europe and Democracy

While tacking back and forth between these participant roles, the High Representative also used publicity to deploy the authorizing discourses of Europe and democracy and thereby to monopolize the ability to define what was democratic or European. Indeed, many OHR statements emphasized Petritsch's role in mediating Bosnia and Herzegovina's movement toward its inevitable European future and contextualized his perspectives and actions as aligned with "Europe" and its attendant positive features: wealth, modernity, democracy, civilization, and normality (see Majstorović 2007). He thus often sought to legitimize his criticism and punitive actions by pointing out the un-European nature of others' actions or inactions. For instance, in his decision to remove the Federation Minister of Finance from his position, the High Representative argued that he had to act because the minister, in the face of a significant scandal, had failed to do "what is expected of any Minister of Finance [found in the same position] in . . . Europe" (OHR 2002a). Elsewhere, in assessing a vote taken in the Federation Parliament that went contrary to what he had called for, the High Representative declared "BiH will not be able to get in to Europe with the current arrangements" (OHR 2003). Through this Europeanization strategy various High Representatives downplayed the exercise of the Bonn powers by deflecting the contradiction surrounding the *means* of "imposing democracy" by emphasizing the inherent good of the *ends* of Europe.

A second and overlapping practice was to invoke the discourse of liberal democracy. Much like the Europeanization strategy, democracy was presumed to be a state of being that Bosnia and Herzegovina had yet to achieve, but one for which there was also no alternative. OHR publicity would thus regularly stage impasses that required international action to break. In this way the High Representative often justified his impositions of law or removals of elected officials as necessary by pointing to the illiberal nature and failed democratic relationship between the people of Bosnia and Herzegovina and their political representatives—Bosnia and Herzegovina's politicians were failing to act democratically and Bosnia and Herzegovina's citizenry was failing to hold them accountable:

> It is with considerable regret that the High Representative and the OSCE Head of Mission announce the removal from office of various public officials. These officials have failed the voters who elected them by pursuing anti-Dayton, anti-peace, anti-reconciliation and extra-legal agendas—especially at the local level where their obstructionism hurts the very people they should be helping. They have consistently refused to take ownership of the laws of their own nation by refusing to obey the letter or the spirit of law, regulation and court rulings. . . . All have snubbed the most basic rule of democracy: the rule of law instead of men. Their removal is not just due; it is past due. (OHR 1999a)
>
> The High Representative Carlos Westendorp today removed Nikola Poplasen from the Office of President of Republika Srpska with immediate effect. . . . President Nikola Poplasen has abused his power and blocked the will of the people of Republika Srpska by hindering the implementation of the election results, refusing to abide by the decisions of the National Assembly as well as by consistently acting to impede the formation of a legitimate government supported by the National Assembly. (OHR 1999c)

Analysis of the OHR's use of democracy as a discourse both authorizing such actions and justifying, on other occasions, the refusal to act, points to both the labile nature of democracy discourse and a recombinant approach to democratization. OHR publicity painted a picture of democracy as disaggregated into multiple logics, values, and principles, any one of which, depending upon the specific situation, may be foregrounded over others. This helps explain how democratic values can be used to authorize and justify ostensibly antidemocratic action. Note how the High Representative invoked the democratic principles of the "rule of law" and "will of the people" to justify removing officials who were, presumably, elected as an expression of the will of the very same people. On another occasion, when the High Representative removed an elected Serb official from office for obstructing the return of Muslim refugees to their prewar homes, he foregrounded a source of democratic authority that focuses on governing purpose (the common good) in order to override another source, one based upon procedural and electoral principles. Yet, as the opening vignette of this chapter demonstrated, he could also appeal to democratic principles to refuse to exercise his powers in certain ways, such as establishing Bosnia as a full protectorate of the international community—even though those demanding that he take this measure argued that such a move would support the democratization of the country.

By maintaining the ability to shift between various authorizing positions, and investing his perspectives and actions with the values of Europe and democracy, the High Representative could project an alignment between the desires of a Bosnian public and an authorizing international community.

Discourse of Evaluation

Tacking between these authorizing positions, however, also created a set of instabilities and vulnerabilities. As noted earlier, Petritsch's claims to act in the name of the people(s) of Bosnia and Herzegovina came with an obvious legitimacy deficit: he was an unelected foreigner whose position stood outside of Bosnia and Herzegovina's constitutional order. Moreover, movement between positions created expectations that required management. As the demands to make Bosnia and Herzegovina a full protectorate showed, being an addressee of Bosnian opinion was not something he could choose. Thus a significant amount of time was spent justifying not only when he could, or should, occupy these positions, but also what it meant to occupy them—to enact sets of relations and define or at least delimit what they could signify. My analysis of OHR publicity shows that Petritsch discursively created a dividing line between himself as an "international" and the rest of the people of Bosnia and Herzegovina. Yet he also blurred that line by evoking a certain intimacy with Bosnian desires when claiming to act according to the interests of Bosnia and Herzegovina citizens. This points to the High Representative's use of a discourse of evaluation, through which he sought to create relations of difference between "internationals" and the people(s) of Bosnia and Herzegovina as well as a distribution of agency and responsibility for those categorized as such.

Similar to what Graan noted in his study of postconflict Macedonia (2010), foreign evaluations of Bosnia and Herzegovina politics and society were distinguished by their pedagogical and paternalistic tone in relation to various Bosnia and Herzegovina publics, a tone that relied, in turn, upon authorizing discourses of liberal democracy and Europe. One effect of these evaluations was to differentiate and structure an unequal relationship between foreigners and Bosnians by presenting the (European) foreign speaker as an expert (on Europe and democracy) capable of rendering judgment and the Bosnian as an immature novice still learning (about democracy and what it means to be European).

In addition to producing a hierarchical relationship between "internationals" and Bosnians, foreign evaluations also created democracy and Europe as the unchanging norms against which to measure all developments in Bosnian politics and society. This reinforced the High Representative's attempt to monopolize the ability to define what democracy and Europe meant. Take the following evaluation, which is part of the case study in constitutional reform that I develop later in this chapter. In an open letter entitled "A Chance for the Republika Srpska," published in the Banja Luka–based magazine *Reporter*, Petritsch threatened to assert his powers in precisely the ways he refused to in his mild exchange with the intellectuals:

> What the Republika Srpska [RS] needs is honest and fundamental reform—deeds, not just words. It is clear that in the 7th year of Dayton, the RS is still a nationalistic mono-ethnic structure, an abnormal model of exclusivity where the rule of law has not taken root. Such a community has no place in the Europe of the 21st century. There are many areas in which the RS authorities can do better in order to genuinely serve their citizens and prove to the outside world that the RS is a legitimate part of Bosnia and Herzegovina, which is trying to live up to the commitments of the Dayton Peace Agreement and the requirements of the modern age. . . .
>
> Constitutional reform provides a unique opportunity for the RS to implement fundamental and positive change and to address the danger of its disappearance. The RS is threatened from the inside because it does not live up to European standards, because it does not treat all its citizens with the evenhandedness they are entitled to expect in a multiethnic Entity . . . this is what delegitimises and weakens the RS. But it can prove otherwise. I would also say that this is also a unique opportunity for the RS authorities to demonstrate the essence of ownership, and show that they have the capacity to forge the sort of compromises which are crucial in a multiethnic society such as BiH. . . .
>
> RS citizens, regardless of their ethnic background, want a normal life. They want living standards that correspond to 21st-century Europe.
>
> . . . Let me make it perfectly clear. Without a serious commitment to constitutional, social, economic, return and human-rights reforms, the RS may face disappearance—the behaviour of its leaders will have rendered the Entity economically and politically unsustainable. (OHR 2001a)

Note how this evaluation constructed a distribution of agency and responsibility designed to catalyze action on the part of Republika Srpska authorities toward a set of specific goals. The role of domestic actors, in this case Republika Srpska authorities, is presented as primary and active: demonstrating ownership, proving their commitment, and so forth. When it came to political issues classified as domestic, the role of foreign agencies and actors is presented as secondary, passive, and temporary, as supervising or mediating the actions of Bosnia and Herzegovina officials. It was only when those officials' conduct failed to conform to their expected role—either through inaction or the wrong action—that the HR was forced to take an active role; he never initiated it himself. (Note the implicit threat that closed the above letter, or the final quote from his reply to the intellectuals cited at the outset of this chapter.)

Such a distribution of agency and responsibility allowed Petritsch to frame the exercise of the Bonn powers as necessary but otherwise an exception to the normal order of things. It enabled him to restate the norms of nation-state sovereignty and democratic representation, as well as to transfer responsibility for any given state of affairs away from foreign actors and onto Bosnians, and thereby deflect calls that he act when addressed by members of the Bosnia and Herzegovina population.

Of course, OHR practices of publicity did not happen in a vacuum. In tacking back and forth between authorizing positions, and in deploying the discourses of Europe, democracy, and evaluation, the High Representative assumed a set of opposing interests that would critique him on any number of grounds.

Competing Interpretive Frameworks

Even as some Bosnia and Herzegovina politicians addressed Petritsch as a responsible political authority and exhorted him to exercise the Bonn powers toward particular ends, others cited his unelected status as making his actions illegitimate. Bosnia and Herzegovina officials thus also authorized their own perspectives and actions with the discourse of democracy, but more often they used the discourse of national self-determination and popular sovereignty; this discourse could be deployed to resist, take up, or resignify OHR statements and demands, depending upon the situation.

Thus OHR publicity was constantly contending with others in framing and reframing their own and others' speech and actions in a series of competitive interpretations: Were the OHR's actions best understood as "neocolonial" and "anti-Serb," or were they instead "securing democracy" and modeling "European standards"? Was a vote in the Republika Srpska National Assembly (RSNA) a "vote against Europe" or "protecting the vital national interests of the Serb nation"? OHR publicity sought to create frameworks of reception and interpretation that anticipated others' attempts to frame OHR speech and actions, and provided arguments against these anticipated counterarguments. Although Petritsch's claims to act in the Bosnia and Herzegovina public interest were often fiercely contested, he maintained a robust ability to both force Bosnia and Herzegovina officials to contend with his representations and demobilize opposition to his actions by investing his voicings with the threat of the Bonn powers and the reward of international recognition. Whenever he justified the exercise of the Bonn powers as necessary to break some sort of political impasse, the High Representative also signaled future sanctions if Bosnian speech and conduct failed to meet international expectations.

As mentioned earlier, the OHR also had to contend with other non-Bosnian attempts to shape international opinion and policy in Bosnia and Herzegovina. This included, for example, international NGOs like the International Crisis Group or think tanks like the European Stability Initiative, both of which had offices in Sarajevo and were often run by foreigners who had formerly worked for the OSCE, OHR, or UN. These organizations carried out their own research in Bosnia and Herzegovina and used the results of their research to produce policy recommendations, which they would circulate through the Bosnian press as well as in the foreign press such as the *Wall Street Journal*, *Financial Times*, *The Guardian*, *Le Temps*, or *Frankfurter Allgemeine Zeitung*. These newspapers also included opinion pieces by individual politicians from powerful state sponsors of the OHR like the United States, the EU, Germany, and the United Kingdom. Those other voices usually urged specific actions on the part of the OHR or pushed for an end to the international mission in Bosnia and Herzegovina. The foreign press thus became another site of intervention encounter as the High Representative was compelled to respond to other representatives of "the international community" voicing competitive interpretations of OHR actions: was the High Representative "facilitating peace and democracy" or "running Bosnia like a Raj"? To add another layer of complexity, OHR publicity often had to speak to both audiences—a "domestic" public and an "international" public—and manage competing interpretive frameworks simultaneously.

This was yet another reason why OHR publicity discursively stabilized rather than elided or denied the ambivalence of the High Representative's position. It was also why the OHR constructed an image of postwar Bosnia and Herzegovina as caught in a transitory temporality, a limited state of exception to the nation-state order of things. By 2000, there was increasing "donor fatigue" on the part of major foreign powers and growing pressure to reduce the expensive international presence in Bosnia and Herzegovina and turn over responsibility for major tasks like running elections to the country's institutions. This pressure created a sense of urgency about the changes needed to collapse the transitory temporality and make the Bosnia and Herzegovina state work on its own. This, paradoxically, suggested an expansion of the High Representative's powers of imposition.

It was at this time that a constitutional amendments process came to figure as a key test of the High Representative's ability to manage and resolve these competing demands. I now turn to a few key episodes in this process in order to track how Petritsch sought to bring the process to a conclusion without *imposing* amendments, thus showing that his policy of promoting rule of law and "local ownership" was working—that Bosnia and Herzegovina was a Europeanizing, democratizing *Rechtsstaat* that did not need foreign supervision. His failure to get what he wanted, and eventual decision to impose the constitutional amendments, point to the limits of publicity as a form of governmentality.

A Controversial Court Decision and (In)Direct Governmentality

In June 2000, the State Constitutional Court of Bosnia and Herzegovina handed down its partial ruling on a case initiated by chairman of the presidency of Bosnia and Herzegovina, Alija Izetbegović in 1998. It became known as the "constitutive peoples" ruling, and it found that the constitutions of Bosnia and Herzegovina's two political entities, the Federation and Republika Srpska, contained language that undermined the right of the peoples of Bosnia and Herzegovina to full equality. The particular problematic passages said to be in disagreement with the State Constitution (which was created by the Dayton Agreement and had priority over the entity constitutions) centered on the issue of "constitutive peoplehood"—the definition and delineation of "the people" whose self-determining capacity was foundational to the state. The ruling focused on Article I of the Republika Srpska Constitution, which stated that the Republika Srpska was a "state of the Serb people and of all of its citizens," and grounded the founding of that state in the "natural, inalienable and non-transferable right of the Serb people to self-determination." The Federation Constitution was identified as problematic on a similar basis, particularly the statement that the Federation was made up of "Bosniacs [*sic*] and Croats as constituent peoples as well as Others."

The plaintiffs had argued that by making the Serbs "constitutive" of the Republika Srpska and Bosniaks and Croats "constitutive" of the Federation, the entity constitutions undermined the meaning and function of the constitutive peoples principle that had been included in the State Constitution and placed "multiethnicity" as a foundational principle of all levels of Bosnia and Herzegovina politics.[12]

The stakes were high. Rightly seeing the case as undermining key terms of the separatist Serb state-building project, Republika Srpska legal experts mounted a vigorous but unsuccessful challenge to the case. In its partial decision, it was clear that the court's central concern was whether or not the entity constitutions created a legal and normative context that would hinder the right of refugees to return, particularly those that would constitute an ethnic minority in the areas to which they were returning (so-called minority returnees). The court's ruling thus directly overturned the exclusive claims to self-determination that underwrote Bosnia and Herzegovina's political entities. More importantly, it also ruled that the entity constitutions needed to be changed to ensure that that Bosniaks, Croats, Serbs, and others were "constitutive" in both entities.

As with all common state institutions provided for in the Dayton Agreement, the Constitutional Court's judicial composition itself reflected the "national key" principle of proportional representation, with international oversight. Controversially, the ruling was taken on a 5 to 4 vote: the Bosniak members voted with the three foreign members of the court, and the court's two Serb and two Croat members dissented.

The reaction in the major Bosnian news outlets came swiftly as political actors sought to frame the decision in the terms of popular sovereignty and threat that underwrote the state projects they advocated. Politicians from the Republika Srpska, in particular, signaled their hostility to the ruling, asserting their opposition as synonymous with the will of the Serb people, a people whose very existence, they claimed, was predicated on the existence of the Republika Srpska as a monoethnic political unit. On a page in the Sarajevo daily *Oslobodjenje* dedicated to discussing the decision (July 5, 2000, 5), Republika Srpska president Mirko Šarović pointed to the split nature of the court's decision and argued that the decision amounted to the political will of two whole nations being "outvoted," an outrage assisted by the international community. Former Republika Srpska president (and later convicted war criminal) Biljana Plavšić echoed this sentiment, stating that the decision was "reminiscent of events in 1992 . . . when a whole people (Bosnian Serbs) did not take part in the referendum in which Bosnia and Herzegovina was voted out of the former Yugoslavia." She suggested that this decision represented a revision of the Dayton Agreement and could lead to the abolishment of the Republika Srpska and thus further violent conflict. This set of positions laid the basis for Republika Srpska officials to basically ignore the ruling's requirement to amend the republic's constitution.

The response of the OHR was initially minimal. On the date of the decision, and reflecting his stated interest in building a functioning state based upon the rule of law, Petritsch issued a press release that framed the issue in procedural terms, noting that the court's decision was binding (OHR 2000a). However, in response to statements like those quoted above, the OHR issued a scolding, paternalistic press release in a bid to police the political speech of domestic officials (OHR 2000b).

Aside from these initial press releases, the OHR was relatively silent, noting occasionally that constitutional reform was one of many issues that needed attention after the countrywide elections took place in the fall. Yet in the two months following the elections of November 2000, aside from the formal creation of otherwise moribund constitutional commissions in the entity parliamentary assemblies, nothing happened to bring the entity constitutions in line with the court's ruling. Thus in January 2001, seven months after the initial ruling of the court, Petritsch exercised his powers in a novel way: he issued a decision in order to incite an enactment of "local ownership" over political processes.

The decision essentially recreated the constitutional commissions in each entity and required them to prepare recommendations for the implementation of the Constitutional Court decision within two months (OHR 2001c). As with other decisions, Petritsch argued in the preamble that he was compelled to act in order to overcome an impasse created by politicians who were failing to respond to the court's ruling. He also claimed to be acting to protect all of Bosnia and Herzegovina's citizens against the discrimination that existed in the absence of constitutional reform.

The decision and its justification embodied an ambivalent logic: it invoked democratic values like the rule of law and involved actors with democratic legitimacy, but it was imposed by an unelected official. The High Representative declared that each commission would have sixteen members, chosen by him from among those elected to sit in the entity assemblies. He emphasized that the creation of these commissions and his assertion over their form and composition were not to be construed as dictating "the way in which the said partial Decision of the Constitutional Court shall be implemented." That was to be decided by Bosnia and Herzegovina officials, not foreigners. He also stressed that foreign intervention into constitutional matters was of a temporary, "interim," and isolated nature. In other words, he went to great pains to cast his role as passively mediating rather than actively dictating. It was the first time that he exercised the Bonn powers in this way, to initiate a governmental process and compose a group of people to carry out the process. Of course, in order for constitutional reform to be a convincing enactment of "local ownership," it required the active participation of Bosnia and Herzegovina officials—neither participation nor the end result could be imposed.

The existence of the Bonn powers influenced the way in which Bosnia and Herzegovina authorities calculated risks and benefits to cooperating with international expectations. The benefits included financial resources and the kind of domestic political capital that came with international recognition. This was clearly the calculation of the Alliance for Change, a disparate collection of nonnationalist parties that had ruled in the Federation and State government since 2000 under the visible sponsorship of key foreign powers. The risks to going against international expectations had been demonstrated by past removals of politicians from office.

But the hazards of cooperation were also present. In this case, the constitutional reform process threatened to erode a core foundation of legitimacy for Republika Srpska politicians, who had thus far taken the process as an opportunity to enact their own ongoing performance of national self-determination by criticizing and then ignoring the court ruling. Publicity was one of the sites and instruments through which these benefits and hazards were negotiated, as became clear in the endgame of the amendments process that played out over the first few months of 2002.

The Stakes Are Raised

Despite the hope that his January 2001 decision would see the amendments outlined and adopted in a swift manner, by year's end no visible progress had been made. With the end of his term as High Representative just half a year away, the issue came to be seen by Petritsch as a referendum on his tenure, and toward the end of 2001 he sought to catalyze action on the amendments process.

One example was the letter "A Chance for the Republika Srpska" quoted above, which was the conclusion of a series of actions and pronouncements that focused attention on the Republika Srpska as the source of obstruction to progress on numerous fronts, including the amendments process. In interviews and press conferences, Petritsch threatened sanctions while relentlessly criticizing Republika Srpska officials for risking isolation from Europe and not following the rule of law. He also sought to contain a familiar counterargument:

> In my discussions with RS officials, I often hear the argument that this or that cannot be done because "the people" are against it. Firstly, I do not believe this. "The people's will" is often used as a convenient excuse for obstructionism that is in the sole interest of officials who want to protect their personal interests. Take, for example, the neutral license plates. When we negotiated them in 1997, RS leaders such as Krajisnik predicted violence and demonstrations by "the people." As it turned out,

"the people" was eagerly queuing up for the new plates once they were launched. (OHR 2001b)

It was in this context that in late January 2002 leaders from the eight largest political parties from both entities met at Mrakovica in the Kozara mountains to discuss the amendments and significant agreement was reached. However, when little progress was made afterward on a few sticking points, and stating that his role was only to "facilitate and mediate," Petritsch hosted what his office called Bosnia's "tryst with destiny" (OHR 2002b), a seventy-hour marathon round of negotiation between the leaders of the eight parties. In an effort to frame this as an exercise in "local ownership" of state political processes, photos of the meetings were made available to the press and showed party leaders (and Petritsch) in various scenes, "working together," "in negotiation," and even laughing. At the press conference announcing the conclusions of the negotiation, photos show Petritsch at a podium, surrounded by the party representatives. Whether these images show him as a leader or a mere mediator is open to interpretation.

As a result of this marathon session, most of the major parties in each entity signed what became known as the Mrakovica-Sarajevo Agreement on "mutually acceptable principles and provisions." Petritsch, the US ambassador, and the Spanish ambassador (representing the EU) signed as witnesses. These principles had to be concretized in the recommendations of the entity constitutional commissions and then presented to the respective entity legislative assemblies to be voted upon. In the Republika Srpska, this process did not play out as the OHR hoped for, and it found itself outmaneuvered and bumping up against the limits of its "ownership" strategy.

"Outvoting" and the Republika Srpska National Assembly Amendments

Almost immediately upon returning to Banja Luka, representatives from the Republika Srpska publicly played down the binding nature of the Mrakovica-Sarajevo Agreement, instead calling it a good starting point for discussion. Having gained international recognition and restated their status as indispensable players in Bosnian politics, they now sought to prevent appearing to have undermined the Serb state project by presenting themselves as having contained the potential damage to the Republika Srpska (International Crisis Group 2002, 8). They also made pronouncements that signaled their continuing opposition to the court's decision, even while claiming they were complying with it.

In the days between the signing of the Mrakovica-Sarajevo Agreement and the session in which the RSNA was to vote on the amendments, the Bosnian media was full of assessments by Republika Srpska politicians and their supporters about what effect the amendments would have on the future of the Republika Srpska. Important justification for resisting the Mrakovica-Sarajevo Agreement was provided publicly by Serb members of the State Constitutional Court. In an issue of *Glas Srpski*, court member Vitomir Popović argued that the principles in the agreement and the corresponding constitutional amendments could have dire economic consequences: "Probably, they will be accompanied by demands to abolish the hymn, flag, coat of arms, and all [state] characteristics of the RS. . . . Besides that, a large number of our people will be left without work in all state and public structures" (*Glas Srpski*, April 4, 2002).

Casting this issue as a potential repeat of the "oppression" against Bosnian Serbs by Bosnian Croats and Bosniaks was clearest in the deployment of the discourse of "outvoting." On one newspaper's opinion page, a member of the RSNA Constitutional Commission, Branko Morait, delegitimized the commission's recommendations by repeating an argument associated with the lead-up to the 1990s war. At that time, Serb nationalist politicians claimed that two of Bosnia's peoples (Croats and Muslims) had "outvoted" the Serb people when deciding the question of Bosnia's independence; Morait argued that the amendments process was threatening to repeat this violation of the "will of the Serb people" and could thus lead to a repeat of the violence of the war (*Nezavisne Novine*, April 4, 2002).

News media also reported upon a set of meetings between Republika Srpska governmental authorities and representatives of Bosnian Serb military veterans. Veteran representatives claimed that the Mrakovica-Sarajevo Agreement dishonored the blood spilt in "the centuries-long struggle of the Serb people for freedom and State independence" (*Glas Srpski*, April 2, 2002). They characterized the agreement in terms that cast Muslims as battlefield enemies and argued that it was not the result of "compromise" by Serb, Muslim, and Croat political parties but was an imposition of the international community. After meeting with veteran representatives, the speaker of the RSNA, Dragan Kalinić, noted that they disagreed with the agreement "offered by the High Representative" and vowed that they would never allow the disappearance of the Republika Srpska.

Having publicly laid the basis for resisting the amendments process as an undemocratic imposition of hostile Bosniaks and their foreign allies, and having sacralized this resistance with the invocation of the blood spilt by Serbs in the 1990s war, the stage was set. In the legislative session on April 4 convened in the RSNA for the specific purpose of debating and then adopting the provisions of the Mrakovica-Sarajevo Agreement, the speaker exploited a procedural loophole to propose an alternative set of amendments, drawn up in secret and signed by all sixty-eight Serb deputies (82 percent of all deputies in the RSNA). The alternative set departed significantly from the Mrakovica-Sarajevo Agreement, and even appeared to violate the Dayton Agreement in the very terms struck down by the Constitutional Court decision (International Crisis Group 2002, 12). In doing so, the majority in the RSNA demonstrated their unwillingness to go along with the expectations created by the OHR's managed process or with the Constitutional Court's decision. When the constitutional commission rejected the alternative amendments (as had been expected), it triggered a procedure whereby both the constitutional commission's draft amendments and the new alternatives came up for a vote and the latter passed without discussion, despite attempts by non-Serb deputies to postpone and later to disrupt the vote.

The Republika Srpska political leadership had, in other words, used an internationally instigated event of democracy at work and local ownership to orchestrate a performance of resistance and collective Serb self-determination. Afterward, various Republika Srpska party leaders publicly cast themselves as having fended off an attack on their state project and as peacemakers for having avoided the violence that such an attack would have inaugurated if it had succeeded, and as having mitigated the anti-European accusations of the "international community" (International Crisis Group 2002, 9).

The strategy of the High Representative to use publicity in tandem with the Bonn powers lay in tatters. One of the governing parties in the Federation who had wholeheartedly supported the Mrakovica-Sarajevo Agreement publicly threatened to withdraw its commitment to it if the High Representative did nothing about the amendments passed by the RSNA (International Crisis Group 2002, 11). Emboldened by the RNSA vote, Bosniak and Croat nationalist parties in the Federation House of Representatives opposed the amendments and thus prevented them from passing in that entity as well. On April 11, Petritsch publicly responded to calls that he take action by stating that the international community wanted only a mediating and not an implementing role (*Nezavisne Novine*, April 11, 2002).

Such statements notwithstanding, a series of events, all conspicuously documented and circulated in OHR press releases, made it clear that plans were underway to impose the amendments. As a signatory and thus self-described "guarantor" of the Mrakovica-Sarajevo Agreement, Petritsch issued a deadline of April 18 for it to be fulfilled by both the Federation and Republika Srpska legislative bodies. On April 10, he consulted with the steering board of the PIC, which gave him its full backing. Two days later, the ambassadors of the United States, United Kingdom, Germany, Italy, and France conveyed to the four party representatives of the Republika Srpska that the RSNA amendments did not fulfill the Mrakovica-Sarajevo Agreement. On April 19, Petritsch was forced to do what he had spent nearly two years avoiding: he imposed the Mrakovica-Sarajevo Agreement amendments upon the Republika Srpska and the Federation constitutions (OHR 2002c).

Conclusion

To some degree, the failure of internationally mediated constitutional reform to deliver a convincing performance of "local ownership" over state processes was rooted in an instability created by the Dayton Agreement, particularly its partial recognition and cobbling together of multiple state projects. The end goal of "democratization" and "local ownership" of the state faltered when the "locals" disputed what state it was they were demonstrating ownership over and in which they were to enact democratic relations of representation and accountability. This was particularly the case here because in demonstrating "ownership" local politicians were required to undermine a core basis for their authority, which was a commitment to a state project that embodied Serb national self-determination.

This instability is the result, in part, of the UN order of nation-states in which Bosnia exists: an order committed to steady state existence, where nation-states cannot (legally) expand their territory and in which all warfare between nations and states, especially wars of conquest, is outlawed. Thus once Bosnia and Herzegovina had gained international recognition as an independent state, the international response to the war in Bosnia and Herzegovina (and ethnic conflict in Kosovo and sectarian violence in Iraq) was international "state-building" under the sign of democracy, where "the people" are supposed to be sovereign. This put the High Representative in postwar Bosnia and Herzegovina in a tricky position as an unelected foreigner pursuing state-building and democratization goals in a context of unfinished state projects, where internationals and locals alike sought to ground their authority in some definition of "the people." What I have shown here are some of the innovations through which the High Representative sought to legitimately pursue these goals in the face of two contradictions—what I have called the democratization and state-building paradoxes.

Publicity was indispensable to this task: It was an instrument to invoke the "international community" as a source of authority; to conjure and contest the authorizing abstractions of democracy and popular sovereignty—the people and its will, public opinion, and so forth; to enact relations of representation and accountability; to define a distribution of "international" and "local" responsibility in relation to political action; to proliferate normative understandings of democracy and nation-state sovereignty even while violating those norms; and to exercise symbolic authority by circulating and attempting to monopolize the authorizing discourses of democracy and Europe. It was also a means of governmentality used to incite actions along prescribed pathways. By focusing on the OHR's practices of publicity, I have uncovered a political logic of ambivalence and outlined its advantages and limits as a framework for transformation.

This analysis thus suggests that any study of international state- or nation-building, or democratization, should include attention to mass-mediated encounters and the practices of publicity that constitute them. Indeed, a brief examination of the online archives of press releases from the Iraq Coalition Provisional Authority and of the Daily Briefings of the UN Transitional Administration of East Timor[13] reveals rich repositories of political communication and governmentality centered on challenges of authority and legitimacy similar to those faced by the OHR.

This leads me to question the easy conclusions behind some of the commonest critiques of international intervention. One explanation for why publicity has been overlooked in studies of intervention lies in how scholars and commentators have related their critique to the paradoxes and contradictions of international intervention. Indeed, most critical writing uses a discourse of (neo)colonialism or (neo)imperialism, taking the twin paradoxes that I detail in this chapter as the endpoint of analysis and beginning of critique. Yet, as Cooper and Burbank (2012, 239) have noted, those evoking the language of empire are often more interested in discrediting, praising, or otherwise influencing such intervention projects and their government sponsors than with understanding what is unfolding on the ground (Chandler 2006; Ignatieff 2003; Knaus and Martin 2003). Such critiques are inherently normative, relying upon the categorical distinctions of nation-state order and its forms of popular sovereignty for their description of "foreign" domination over "domestic" populations. They are thus likely to look past instances like the opening vignette about a Bosnian desire for the suspension of ostensibly democratic institutions and duly elected representatives because they do not easily fit the narrative of (neo)imperial domination. Such forms of critique entail categorical and normative assumptions about how "democracy" and "the state" should function and quickly conclude that Petritsch's rejection of international responsibility for Bosnian politics must be an instance of "empire in denial" (Chandler 2006), a rhetorical smokescreen or psychological blind spot that renders the exercise of power unaccountable. To focus on paradox or contradiction in this way is to hurry to the *ought* rather than to dwell with the *is*. I would argue that it is much more revealing to take seriously Petritsch's concerns about the contradictions of his position, which he regularly reflected upon, and explore how he attempted to manage them. I suggest here that rather than taking contradiction and paradox as the engine of a normative critique (and thus the end of the story of how to understand international intervention), we should see them as the engine of pragmatic action—that is, the beginning of an account of international intervention. After all, it was in confronting and managing these contradictions that the actual politics of intervention unfolded and political innovations were produced.

If operating according to the logic of ambivalence was one innovative attempt to accommodate the contradictions and tensions of Petritsch's position in intervention encounters, then another was what we might call recombinant democratization. This refers to the way in which the High Representative promoted the democratization of Bosnia and Herzegovina by appealing to one principle, value, or logic associated with democracy in order to justify actions that would appear to violate other democratic principles, values, or logics. In one way, it shows how the High Representative sought both to make the discourse of democracy hegemonic and normative and to maintain a monopoly over how that discourse was used. It is a sign of its hegemonic status that while the issue of whether the High Representative's actions were democratic or not was fiercely contested, rarely if ever did anyone question whether democracy ought to be the normative standard by which the legitimacy of political action was measured.

Interestingly, others concerned with international democracy promotion have argued for a recombinant approach to match what they call "recombinant authoritarianism" (Heydemann and Leenders 2011). This is a term used to describe the resilience of authoritarian regimes, the way those regimes can accommodate contradiction and how they remain in power despite international democracy promotion efforts in places like Iran and Syria. They suggest that the limits of such efforts are the result of normative Western political frameworks and the way that they posit, for example, the separation of state and society. They argue that such frameworks turn out to be poor indicators of actual political relations in these countries, and how what might appear to be contradictory to a Western observer may not be so to those socialized in such a system. Thus, democracy promotion efforts that follow such normative frameworks will have only a limited impact. Instead, they suggest that international institutions should not shy away from pursuing democratization efforts by combining principles and practices that may appear (normatively) contrary—under such circumstances democracy promotion requires a flexibility commensurate with that of authoritarian regimes.[14]

Of course, what I have described here are a set of OHR practices that contain just such a flexibility and were resilient in the face of normative contradiction—but rather than taking place in a political context which international efforts needed to penetrate and transform with more democracy, this international recombinant politics was pursued in the very name of democracy. As it turns out, it was a limited innovation.

One thing all post–Cold War interventions share is a stated commitment to the temporary nature of foreign administration (Zaum 2012). The production of a time-space of suspension is not uncommon in arguments that seek to legitimize relations of rule on the grounds of necessary transformation. As Chakrabarty reminds us, imperial warrants to rule were based upon claims that "some historical time of development and civilization (colonial rule and education to be precise) had to pass" before colonized peoples were ready for self-rule, and this consigned the colonies to an "imaginary waiting room of history" (2000, 8), always caught up in a temporality of "not yet." Povinelli (2011) noted the "temporal structure of limbo" that underwrote a settler-state program to transform Aboriginal life in late liberal Australia, in which the hardship and suffering instigated by the Intervention (as the state program was called) was discursively and ethically bracketed in the present, and legitimized as a necessary sacrifice when measured from the perspective of a future in which the transformation will have been completed.

The transitory temporality constructed by OHR publicity shared qualities with both of these contexts: the paternalistic tone and the vocabulary of deficiency inherent in much foreign evaluation are strongly reminiscent of justifications for imperial relations of rule. And like Povinelli's case, the means/ends contradictions of the OHR's use of the Bonn powers were not so much to be overcome or resolved as to simply disappear. Once transformation had taken place, the OHR's position would be obsolete and the contradictions would disappear with the OHR.

But such "states of exception" and transitory temporalities are achievements, produced by practices that include their own instabilities and performative requirements. Moreover, in a point mostly overlooked in the critical literature, once states of exception are posited and brought into being, they can be hard to undo. Petritsch needed the participation of elected politicians as the normative representatives of the popular will in state government for the performances of local ownership and democracy at work. If successful, such performances would demonstrate that Bosnia and Herzegovina was a state that could work on its own and permit the withdrawal of the international community and collapse the state of exception. His stick was the Bonn powers and other forms of international disapproval, and his carrot was international recognition, financial resources, and the promise of "joining Europe."

Some Bosnian politicians, however, decided that dwelling in such limbo had its advantages, and they worked within it to create a distribution of political responsibility to their own benefit. Under these conditions they worked through repeated encounters to gain or maintain recognition as indispensable players in Bosnian politics. When participation threatened their base of authority or power, however, they could and did refuse to cooperate and instead cast themselves as defenders of the popular will and national self-determination against foreign oppressors or the state projects of hostile ethnic Others. More recent examples suggest that such performances of resistance have become a routinized part of Bosnian politics, making the international community a useful, if not indispensable, antagonist for Bosnian politicians seeking legitimacy (see Leroux-Martin 2014;

Toal 2013). Moreover, such resistance worked to keep the question of state form and thus the transitory temporality open, despite attempts to bring it to a close. Each collapsed internationally supervised effort, and each exercise of the Bonn powers, was an implicit restatement of the need for an international presence.[15]

But occupying this suspended temporality could not go on indefinitely. In important ways, to declare a state of exception is to maintain a norm. In postwar Bosnia, the way in which the OHR used publicity to produce this state of exception contained its own eroding condition as a position of legitimacy and thus shrinking temporal horizon as grounds for action, since to maintain norms in this way was to draw attention to their violation. Indeed, although the position of High Representative remains in Bosnia and Herzegovina at the time of this writing, and the OHR continues to be a presence in Bosnia's news media, the exercise of the Bonn powers has basically ceased. Since 2009, the few decisions that have issued from the OHR have been to terminate, repeal, or suspend the application of earlier decisions. Ambivalence had become unsustainable.

2

THE USES OF HISTORY

Recontextualization and International Intervention

What would post-Dayton Bosnia-Herzegovina be without the foreign factor? It would not exist at all.

—Nerzuk Ćurak

On March 29, 2001, the OHR issued a press release entitled "HDZ again Rejects Offer for Dialogue." In it, Petritsch expressed concern that his attempts to engage the Croatian Democratic Union of Bosnia-Herzegovina (*Hrvatska Demokratska Zajednica* or HDZ), the largest Bosnian Croat political party, had been rejected. Most prominently, he pointed out that the HDZ had thus far refused his request to nominate candidates for two vacant Croat seats on the Federation Constitutional Commission which he had created two months earlier—seats he had been holding open for them. The press release reminded readers that these commissions were set up in January to "draft proposals for the implementation of the Decision of the BiH Constitutional Court on the constituent status of all three BiH peoples in both Entities," noting that "This groundbreaking ruling will ensure that the rights of Croats and Bosniaks in Republika Srpska, and the rights of Serbs in the Federation are respected." The press release continued:

> As the High Representative has stated many times, he is mandated to, and takes a personal interest in discussing all issues of concern with BiH Croats, including HDZ officials who abide by the law and the constitutions of this country. He refuses, however, to enter into any dialogue with representatives of extra-legal, unconstitutional structures.
>
> While the HDZ tries to make the public believe that it is ready for dialogue, it thus far has used every opportunity to prevent any meaningful discussion. In the same manner, it claims that its elected repre-

> sentatives have been prevented from taking up their seats in the legal institutions, while the HDZ itself has decided to boycott the legal institutions of the Federation and the State of BiH.
>
> The essence of every democracy is the resolution of problems through discussions and negotiations within the legal and constitutional institutions. The implementation of the Constitutional Court's ruling will entail changes to the internal structures of the two Entities. The HDZ has consistently claimed this to be its goal. However, in practice the party has refused to participate in the ongoing legal process. As its activities show, it is ready to sacrifice the economic and social future of its constituency because a few within its ranks find the lack of law and order to be more profitable than rule of law.
>
> The High Representative calls on all HDZ officials to start sincerely representing the interests of their constituency. (OHR 2001e)

Even with its strong critical wording, the press release only hinted at the political crisis Petritsch was facing. The HDZ was, in fact, in open rebellion against the OHR, claiming that it and the Dayton structures it supervised were "anti-Croat"; it was engaged in a boycott of state and entity institutions and refused to recognize their authority; and it had set about creating parallel parastate institutions of "Croat self-rule." It had even persuaded or intimidated Croat members of the Federation military to leave their barracks and pledge loyalty to these new institutions.

In his attempts to put down this rebellion, Petritsch consistently referred to the constitutional commissions that he had created. Drawing attention to these commissions not only allowed him to contest the claims by the HDZ circulating in the press that the international community and the state and entity institutions were anti-Croat. It also allowed him to make the counterclaims that it was the HDZ that did not care about Croat interests because it did not participate in a process designed to secure those interests, and that its actions were not only illegal but also illegitimate because contrary to the values of democracy and the rule of law (values represented by the constitutional commissions that Petritsch had set up).

Such claims and mass-mediated encounters should be familiar by now, another example of publicity which shows rather starkly how the High Representative had to pursue goals of transformation like promoting democracy and "local ownership" in a context filled with others pursuing their own political objectives. Sometimes these goals overlapped, but more often they clashed—sometimes violently. Here was an instance of a political party that did not want "ownership" over political institutions if it was excluded from government (which it had been for the first time since it formed and contested elections in 1990). Instead, it would create its own institutions to exercise ownership over. The HDZ leadership and the High Representative were thus engaged in a struggle over the authority and legitimacy—and existence—of the Dayton state-form.

I have already described how the High Representative had to constantly work to persuade others of the legitimacy of his perspectives and his actions, and the illegitimacy of the perspectives and actions of his opponents. One of the ways he did this, as illustrated above and in chapter 1, was to discursively align his perspectives and actions with the positive values of democracy and Europe, or align the speech and action of his opponents with the absence or violation of such values. As I argued in the previous chapter, this was part of an ongoing attempt to exercise symbolic power by monopolizing these authorizing discourses, to hold for himself the ability to define what was and was not democratic and European.

This kind of symbolic politics, this struggle over how to interpret the meaning of speech and action, points to another source of uncertainty and instability that shapes the practice and outcomes of intervention encounters in Bosnia and elsewhere: foreigners like Petritsch often had to pursue their goals using cultural forms and historical materials—and according to a timeline—not of their choosing. The notion of *konstitutivnost naroda* (the state-constituting capacity of a nationally-defined people) was just such a historically and culturally specific principle, one that Petritsch ended up using in his efforts to promote political reform and "local ownership," and to undermine local nationalist separatists. But such concepts can bear the traces of their former contexts, opening up their use to multiple interpretations; this can complicate the attempts of foreigners like Petritsch to redefine them more narrowly for specific purposes. This serves as a reminder of how intervention encounters are sites of cultural creativity, but unpredictably so: taking a principle like *konstitutivnost naroda* out of one historical, interactional, or institutional context and repurposing it for use in another can serve to alter the Bosnian social and political landscape, just not always in the ways hoped for.

My point is not simply to point to an instability in intervention encounters, one that limits or affects the ways in which they unfold, it is also to offer a method to understand how and why things unfold in the ways that they do. For this, I draw upon a framework used by linguistic anthropology to study "texts in context," particularly the processes of *decontextualization* and *recontextualization*—that is, the extracting of discourse from one setting or context to fit it into another. I proceed from the insight that texts (or other discursive units) gain their meaning only in relationship to their situational (interactional, sociohistorical) contexts, and that such contexts themselves are constituted meaningfully only in relationship to such texts. Such texts are often lifted out of or detached from their interactional (or sociohistorical) setting—decontextualized—and then made to fit elsewhere, or recontextualized (Bauman and Briggs 1990; Silverstein and Urban 1996).

For linguistic anthropologists, tracking this process provides a way to understand "what the recontextualized text brings with it from its earlier context(s) and what emergent form, function, and meaning it is given as it is recentered" (Bauman and Briggs 1990, 75). As Gal has shown, those who recontextualize a text "can make sure that the earlier context leaves its mark, a trace of where the text has been. The gap between the earlier context and newer—the earlier form of the text and a later (always partial) repetition or imitation of it—can be highlighted or denied, can be valorized or denigrated" (2003, 96–97). This, in turn, has effects on the degree to which such texts can persuasively serve as the basis for various kinds of social action.

It is also important to note that recontextualization processes do not only change the meaning of the text. As others have shown, when texts move like this, both text *and* context are transformed (Bauman and Briggs 1990; Gal 2003).

Focusing on decontextualization and recontextualization processes in international intervention offers a method for investigating what happens when the agents of intervention attempt to use a historically and culturally specific form and, in essence, repurpose it to serve particular ends. In this case, Petritsch was using *konstitutivnost naroda* to authorize his speech, actions, and specific goals of political transformation. In this chapter, I revisit the constitutional reform process of the previous chapter as a study in the possibilities and limits of recontextualization as a mode of political transformation.

Doing so, however, means investigating how, where, and when concepts come to mean what they mean; it means delving into details of history, culture, and politics, precisely the kind of knowledge that many agents (or scholars) of intervention do not prioritize or have much patience for. And yet, I argue if we want to understand the complexity of intervention encounters and their effects, we need to be willing to confront the social, cultural, and political nature of encounters and projects that is otherwise erased in a technocratic framework. In the case under investigation here, this means locating the *konstitutivnost naroda* principle in the cultural and political context of Bosnia's recent past, first turning to the Second World War and the socialist era that it inaugurated, when the *konstitutivnost naroda* concept legitimized the statehood of a common, multiethnic, socialist Bosnia-Herzegovina within a multiethnic socialist Yugoslavia. Here the concept was contextualized within a socialist master narrative that defined the state as (1) founded through the joint struggle and sacrifice of a multiethnic, antifascist partisan force; (2) co-constituted by the joint self-determination of Serbs, Croats, and Muslims; and (3) expressing a dual form of popular sovereignty—that of its nations and working peoples, with pride of place given to the latter.

Equally important is to then turn to a second historical moment, the lead up to the 1990s war, when Bosnian Serb politicians attempted to repurpose the concept to legitimize a monoethnic separatist state project—that is, to attempt their own decontextualization and recontextualization, with mixed results. Investigating these processes allows me to identify the various semantic associations the term carried into the postwar period, and the stakes of the constitutional court's decision. I then show how and why it became unexpectedly entangled with international intervention processes of transformation, and with what consequences, both for the meaning of *konstitutivnost naroda* and for post-Dayton Bosnian politics. In particular, the gap between Petritsch's interpretation of the *konstitutivnost naroda* principle and amendments process and other interpretations grounded in the constitutive people principle's former contexts created a space for critical perspectives that revealed the limits of foreign authority in this mode. These other perspectives were often antithetical to those that the High Representative intended. Exploring them helps explain how although Petritsch tried to turn the *konstitutivnost naroda* principle and the amendments process into symbolic indexes of democratic and European standards, the principle today has been widely recognized as one of the greatest obstacles to the country's democratization and its "path to Europe."

"The Most Complicated Country in Europe": The Genesis of the Socialist State of Bosnia and Herzegovina in the Second World War

The Second World War was the core foundational and legitimizing event in the creation of socialist Yugoslavia, and Bosnia and Herzegovina played a prominent role in that event. It was in Bosnia that Josip Broz Tito's communist-led Partisans made their first significant gains against German, Italian, and Fascist Croatian forces, and it was from Bosnian territory that Tito coordinated much of the Partisan uprising in other parts of Yugoslavia. It was in Bosnia, as "liberated territory" under Partisan control, that the first Revolutionary Parliament of the Yugoslav Peoples took place in 1942 to establish the "authority of the Yugoslav peoples" under Communist Party leadership. This was followed with a meeting in 1943 in central Bosnia, where the political and legal foundations were laid for the socialist state of Yugoslavia.

It was also in Bosnia, because of its ethnically diverse population and the interethnic violence of the early part of the war, that the "brotherhood and unity" solution to the "national question" was formulated. As one Slovenian representative put it at the first meeting of the Anti-Fascist Council for the National Liberation of Bosnia-Herzegovina in late 1943,

> Bosnia is the true center of a Yugoslavia which will be an independent, democratic, federal country. Bosnia is the source and center of a policy that will have to be realized in a future, free Yugoslavia. Bosnia is a country where three peoples from three faith traditions live: Catholic, Islamic, and Orthodox. It is the most complicated country in Europe, but if the brotherhood of Serbs, Croats, and Muslims can be realized here, it will not be hard to realize the same between Serb, Croats, Slovenes, [and] Macedonians [in the other republics]. (Josip Vidmar quoted in Babić and Otašević 1970, 62)

The complicated nature of the national question in Bosnia was a reference not just to its ethnic diversity but to its recent experience of interethnic violence. At the beginning of the Second World War, the territory of Bosnia and Herzegovina was formally annexed as part of the Nazi German and Italian-installed Fascist Independent State of Croatia (*Nezavisna država hrvatske*, or NDH), whose rulers and followers were more popularly known as the Ustaše. NDH modes of rule and ideology were heavily influenced by Nazi race theory, and those of the Serb nationality and Orthodox faith (as well as Jews and Roma) were deemed dangerous to the purity of the Catholic Croatian national body. Jews were targeted for extermination and Serbs or Orthodox Christians were given the possibility of "converting" to Catholicism or being subjected to forced deportations and mass killings. Muslims in Bosnia were deemed to be "Croats of the Islamic faith" and the "flower of the Croatian nation." Although Muslims were supposedly equal partners in the new order of the NDH, the reticence if not opposition by Muslim elites to certain aspects of Ustaše practices eventually led to their falling out of favor with the NDH.

There were two domestic armed groups resisting Axis forces in Bosnia and the rest of Yugoslavia: the communist-led Partisans, and the Serbian Četniks, representatives of the royal Yugoslav government-in-exile. While there was some early cooperation between the two groups under pressure from Allied forces, the Četnik leadership saw the greater threat to their aims in Tito's communists, and eventually collaborated with the Italians, German, and even Ustaše forces against the Partisans. Together with a commitment to a Serbian nationalist ideology that led to the wholesale slaughter of Muslims in Eastern Bosnia when it fell under their control, this collaboration with Axis forces made the Četniks—together with the Croatian Ustaše—the iconic domestic representatives of the fascist enemy against which the Partisans defined their popular revolution of "brotherhood and unity."

Given the NDH targeting of the Serb population in Bosnia, the Partisan ranks were at first filled largely by Bosnian Serbs, but soon came to attract large numbers of Muslims and some Croats. In particular it was the antifascist "brotherhood and unity" rhetoric—made persuasive by the multiethnic organization of Partisan leadership positions and a conscious refrain from attacks on Muslim or Croat populations that fell under Partisan control, in striking contrast to both Ustaše and Četnik actions—that offered the inhabitants of Bosnia and Herzegovina the most compelling way out of the fratricidal mass killings that gripped the country in the early 1940s. References to Ustaše and Četniks as domestic adversaries were part of a critical position taken by the Partisans to define the enemy *ideologically* rather than *ethnically*, opening the doors for anyone—even some who fought with the Ustaše and Četniks—to join their ranks.

Constituting Statehood for Bosnia and Herzegovina after the Second World War

As the groundwork for the political and territorial form of socialist Yugoslavia was being laid during the Second World War, a series of key positions regarding the status of Bosnia and Herzegovina were articulated by the Communist Party leaders of the Partisan movement. The first linked the self-determination of Muslims, Serbs, and Croats in Bosnia and Herzegovina—and the existence of Bosnia and Herzegovina itself as a single political unit—to their participation in the Partisan cause and membership in the socialist community of Yugoslav peoples. In what became a common (and convenient) interpretation, communist leaders argued that membership in a communist state as part of Yugoslavia was, in fact, what the people of Bosnia had already shown that they desired, through their "mass participation" in the People's Liberation Struggle, as the Second World War came to be called. At the Jajce meeting, where the political and legal shape of socialist Yugoslavia was formulated, delegates from Bosnia argued that the "mass common participation" of Serbs, Croats, and Muslims in the "armed, revolutionary, antifascist struggle" constituted an "armed revolutionary plebiscite" that definitively affirmed the desire for a "common life" in Bosnia and Herzegovina, and that their "common mass participation" protected the equal position of the country with the other national units of the Yugoslav federation. As one state-sanctioned history of the period put it,

> it was by supporting without reservation the solution of the position of BiH with their mass participation in the People's Liberation Struggle that BiH became, together with Serbia, Croatia, Slovenia, Macedonia and Montenegro, an equal [*ravnopravan*] unit of the socialist community of

> peoples of Yugoslavia. Only in that way was the sovereignty of the Serb, Muslim, and Croat peoples guaranteed in this area. (Babić and Otašević 1970, 11)

As the end of this quotation suggests, it was also at these early meetings that the solution to Bosnia's "national question" was defined and affirmed as the will of its constituent or state-making peoples. A resolution taken at the first meeting meant to lay the political representative framework for postwar Bosnia included a formulation (highlighted in italics) that spells out key terms of constitutive peoplehood for an independent, socialist Bosnia:

> The peoples of BiH through their sole political representative, ZAVNOBIH [*Zemaljsko antifašističko vijeće narodnog oslobođenja BiH* or Anti-Fascist Council for the National Liberation of Bosnia-Herzegovina] desire that their country, *which is neither Serbian, nor Croatian, nor Muslim, but rather equally Serbian and Muslim and Croatian*, to be free and united as blood brothers [*zbratimljen*], in which the full equality and unity of all Serbs, Muslims, and Croats will be secured. (Babić and Otašević 1970, 67)

Images of death and struggle shared by Serb, Muslim, and Croat Partisans during the Second World War should not be underestimated when it comes to understanding the meaning of "brotherhood and unity," as well as the constitution and representation of a united political will that grounded common Bosnian statehood. Lives sacrificed in the Partisan, antifascist cause, and their subsequent narrativization, were powerful for the Communist Party in legitimizing a common Bosnian state and socialist revolution—and in delegitimizing other, monoethnic, nationalist, fascist, or capitalist notions of statehood or political organization. Denitch argues that there was a genuine revulsion against the politics of the prewar elites and leaders, morally discredited because of the fratricidal massacres, among the youth who filled the ranks of the Partisans during the Second World War (1976, 43–46), and in his study of the national question in Yugoslavia, Shoup details how fighting together in the war was crucial to the foundation of a common, multinational Yugoslav (and Bosnian) generation:

> The Partisan movement reared a whole new generation of local and regional cadres, whose first loyalty was to the Yugoslav Party, persons with strong local roots but ready to follow the Party in its essential unitary approach to the national question. In this lay the real secret of the ability of the Communists to overcome the deep contradiction between regional ties and loyalty to Yugoslavia which had been at the root of so many problems of the prewar system. (1968, 91–92)

Securing the Right to National Self-Determination

The affirmation of the right to national self-determination lay at the core of the Yugoslav socialist system. During the Second World War it was decided that the postwar order would replace the prewar Serbian monarchy with a federal system that recognized the separate existence of Yugoslav nations and their sovereign rights. In a neat fait accompli that paralleled the approach to Bosnia, Tito both recognized people's right to national self-determination and sovereignty and the right to secede as having been achieved through the resistance to occupiers, but that that same resistance simultaneously constituted their desire to unite in brotherhood and unity in a common federal state.

Audrey Helfant Budding argues that the key to understanding Yugoslav constitutional language on self-determination or constitutive peoples is that it was intended to legitimate the party's leadership and the state form it created; it never imagined the end of such a state or party (2008, 109). Thus, while we find socialist Yugoslavia's founding document citing "the right of every people to self-determination, including the right to secession or to unification with other peoples" (96), Budding points out that the party never sought a clear definition of peoplehood, and that in official documents and discussions there was a "deliberate vagueness and slippage between territorial ideas of nationality and personal or cultural ideas" (108). So while, on the one hand, five of the six republics of the Yugoslav federation (Croatia, Macedonia, Montenegro, Serbia, and Slovenia) could be considered the main homeland of one of Yugoslavia's many nations (Croats, Macedonians, Montenegrins, Serbs, and Slovenes), the "inclusion of Bosnia-Herzegovina and (often) Vojvodina—two regions with heavily mixed populations and no national majority—in its programmatic statements [the Communist Party of Yugoslavia] indicated that in [its] view the 'people' entitled to self-determination could be defined by historic factors as well as ethnonational ones" (95). This indicates the multiple meanings contained in the term *narod* as it appeared in Yugoslav state socialist rhetoric. On the one hand, it refers to "a people" ethnonationally defined. On the other, depending on the context, it can refer to "a people" united by shared historical existence on a territory ("the people of Bosnia and Herzegovina"), common political struggle (*Narodno-oslobodilačka borba*, or "People's Liberation Struggle"), or economic relations (as we will see below in the reference to *radni narod* or "working people").

Any notion of "constitutive peoples" after the Second World War must be understood in the context of legitimizing communist party rule. Given that prewar Yugoslavia had been ruled as a dictatorship by a Serbian monarch, the party had a particular burden to prove that it would counter Serb (or any other) national dominance. This was formally institutionalized at the federal level (and less formally elsewhere) in a proportional representative system that was governed by a principle called the national or ethnic "key" (*nacionalni ključ* or *etnički ključ*). This meant both that each republic (and each constituent people within each republic) was represented on an equal and rotating basis within federal bodies and that each constituent people was represented in the party leadership at the republican and federal levels, in other public institutions within republics (like the university), and within the leadership of those bodies that cut across the republics, like trade unions.

The "national key" was thus designed to remove ethnonational difference as a source of political division, organization, or mobilization. Within Bosnia, this amounted to a rotation of leading positions in government and other public institutions among Muslims, Croats, and Serbs. The rules governing this rotation were largely unwritten but were all part of a conspicuous attention to national equality that was observed by the party. By many indicators, it enjoyed broad popular support.[1]

It would be a mistake, however, to understand the national key concept in socialist Yugoslavia as a quota system with individuals slotted in positions as ethnic representatives. Rather, it was a system designed to demonstrate the commitment to the equality of nations and the multiethnic legitimacy of the Communist Party, particularly in the leadership's structure—individuals were never *ethnic* representatives or representatives of "national interests," but *party* representatives and it was party membership that was the key to their holding of government posts (Andjelić 2003, 39–40).[2]

Insofar as anyone thought about it, then, all people in Bosnia enjoyed the status of constitutive peoplehood. Indeed, the very concept of minority or majority came to be considered illegitimate (Budding 2008, 107). But it would be a significant oversight if we left the story of sovereignty and the achievement of equality and freedom in socialist Yugoslavia to lie solely with ethnonational self-determination.

The War of Liberation as Socialist Revolution: Securing Self-Determination for Working Peoples

The "liberation" achieved in the Second World War was conceived by the party as applying as equally to "working peoples" as to Croats, Muslims, Serbs, and so on. Indeed, the Communist Party of Yugoslavia saw the war as a vehicle for the creation of a new social(ist) order and a revolutionary movement. Propaganda from the war period that targeted the youth in the Bosnian Krajina illustrates how the fight for brotherhood and unity was merged with the struggle for more familiar socialist goals. It also shows how the freedom and self-determination that came to Bosnia's national peoples through "brotherhood and unity" was discursively associated with the freedom and self-government of its working peoples:

> Through their current political activities, their voluntary labor, and new forms of labor, the youth of Yugoslavia are guarding and strengthening the brotherhood and unity of our peoples—the lasting heritage of the People's Liberation Struggle. They will fight against all who would weaken and destroy that unity in any way, or who would trample down or expropriate the right of the working class to self-rule. It is solely upon these foundations that the material basis and defensive force of our self-governing society can be built and further strengthened, and the right to self-government and a better life of working people can be realized. (Quoted in Kapetanović 1972, 73)

As the 1974 Yugoslav constitution shows, the system envisioned a form of *dual* sovereignty, the bearers of which were the "working class and all working people," on the one hand, and the "nations and nationalities" of Yugoslavia, on the other. Moreover, the preamble to the 1974 constitution of the Socialist Republic of Bosnia and Herzegovina makes clear that pride of place was given to "working peoples and citizens" and "self-managing socialism" as the social body and principles whose authority comprised the legitimacy of the constitution:

> The Socialist Republic of Bosnia and Herzegovina is a socialist democratic state and socialist self-management democratic community of the working class and citizens, the nations of Bosnia and Herzegovina—Muslims, Serbs, and Croats, and members of other nations and nationalities, that live within it, based upon the authority and self-management of the working class and all working people and on the sovereignty and equality of the nations of Bosnia and Herzegovina and the members of other nations and nationalities living within it. (quoted in Hayden 1999, 89)

As Hayden notes,

> while [the 1974 constitution of Bosnia] guaranteed "proportional representation in the assemblies of social-political bodies" to "the nations of Bosnia and Herzegovina—Croats, Muslims, and Serbs and members of other nations and nationalities," the governing bodies established by the constitution paid primary attention to representation by "the working class and all working people" under the leadership of the League of Communists of Bosnia and Herzegovina. (1999, 90)

Thus, not only did the peoples of Yugoslavia have rights to express their nationality and culture freely, but all citizens employed in the vast public sector had rights of self-management to participate in the running of their workplaces and to be politically represented through elected delegates from their workplace in legislative assemblies. Moreover, despite the extensive autonomy of the republics and provinces, the real center of this system and its concept of self-determination was the idea that individual workers and citizens, in association, would govern their workplaces and local communities. The operational principle of sovereignty and public participation was thus simultaneously political and economic, layered and shared through the federal state, the republics, municipalities, unions, local communities, and the military (Woodward 1995, 29–41).

The meaning of *konstitutivnost naroda* or state-constituting capacity of a nationally defined people during the socialist period was thus contextualized within a state-provided master narrative that defined the socialist republic of Bosnia and Herzegovina as (1) founded through the joint struggle and sacrifice of a multiethnic, antifascist partisan force under Communist Party leadership; (2) coconstituted by the "brotherhood and unity" or joint self-determination of Serbs, Croats, and Muslims, and secured by a system of rotation in leadership positions that demonstrated the Communist Party's commitment to equality among its peoples; and (3) expressing a dual form of popular sovereignty—that of its nations and *working peoples*, with pride of place given to the latter. Despite the uneven realization of these rights to self-management, most of the population experienced a significant rise in living standards and social mobility in the decades following the Second World War. This, together with the scrupulous attention paid to ethnonational equality, made the system broadly legitimate for most of the population.

But as Budding notes, in all of this the Communist Party never thought that Yugoslavia would outlast it. Its constitutional system was designed to secure the party's legitimacy and that of the state rather than facilitate its peaceful dissolution (2008, 109). The end of one-party rule left unresolved tensions between competing concepts of self-determination. It is thus not surprising that once the European Commission began to arbitrate the break-up of Yugoslavia in the early 1990s, the term *konstitutivnost naroda* was (re)introduced into political discourse as part of the struggle over future state forms and borders (Mujkić 2007).

Konstitutivnost Naroda Redux

By the close of the 1980s Yugoslavia's party leadership(s) had been unable to reach consensus upon what was by then a decade-long crisis. What had begun as an economic crisis initiated by the need to service Yugoslavia's foreign debt transformed into a political crisis as the Communist Party elites of various republics—particularly Serbia and Slovenia—clashed over the best way to reorganize the political economic system. Serbia favored greater federal centralization, while Slovenia favored decentralization to individual Yugoslav republics, extending a process already begun in the late 1960s and 1970s. As Woodward argues, this confrontation did not become public until 1988–1990 because events leading up to it proceeded upon two parallel tracks:

> On the one hand was a gradual but insidious breakdown of the old order, particularly its system of multinational guarantees and federal contributions to social welfare. On the other hand were the increasingly open resort by republican politicians, from Slovenia to Serbia, to nationalism in their fight over constitutional reform. (1995, 73)

At this time, republican leaderships in Slovenia and Serbia initiated a redefinition of the polity in ways that served their contrary positions, but were united in undoing the socialist Yugoslav commitment to national equality. Slobodan Milošević of Serbia resorted to using huge mass demonstrations to intimidate or replace rivals within the party and appealed to popular resentment of the federal austerity measures throughout Serbia to eventually "restore the constitutional integrity" of the Republic of Serbia in 1988 by ending the extensive autonomy that had been granted to Kosovo and Vojvodina in the 1974 constitution. Because the decision to grant extensive rights to self-rule to Kosovo and Vojvodina was made in part based upon their ethnonational make-up (Kosovo with a large Albanian population, and Vojvodina with a history of ethnic diversity that included Hungarians, Croats, Slovaks, and Romanians), the leadership in other republics increasingly viewed calls for greater federal centralization from Belgrade as cover for attempts at Serb domination within Yugoslavia. Moreover, as head of the party in Serbia, Milošević began to pursue his hold on power and the goal of a stronger federal structure centered in Belgrade by appealing to *individual* Serbs rather than to the population of the Republic of Serbia.

It was in this context, in efforts to shore up the legitimacy of republican elites and the sovereignty of the republics in which they ruled, that the first multiparty elections and a wave of constitutional revisions took place. The constitutions of Croatia, Slovenia, Macedonia, and Serbia were all rewritten or amended in ways that transformed the notion of rights, citizenship, and participation by claiming the majority ethnonational population in that republic to be the source of the sovereignty of that republic, complete with the rights to self-determination and secession that nationhood implied (Hayden 1999, 69–73).

These changes redefined the meaning of national identity and its accompanying political rights, thus transforming people who were not of a republic's majority nation to the status of minorities. It also opened up the question of constitutive peoplehood: "Persons who found themselves thus demoted to minority status without rights they had held for forty years also took their turn to claim (as in the case of Serbs in Croatia) or to assert (as in the case of Albanians in Kosovo and Macedonia) *their* rights to national self-determination with political autonomy" (Woodward 1995,143). Thus, even though much of this constitutional rewriting was in the service of shoring up the sovereignty of the republics against the federal government, the declarations of ethnonational sovereignty by the new leaderships in Slovenia and especially Croatia made it possible for those of other nationalities to "now claim the right to redraw borders in the case that the republics followed through on their assertions [of independence from Yugoslavia] on the grounds that the right of self-determination in the constitution belonged to nations, not republics" (143).

For Bosnia and Herzegovina, with no majority nation, with a Communist Party leadership intolerant of expressions of nationalism, with probably the strongest popular commitment to the revolutionary tradition of the People's Liberation Struggle, where the principles of "brotherhood and unity" were most deeply woven into the institutional fabric of the republic, and with nationalist politicians in Serbia and Croatia making appeals to coethnics across republican lines, navigating this increasingly chaotic terrain proved extremely difficult.

Reshaping Bosnia's Political Will(s): Multiparty Elections in Bosnia and Herzegovina

It is critical to understand how contingent the development of nationalist politics in Bosnia was on developments elsewhere in Yugoslavia and how unwelcome it was for a wide swath of Bosnian society. I foreground this in order to make clear the lengths that nationalist politicians in Bosnia had to go to in order to redefine the Bosnian polity along monoethnic lines and cast themselves as legitimate spokespersons for the "political will" of "their" nations—and how they used the principle of "constitutive people" to further these aims.

With multiparty elections in Croatia and Slovenia planned for April and May of 1990, the Bosnian government had little choice but to follow suit and announced their own elections for October of that year. Still, the Bosnian communist leadership had not yet decided how competition for seats in the republican parliament and in municipal governments would be contested. The party did allow the formation of opposition parties, but in March of 1990 it banned political organization on the basis of nationality. By a number of measures, this was not an unpopular move. For example, one survey carried out in Bosnia's three largest cities in April and May of 1990 showed strong majority support for the ban on ethnic or nationalist parties, as well as even larger support for keeping Bosnia within a federal Yugoslavia (Andjelić 2003, 141). Eventually, however, the ban on ethnic parties was declared unconstitutional and undemocratic, and ethnonationalist parties emerged to contest the elections alongside a host of other nonnationalist parties.

In anticipation of the October elections, the communist republican parliament turned to amending the Bosnian constitution to provide for a multiparty system. Against the backdrop of the politics of ethnic exclusion emerging elsewhere in Yugoslavia, and because the institutions that guaranteed and embodied national equality relied upon one-party rule (Budding 2008, 107), the overriding concern was to secure the equality of all peoples living in Bosnia and to make domination by one (or two) ethnic group(s) impossible. In their focus on the question of national equality, the members of the parliament undermined the notion of dual sovereignty by removing the references to "the working class and all working people" in the preamble to the republican constitution (even as it continued to characterize the state as socialist):

> The Socialist Republic of Bosnia and Herzegovina is a democratic sovereign state of equal citizens, the nations of Bosnia and Herzegovina—Muslims, Serbs, and Croats and members of other nations and nationalities who live within it.

Proportional representation of Bosnia's nations and nationalities in all "assemblies of social-political organizations, organs that they appoint, the Presidency of the Socialist Republic of Bosnia and Herzegovina and other state organs" was guaranteed by another amendment. Finally, the equality of the country's peoples was to be protected through a "Council for Questions of the Establishment of Equality of the Nations and Nationalities of Bosnia and Herzegovina" in the republican parliament (which was never formed).

The effect was subtle but significant: the arrival of the first multiparty elections occurred at the same time that the sovereignty and self-government of working peoples were eliminated, subordinating questions of economic security and social rights to questions of ethnic belonging. A systemic focus on the equality of nations and the expectation that political conflict could fall along the axes of ethnic difference made national identity the primary idiom of political subjectivity and made appealing to national constituencies all the more powerful.

The campaign season was a chaotic one, with three major ethnonationalist parties attempting to attract known (Communist Party) politicians to be included in their party lists. These parties were the predominantly Muslim Party for Democratic Action or SDA, the Serb Democratic Party or SDS, and the Croatian Democratic Union or HDZ. Across the board they appealed to ethnic constituencies, but also openly cooperated with one another against the reform communists and other multiethnic parties. They also appealed to values strongly associated with the state socialist master narrative. At one event held in a suburb of Sarajevo, candidates for the SDA and SDS accused the reform communist Social Democratic Party (SDP) of fostering ethnic strife, and cast themselves as the true defenders of "brotherhood and unity":

> [the communists] taught us how we must be estranged from our spiritual and national culture, leading to the uncomfortable feeling this evening as we seek to be together. This evening's meeting begins the creation of a new common life of Serbs, Muslims, and Croats. (Quoted in Donia 2002, 37)

Strong dissatisfaction with the Communist Party and the effects of the now decade-long economic crisis, rising fear of ethnic politics coming from Croatia and Serbia, the looming breakup of Yugoslavia, plus the fact that the only real noncommunist alternative were national Serb, Muslim, and Croat parties, combined to result in a strong victory for these three ethnic parties in the October election;[3] they partnered to form a government at the republican level.

The election campaign and results thus went a long way to bestowing ethnic spokesperson status on the leadership of these parties and creating the image of fundamental ethnic cleavages in the polity. This was demonstrated and made substantive by a radical shift in the meaning of the national key, as the parties in coalition used the key to initiate a purge of the republican administration, replacing those cadres still loyal to the Titoist system with persons loyal to the nationalist parties. The national key was thus no longer part of a system committed to multiethnic common life and to preventing ethnicity from being a source of political mobilization; it was now a way for the three major ethnic parties to enhance their power by creating patron-client relations along ethnic lines.

The new coalition government was haunted from day one by the question of Bosnia's future and upon what basis it would be decided. During the campaign season there were no calls for Bosnian independence from Yugoslavia from any major party, but with events in the region accelerating toward Slovenian and Croatian independence, Bosnia's new national parties began to articulate different positions on the question of Bosnia's future. In this context, the *konstitutivnost naroda* principle was mobilized by the Serb SDS at a moment of political impasse to consolidate its legitimacy and authorize a set of political positions that undermined the territorial integrity of Bosnia and Herzegovina and the principle of equality of nations and nationalities.

Reshaping Bosnia's Political Will(s): The Question of Independence

Right up until the war broke out there was significant ambivalence within Bosnia across all social cleavages regarding the question of independence. Like Andjelić, Gagnon (2004) cites pre-election polling data taken in May of 1990 to suggest that the overwhelming majority of respondents desired a maintenance of the status quo, that is, 94 percent favored "a sovereign Bosnia-Herzegovina with existing external and internal borders, within the framework of Yugoslavia" (43). Even after the elections, when the question of independence was being hotly debated in Sarajevo, with war raging in Croatia and the nationalist parties already discussing a de facto division of Bosnia, a poll of Bosnian students found 67.6 percent opposed the idea of regionalization of the republic along ethnic lines—95.5 percent of Muslims, 72.4 percent of Croats, and 67 percent of Serbs (43).

Debate on the question of independence, however, was not a matter for public opinion, but for the nationalist parties in government. The first major clash came in October of 1991 when two competing memoranda were submitted before the republican parliament on the question of Bosnia's sovereignty. The first was submitted by the Muslim SDA with support of the Croat HDZ and it exhibited reluctance to remain within what the two parties were by then calling a "Serb-dominated" Yugoslavia without Croatia and Slovenia. The memo stated that Bosnia and Herzegovina would participate in federal Yugoslav bodies only if all other federal units did, and would not regard as binding any decisions taken by federal organs without the participation of all federal units. The Serb SDS submitted a competing memorandum stating that Bosnia and Herzegovina would participate in the federal parliament and presidency, but that if Croatia were to secede from Yugoslavia and gain international recognition, a process would begin to initiate a "mechanism for the realization of the right of self-determination including secession of the constituent nations of Bosnia and Herzegovina (Muslims, Serbs, and Croats)" (Hayden 1999, 93). In other words, the SDS appealed to the constitutive people principle to raise the political stakes of opposing them on the question of participating in federal Yugoslav structures—to disagree with them was now to risk common Bosnian statehood. It was at this point that Radovan Karadžić, head of the SDS, made his much-quoted statement that the Muslim people risked extermination if they voted for independence. The SDA measure, a "Declaration of Sovereignty," was then adopted in the parliament by majority vote, but without the support or even the presence of any Serb deputies. The SDS subsequently declared such "outvoting" illegal and against the spirit of the recent constitutional amendments, and argued that such actions both undermined the constitutive people status held by the Serb people and made palpable the threat that Serbs would face as a "minority" in an independent Bosnia. As representative of the Serb "constitutive people," the SDS stated that it would not recognize any decision as binding that did not get passed with its approval and participation.

After the "Declaration of Sovereignty" imbroglio, and facing a hostile majority to its position within the republican parliament, an SDS advisory committee met to discuss strategy, including the formation of a separate Serb assembly of Bosnia and Herzegovina and the staging of a plebiscite asking Bosnian Serbs if they wished to remain a part of Yugoslavia. This move was designed to further the separation of the population into monoethnic polities, to offer a public representation of a united and distinct Bosnian Serb political will, and to buttress the positions of the SDS with democratic legitimacy. Few Muslims or Croats voted in the SDS-organized plebiscite, and the vast majority of Serbs who took part voted to reject independence for Bosnia and Herzegovina and to remain in Yugoslavia.

In response to the SDS-organized plebiscite, and to the invitation of the Badinter Arbitration Commission of the European Community for applications from republics seeking independence from Yugoslavia, the Bosnian presidency headed by SDA leader Alija Izetbegović voted on December 20, 1991, to apply for Bosnia and Herzegovina to be recognized by the European Community as an independent state. In response, the next day a self-styled Serb assembly met and approved "preparations for the formation of a Serb Republic." On January 9, 1992, these "preparations" became reality as the Serb Assembly of Bosnia and Herzegovina proclaimed the Serb Republic of Bosnia and Herzegovina and its secession (Donia 2002, 62). The Bosnian government declared this proclamation illegal and it received no international recognition.

This kind of brinkmanship extended into late January when, following a marathon open session of the parliament, the proposal to organize the referendum on independence was passed by a majority of (SDA and HDZ) deputies but without the presence of SDS deputies. The referendum was scheduled for February 29 and March 1 of 1992. The day before the referendum was to be held, the parallel Serb Assembly of Bosnia and Herzegovina met and voted to substantiate its earlier declaration of a Serb republic by creating a constitution. In its preamble and primary articles the constitution offered an affirmation *and* reinterpretation of the links between the Second World War and notions of freedom, self-determination, and constitutive peoplehood to legitimize the foundation of a Serb state of Bosnia and Herzegovina:

> Beginning with the inalienable natural right of the Serb people to self-determination, self-organization, and association, on the basis of which

> it freely determines its political status and protects its economic, social, and cultural development
>
> Respecting its centuries-long fight for freedom and readiness to live with other peoples in relations of mutual respect and equality,
>
> Having in view its decision taken in the course of the Second World War to constitute with other peoples, Croats and Muslims, the Republic of Bosnia and Herzegovina within the federal state community of Yugoslavia,
>
> Expressing its resolution to decide its destiny independently and carrying out its firm will to create its sovereign and democratic state, established on national equality, honor, and the guarantee of human rights, social rights and the right to rule,
>
> Article 1: The Serb Republic of Bosnia and Herzegovina is the state of the Serb people and the citizens that live in it.
>
> Article 2: The territory of the Republic refers to the area of autonomous units, municipalities, and other Serb ethnic totalities, including areas in which genocide was committed against the Serb people in the Second World War.
>
> Article 3: The Republic belongs to the state of Yugoslavia.
>
> Article 4: The Republic may enter into a community with state entities of other constitutive peoples of BiH. (*Službeni Glasnik* 1992, 1)

Note how subtly the text tacks between the "brotherhood and unity" language of previous constitutions—"living with other peoples in relations of equality" and "constituting with Croats and Muslims the Republic of Bosnia and Herzegovina"—and new language that reserves the right to secession, and turns war crimes during the Second World War into a pretext to extend the territoriality of a new Serb state to possibly include all of Bosnia. Not only does this ambivalence reflect a recognition that the status of Bosnia and Herzegovina was still undecided and dependent in part upon the goodwill of foreign (European) powers, it suggests the continuing popularity of elements of the socialist master narrative about the Second World War and the general desire among Serbs and their neighbors not to see Bosnia break up. In particular, Article 4, holding out the right to "enter a community with state entities of other constituent peoples of BiH," reflects this ambivalence.

The referendum on independence was called illegal by the SDS, who urged Serbs to boycott it. When it was voted upon and passed by a significant majority of those voting, it was largely without the participation of the Serb population (who either heeded the SDS's call for a boycott or were prevented by Bosnian Serb authorities from voting). Still, the majority result led the European Community to announce that it would recognize Bosnia and Herzegovina as an independent state effective April 6, 1992. This resulted in a hardening of the SDS position. Thus, less than two years after praising Muslims as the "best brothers of the Serb people" and stating, "I believe in the great potential of the Muslim nation, I believe in its simple human good," during the 1990 campaign season, SDS leader Karadžić came to insist that Muslims and Serbs could not live together. He went to war to make sure of it.

It is not surprising that it was precisely on the question of the future status of Bosnia-Herzegovina, whether sovereign and independent of Yugoslavia or with a form of sovereignty within Yugoslavia, that the *konstitutivnost naroda* concept would (re)appear. That this question was being decided under a new ethnicized multiparty system, made up of self-styled ethnic spokespersons without an effective consensus model or an institutionalized commitment to national equality, made it possible for the SDS to equate being "outvoted" in parliament with the persecution of the Serb people. Under these circumstances, the "constitutive people" principle offered the grounds upon which the SDS could reject the democratic majority decision in the republican parliament (because it had been taken over the objections of the representatives of one of the country's "constitutive peoples"), shore up its authority to speak in the name of all Serbs, authorize its party's position on independence, and legitimize its separatist state actions. Nevertheless, this did not automatically translate into a desire for separatism on the part of Bosnia's Serb population, and as events would make clear, it was not so easy to disassociate the notion of constitutive peoplehood in Bosnia from its socialist-era context.

Decontextualizing Constitutive Peoplehood

The efforts of nationalist parties, from the formation of parallel institutions to purges of governmental positions, were met with resistance from many intellectuals committed to nonnationalist democratic ideals as well as from communists loyal to the creed of "brotherhood and unity." Even within each main nationalist party, there were factions that differed on the future and shape of the Bosnian state. Burg and Shoup (among others) refer to opinion polls to suggest that, outside the leadership of the nationalist parties, many if not most Bosnians were not convinced nationalists nor did they want to live separate lives, particularly if that meant war (1999, 64–69). This was reflected in the numerous examples of ordinary citizens risking their own lives to resist ethnic violence and efforts to divide their communities (cf. Burg and Shoup 1999, 129–130, 174–476), or to protect or shelter those in vulnerable situations (Broz 2005; Hukanović 1996; Thorpe 2005).

The claim that Muslims and Serbs could not and should not live together in one state not only butted up against demographic reality on the ground, it also had to contend with what appeared to be the desire of the majority of Bosnians, based upon nearly half a century of lived experience of "brotherhood and unity" and pride in the revolutionary tradition of the Second World War, to do just that, to live in a state that was "neither Serb, Muslim, nor Croat but rather equally Serb, Muslim, and Croat" (albeit divided over the question of whether that state should remain in Yugoslavia or not). In order to make the claim of Muslim, Serb, and Croat irreconcilability meaningful thus required more work than simply arguing it. The separatist state-building strategy of the SDS was thus pursued along two tracks. The first was to stage acts of ethnic violence and stoke fear in order to remove non-Serbs (and any sign of them) from territory claimed as part of the Bosnian Serb state. Such violence was also aimed at discrediting or rendering irrelevant socialist narratives about "brotherhood and unity," and detaching the constitutive people concept from association with common sacrifice for a multiethnic state of Bosnia and Herzegovina. The constitutive people principle may have had an impact on this strategy: an International Crisis Group report quotes Milan Lukić, a participant in "Muslim cleansing" around the Višegrad area as stating that "the Serbs' aim was to drive the non-Serb population down below 5 per cent, since a people who fell under that threshold could not be 'constituent' according to Yugoslav law" (2002, 2n5). The second track was to offer a master narrative that would make sense of and legitimize that violence and the homogeneous form of the state project (see Gilbert 2013).

The New Master Narrative

The basic contours of the master narrative of the Bosnian Serb state project were already plain in the preamble and first articles of the 1992 constitution listed above, as well as later iterations of the Republika Srpska constitution. The Second World War went from being the "People's Liberation Struggle" or "armed, revolutionary, antifascist struggle" fought for Yugoslav nations and working people, from a "socialist revolution" for "a self-governing society" and for "the right of workers to self-rule," to just one of the many instances where Serbs resisted "the genocide against the Serb nation in the 20th century." This view of the twentieth century became part of the "centuries-long struggle of the Serb people for freedom and State independence," "expressing the will and determination of the Serb people from the Republika Srpska to link its State completely and tightly with other States of the Serb people."

Similarly, although the term "genocide" had been a part of some socialist-era narratives about the Second World War, it was portrayed by the socialist state as an outgrowth of the political ideology of fascism. By emphasizing the war as a struggle against genocide rather than against fascism, the new master narrative emphasized the ethnic identity rather than the political identity of the participants, and thus separated them into absolute collective ethnic categories of innocent victims and perpetrators, and erased the political differences between Serb fighters. This was perhaps clearest in the SDS-led revival and rehabilitation of the Četniks and their commensuration with Serb Partisan fighters and (eventually) fallen Serb soldiers in the 1990s war as all having fought against genocide and for Serb state independence. Framing conflict in terms of genocidal violence helped to underscore the claim that Serbs, Muslims, and Croats could not live in the same state and was above all aimed at undermining the dominant trope of "brotherhood and unity."

The "constitutive people" notion was thus recontextualized as part of the separatist state-building projects of the war (particularly the Republika Srpska) and, rather than a commitment to equality grounded in common statehood, came in part to index the belligerent politics of ethnic difference and tactics of ethnic cleansing through which these projects were pursued. Of course, the ways in which Serb nationalist elites made this principle "fit" their political aims changed the meaning of that principle, as well as the context into which it was (re)inserted.

The ability of Serb separatists to successfully recontextualize the meaning of *konstitutivnost naroda* was only partial because it bore the traces of its former context, which opened it up to other uses. Take, for example, the attempts to draw commensurabilities between Serb Partisans and Četniks. The Partisan revolutionary tradition offered those fighting Bosnian Serb forces in the name of a united Bosnia and Herzegovina the opportunity to draw easy parallels between the Četniks of the Second World War and the Bosnian Serb separatists of 1990. Moreover, many prominent living Serb Partisans themselves resisted comparisons between the Četniks and Partisans, and condemned the war in Bosnia in the same moral, antifascist terms used during the Second World War. An early example was the "Appeal for Peaceful Coexistence by the Peoples of Bosnia-Herzegovina" issued in Belgrade on April 30, 1992, and signed by seventy Partisan veterans, including Bosnians of all nationalities. It condemned the "external and internal aggression" on the "sovereign and internationally recognized state" of Bosnia-Herzegovina and the "national-chauvinist doctrine" according to which the "coexistence of people of different nationalities" was not possible (cited in Hoare 1999). Hoare offers numerous examples of Bosnian Serb Partisan veterans who, despite their advanced age, were active in pressing to lift the siege of Sarajevo, and who in press releases defended the unity of the Bosnian state for all its peoples.

The continued coexistence of Serbs, Croats, Muslims, and others in cities like Tuzla and Sarajevo during the war belied the claims that they could not live together. And by referring to their adversaries as Četniks rather than Serbs, those fighting for a united Bosnia resisted a definition of their enemies in ethnic terms (as Serb separatists would have it) but rather in ideological terms.

This, combined with the terms of the Dayton Agreement—which partially recognized the Serb separatist state project but kept it within a Bosnia and Herzegovina whose state constitution held that it was determined by "Bosniacs, Croats, and Serbs as constituent peoples (along with Others)"—meant that the meaning of *konstitutivnost naroda* would continue to be contested. This made the stakes particularly high for the constitutional court case, which in essence sought to contest the ability of proponents of the Republika Srpska to use that principle to legitimize its monoethnic basis.

Back to the Future

Recall that in June of 2000 the Constitutional Court of Bosnia ruled on what was perhaps the most significant case brought before it since its creation as part of the Dayton Agreement. The case had been initiated in 1998 by then head of the collective presidency and leader of the SDA, Alija Izetbegović, which contested the constitutional basis of Bosnia's divided postwar status quo. It challenged the constitutional language of Bosnia's two main political "entities," the Republika Srpska and the Muslim-Croat Federation, on the grounds that they were not in harmony with the Bosnian state constitution created at Dayton, particularly in insuring full equality or constitutiveness for the three main ethnic groups throughout the territory of Bosnia and Herzegovina. The case also singled out the language in the Republika Srpska constitution upon which its separatist state project was built, such as its claim of competencies that were the prerogative of the State of Bosnia and Herzegovina, calling itself a state, and regulating "its" citizens' relations with other states. The case also challenged the constitutionality of provisions that appeared to be antithetical to participation in common Bosnia and Herzegovina institutions, such as Republika Srpska's holding for itself the right to protect its interests against those of the Bosnian State and the Federation entity.

The particular problematic passages said to be in disagreement with the state constitution had to do with the issue of "constitutive peoplehood" and lay at the heart of the Republika Srpska state master narrative described above. These included Article I of the Republika Srpska constitution, which stated that the Republika Srpska was a "state of the Serb people and of all of its citizens," and grounded the founding of that state in the "natural, inalienable and non-transferable right of the Serb people to self-determination on the basis of which that people, as any other free and sovereign people, independently decides on its political and State status." The Federation constitution was also identified as problematic on a similar if less elaborate basis, particularly the statement that the Federation was made up of "Bosniacs [*sic*] and Croats as constituent peoples as well as Others."

The plaintiffs thus argued that by making the Serbs "constitutive" of the Republika Srpska and Bosniaks and Croats "constitutive" of the Federation, the entity constitutions undermined the meaning and function of the constitutive peoples principle in the Dayton State Constitution, which placed "multiethnicity" as a foundational principle of all levels of Bosnian politics.[4]

Rightly seeing this as undermining the terms of the separatist Serb state-building project, legal experts from the Republika Srpska mounted a vigorous challenge to the case. They first disputed the court's right to review the republic's constitution, and then argued that because the Dayton State Constitution recognized the ethnonational right to self-organization based upon the territorial separation of the entities, Serbs, Muslims, and Croats *were* in fact "constitutive" in Bosnia and Herzegovina: Serbs in the Republika Srpska, and Muslims and Croats in the Federation. They also argued that calling the Republika Srpska a "state" did not take away from the Bosnia and Herzegovina state, and grounded the Republika Srpska claim to statehood in "the expression of her original, united, historical national movement, of her nation which has a united ethnic basis and forms an independent system of power in order to live really independently, although as an independent entity in the framework of a complex state community" (Constitutional Court of Bosnia and Herzegovina 2000, 7).

In its partial decision on the case, later known as the "constituent peoples decision," the court rejected the arguments that it had no right of review as well as the right of the Republika Srpska to be called (or considered) a state. It also dismissed the notion that the state constitution allowed any room for sovereignty for the entities or a right to national self-organization on the basis of territorial separation. Indeed, they argued that separation and segregation were not legitimate aims of a democratic society, and that territorial delimitation could not be used as an instrument of ethnic segregation (Constitutional Court of Bosnia and Herzegovina 2000, 17).

In chapter 1, I indicated that the central concern in the court's decision was whether or not the entity constitutions created a legal and normative context that would hinder the right of refugees to return, particularly those that would constitute an ethnic minority in the areas to which they were returning (so-called minority returnees).[5] The court's ruling stated that the current preamble to the

Republika Srpska constitution created two distinct categories of persons (Serbs and non-Serbs) that led to the automatic exclusion of non-Serb persons and prevented the return of refugees.

With that, the court directly overturned the exclusive ethnic claims to sovereignty of Bosnia's political entities. It ruled that the challenged language was unconstitutional and was to be immediately stricken from the entity constitutions, and that substantive positive measures needed to be taken to make manifest the constitutive peoples principle across Bosnian society and politics.

Not surprisingly, the decision was controversial: as with all common state institutions provided for in the Dayton Agreement, the court's judicial composition reflected the national key principle with international oversight. It thus modeled not only the principle it instituted through the constitutive peoples decision (there were two judges from each of the three main ethnic groups and three foreign judges) but also the divisions that the constitutive peoples principle aimed to overcome at the very moment that it institutionalized them: the decision was taken on a five-to-four vote, with the Bosniak members voting with the foreign members of the court and the court's two Serb members and two Croat members dissenting.

The reaction in the major Bosnian print outlets included themes that would come to later dominate how the constitutional court decision would be taken up and circulated in the public sphere. As discussed in chapter 1, politicians from the Republika Srpska in particular signaled their hostility to the ruling. On a page in the Sarajevo daily *Oslobodjenje* (July 5, 2000, 5) dedicated to discussing the decision, several argued that the way the decision had been passed was in fact evidence that legitimized their claim that a separatist state was necessary to protect Serbs in Bosnia, and that the decision constituted a threat to the existence of the Republika Srpska and thus the freedom of the Serb people in Bosnia. For example, SDS leader Mirko Šarović raised the specter of ethnonational domination, arguing: "It is very problematic in this part of the world to outvote one people, and in this case two peoples—Serbs and Croats—and it is inevitable that the decision of Constitutional Court of BiH will face problems when it comes to implementation." Former Republika Srpska president (and later convicted war criminal) Biljana Plavšić echoed this sentiment, drawing parallels between this ruling and the independence referendum from 1992, and raised the possibility of further violent conflict.

In contrast to the periodization referred to by these politicians that drew attention to the immediate prewar period and the foundation of the Republika Srpska, the same page carried a statement by SUBNOR BiH, the Partisan veterans' organization of Bosnia, which cast its comparative eye to a more distant temporal horizon. It read that SUBNOR supported the decision "in the name of the fighters who from 1941–1945 fought for the Republic of BiH, a state of free and equal peoples . . . in this decision we see the renewal of the principal of the Declaration of AVNOJBIH [Bosnia-Herzegovina Anti-Fascist Council for the National Liberation of Yugoslavia]." On one newspaper page, then, we find encapsulated the fact that the struggle over the meaning of the *konstitutivnost naroda* principle was a continuation of the struggle over state form in the immediate prewar period.

Recall, however, that nothing really happened after the formal creation of otherwise moribund constitutional commissions in Bosnia's two entity parliaments. The constitutional court had declared in its ruling that the full equality of Bosnia's citizens could not be protected in the absence of substantive changes to the constitution, thus the longer that no action was taken the longer it seemed that such a condition was of no real concern to Bosnia's political classes or its foreigner supervisors. This became intolerable for the international community, but any direct steps taken dictating constitutional reforms could undermine its legitimacy. Hence, in an effort to spur movement on the "constitutive peoples" decision, the OHR began to more actively intervene in the process at the beginning of 2001. In one prominent step designed to bring the authority and legitimacy of "Europe" to bear upon the process, Petritsch formed a task force made up of representatives of OHR, OSCE, and the European Commission for Democracy through Law of the Council of Europe (also known as the Venice Commission). Its task was to prepare concrete proposals for the amendments required to implement the court's decision. In addition to this, the Venice Commission was requested by Bosnian State authorities and the High Representative to offer its opinion on the implications of the court's decision.[6]

Most prominently, the High Representative exercised the Bonn powers to issue a decision on January 11 (OHR 2001c) that required the entity constitutional commissions to prepare recommendations for the implementation of the constitutional court decision according to a specific deadline. In chapter 1, my aim in drawing attention to this decision and the amendments process was to analyze it as an attempt to orchestrate an enactment of "local ownership" and "democracy at work" that would provide evidence that the presence and powers of the international community in Bosnia were indeed temporary. Here my aim is to describe how the amendments process and the *konstitutivnost naroda* principle came to be contextualized as part of the High Representative's broader efforts at political transformation and how, to put it mildly, this happened under circumstances and according to a timeline not of his choosing.

His January 11 decision revoked the previous rules and procedures regarding the composition of the commissions. In the place of these rules, the High Representative declared that each commission would have sixteen members and, following the national key principle established in the Dayton Agreement, that it "be composed of an equal number of delegates coming from each of the constituent peoples of Bosnia and Herzegovina along with Others." Moreover, the High Representative would name the actual delegates to the commissions from among those elected to sit in the entity assemblies (as nominated by their parties), as well as appoint the chairperson. In addition to their duties in proposing the changes to the entity constitutions and bringing them in line with the court's decision, the commissions were given the power to review any new legislation proposed by the legislatures of the Republika Srpska or Federation.[7] If any of the representatives of the commissions felt that new legislation violated or threatened the "vital national interests" of one of Bosnia's constitutive peoples, they could hold it up. The decision also mandated that if there were irreconcilable disagreements within the commissions, the High Representative would act to resolve them. The political parties in the entity parliaments were requested to forward nominations by the end of January.

In chapter 1, I emphasized the care that Petritsch took to describe foreign intervention into constitutional matters as an "interim" measure and to background his own role in the reform process as passively mediating rather than actively dictating. In its conclusion, the language of the Decision exhibited a decided ambivalence about Petritsch's role in playing such a heavy-handed part in the process of constitutional change. Yet soon thereafter it became quite useful to emphasize his role in the constitutional reform process. This is because before the commissions could be composed, the OHR found itself in the midst of a major political crisis and challenge to its authority. The constitutive peoples decision would feature centrally in the way it responded and crystallized the terms in which the OHR would subsequently promote the amendments.

HDZ and the Challenge to the Dayton State

In the parts of Bosnia and Herzegovina where Croats predominated numerically, particularly Herzegovina, the nationalist HDZ had ruled since the outbreak of war as a party indistinguishable from the government. It attracted the overwhelming majority of Bosnian Croat votes in the first three multiparty elections in Bosnia (1990, 1996, 1998) and together with its main Bosniak coalition partner, the SDA, comprised the government in the Federation. It had access to major financial aid from the HDZ-dominated government in neighboring Croatia that allowed it to provide resources to a vast majority of the Bosnian Croatian population in return for their support.

However, as Hannes Grandits (2007) describes, by 2000 the elite within the HDZ was threatened with a loss of faith on the part of the Bosnian Croat population. This was due to the obvious enrichment of the party leadership, increasing economic inequality between the party leaders and average Croat citizens, and an increasing sense of social insecurity that was taken as evidence of the unfulfilled promises of improved social welfare. Moreover, the new post-Tudjman/post-HDZ government in Croatia cut off a large amount of financial assistance to Herzegovina, and this loss was felt by most of the ordinary population. By the general elections of November 2000, the HDZ's dominant position was threatened for the first time as former HDZ members joined Croat opposition parties. Additionally, the OSCE changed the election rules to allow Bosniaks or Croats to vote for Bosniak and Croat candidates for the Federation House of Peoples, rather than having them chosen only by members of the same ethnic group, which had been the practice up until then. Grandits notes that the HDZ leadership rightly saw this as a threat to their position: "The new rules, which were intended to dilute the influence of the nationalist parties . . . seriously endangered the future predominance of the HDZ among the allotted Croat members of this chamber" (2000, 117).

The HDZ, led by its president, Ante Jelavić (who was also the Bosnian Croat member of the Bosnian presidency), responded by accusing its Croat political opponents of being traitors, and by charging the international community of systematically discriminating against Croats. Campaigning with the slogan "Self-Determination or Extermination," the HDZ issued demands for the creation of a third "Croat" entity in Bosnia and Herzegovina by pointing out that the Serbs had one and that Croats had no chance against the overall Bosniak majority in the Federation. The removal by the High Representative of several candidates from the HDZ candidate list for obstructing refugee return, discriminating against minorities, and spreading ethnic hatred, was presented by the HDZ as evidence of the international discrimination against the Croat people.

With two weeks to election day, the HDZ moved to reestablish itself as the dominant representative of Croats in Bosnia and Herzegovina by organizing a so-called Croat National Assembly of "all patriotic parties and institutions," with Ante Jelavić as its inaugural president. War veterans associations and cultural associations close to the HDZ organized mass protests aimed at the OHR and OSCE, with the result, according to Grandits, that this "'patriotic' wave overpowered all earlier grievances against the HDZ" (2007, 118).

In a final move to shore up the legitimacy of its position as representing the united will of the Croat people, a "referendum" was called, to be held on election day, in which Croats were to support or reject the plans of the Croat National Assembly. The OHR and OSCE, among others, were strongly critical of the referendum, arguing that it was illegal and violated the election law and the Dayton Peace Agreement, and threatening the HDZ leaders with dire consequences.

Nevertheless, come election day the referendum was held and, according to the voting results, the HDZ remained by far the strongest party among Croat voters.

Despite this success, the multiethnic postcommunist Social Democratic Party (SDP) and the Party for Bosnia-Herzegovina (SBiH) won considerable support among Bosniak voters at the expense of the SDA, the HDZ's coalition partner in the Federation. Together with smaller Croat parties, the SDP and SBiH formed a new governing coalition called the Alliance for Change. Thus despite their strong electoral showing, the HDZ found itself excluded from the reins of power for the first time. As a result, Ante Jelavić and other HDZ leaders refused to recognize the situation, accused the international community of trying to manipulate the elections results, and called the Alliance government illegal because it was formed without the largest Croat party, and was "therefore against the will of the majority of the Croat people."

It is in this context that the High Representative began using the constitutive peoples decision to publicly counter the charges that Croats were "endangered" in Bosnia and the attendant demands for a third Croat entity. He also disputed the claim that the international community discriminated against Croats by referring to his decision establishing the constitutional commissions, and by pointing to the commissions' ability to protect the "vital national interests" of any constitutive people. In the February decision in which he formally named the members of the two constitutional commissions, Petritsch used the HDZ's refusal to nominate members as an opportunity to challenge their claim to represent Bosnian Croat interests as hypocritical, to characterize their boycott as anti-European, and at the same time safeguard the legitimacy of the commissions he had set up:

> . . . despite numerous requests to the HDZ to forward candidates for these important bodies for ensuring the rights of the constituent peoples, the HDZ has failed to rise to the task of defending the interests of the Croat people of Bosnia and Herzegovina. It seemingly does not care about protecting Croat interests in the Federation or in BiH as a whole. The Croat positions have thus been filled with BiH Croats from other parties.
>
> The High Representative is astonished by the contrast between the rhetoric of the HDZ on the need to defend the interests of the Croat people and the behaviour the party displays when it actually supposedly comes to their defence. This is nothing short of negligence toward the BiH Croat people. . . .
>
> The High Representative and his staff look forward to working with the Commissions to take Bosnia and Herzegovina towards a European

> future where individual as well as group rights and other freedoms are guaranteed and enforceable. (OHR 2001g)

The HDZ responded to being shut out of the government with a challenge to the existence of the Federation entity and Bosnian State by publicly calling for a boycott of all state and entity institutions (by refusing to take their seats), and actively using all means at their disposal to actively obstruct their functioning. On March 2, 2001, the day before a meeting of the Croat National Assembly in Mostar, the High Representative continued his line of argumentation, displaying sympathy for the vulnerability of Croats as the "smallest" constitutive people in Bosnia and magnifying the importance of the court's decision:

> the implementation of the groundbreaking Constituent Peoples case represents a unique opportunity to affirm the rights of the Croat people both as individuals and as a collective in the Federation, but more significantly in the Republika Srpska, where the position of Croats is genuinely difficult. . . . Indeed, of the three constituent peoples the Croat people, due to their size, should perhaps have the greatest interest in their representatives fully embracing those institutions at the Federation and State level which provide for the protection of their vital interests. (OHR 2001j)

After attempting to defuse the accusations that the current Federation and State governments were "anti-Croat," the statement continued to reject the calls for a boycott of State and entity institutions and cast participation in the constitutional commissions as a matter of democracy and human rights, thus a prerequisite for joining "Europe," and making nonparticipation not only undemocratic but also collectively dishonorable:

> As Bosnia and Herzegovina moves towards Europe and integration into European structures, every constituent people in Bosnia and Herzegovina needs to take care to ensure its democratic honour. Europe is only ready to accept developed states and peoples with a high degree of political maturity and a proven record of respect for basic democratic principles and human rights. (OHR 2001j)

On March 2 and in language reminiscent of the immediate prewar period, the 528 delegates of the Croat National Assembly declared Croat "self-government" to cover all areas populated by Croats. The seriousness of this challenge was underscored by the fact that the HDZ persuaded Croat soldiers in the Federation military to leave their posts. They were able to do this because members of the HDZ had privileged access to the funds of the Hercegovačka Banka, the

Mostar-based bank through which the government in Croatia funneled financial support to its sister organization in Bosnia and Herzegovina (totaling 647 million German marks over three years). Over one million marks were used to buy the loyalty of Croat soldiers, promising them future salaries paid by the Croat National Assembly.

Petritsch responded by removing Ante Jelavić from the Bosnian presidency and banning him from serving in any official political capacity in the future, for "failing to uphold the Constitutional Order of the country." In the press release explaining his actions, Petritsch continued his line of reasoning, using the constitutive peoples decision and amendments process to argue that if Jelavić's claim that the "Federation was no good for Croats" was true, then he should have participated in the work of the constitutional commissions, "which offer the Croat people the historic opportunity" to amend the constitution and "secure their constituent status across the whole of Bosnia and Herzegovina." Jelavić's refusal to participate, Petritsch argued, belied his claims and only further justified his removal.

> [L]aw and order are slowly taking root in BiH. . . . People like [Jelavić] do not want normality, the rule of law, economic prosperity for everybody. . . . I asked Mr. Jelavic and other HDZ officials time and again to nominate members to the Constitutional Commissions. . . . Mr. Jelavic consistently blocked and refused . . . I continue to stand ready to listen to all genuine concerns that the Croats of BiH have . . . But it needs to be clear to the Croat people in BiH that this I can do only with Croat officials who are sincerely interested in making Bosnia and Herzegovina a normal, law-abiding European country. (OHR 2001i)

In multiple interviews and statements following Jelavić's dismissal—an action that the HDZ pointed to as evidence of the OHR's anti-Croat position—Petritsch pointed again and again to the constitutional commissions to contest such criticism.

The OHR also moved to dismantle the financial power base of the HDZ, primarily by placing the Hercegovačka Banka under international control with the justification that the financing for the illegal and parallel Croat "self-government" structures was being channeled through this bank. This resulted in HDZ-related forces escalating street violence in opposition to international organizations in Herzegovina, as well as attempting to find other sources of funding by extracting money from Croat business owners under threat of violence. In his continuing attempt to manage the situation, Petritsch took the occasion of Easter to offer a message of peace and drive a wedge between the leadership of the HDZ and ordinary Bosnian Croats by casting himself and the entire "international community" as more committed to helping Bosnia's ethnic groups and citizens than its ethnic representatives:

> this is an irrational and baseless dispute put forward by a handful of people who are in danger of losing the privileges they have enjoyed for so long, and are arguing with the entire international community, which is trying so hard to make Bosnia and Herzegovina work - work in a way so that all its constituent peoples and citizens can say "yes" to it. (OHR 2001d)

He warned that Croat self-rule would be a "ghetto," having been rejected by "the entire international community, from its representatives in Bosnia and Herzegovina, to Croatia, to the European Union and every other powerful country in the world. Those who would live under its rule would inevitably become increasingly isolated and impoverished." Finally, he noted that there were still two empty Croat positions on the Federation Constitutional Commission, evidence of the international community's desire to have them filled by HDZ representatives, and he expressed the hope that "responsible Croats" would take them up soon. In the end, he had to appoint two non-HDZ Croats to the position, and he lamented this by casting the HDZ as having failed its democratic obligation for having "thrown away the historic opportunity to engage in the process of constitutional reform and to contribute to securing the rights of the Croat people in the future institutional framework of the Federation of Bosnia and Herzegovina" (OHR 2001f).

In the end, the HDZ attempt to mobilize the Croat population failed in its confrontation with the OHR and OSCE. Grandits argues that this was in part because the HDZ could not pay the Croat soldiers who had deserted their posts, and just a few weeks after they left negotiations began for their return (2007, 120). All told, Petritsch removed, suspended, or otherwise banned eight HDZ officials from their government positions. More importantly, however, Grandits argues that many Croats feared the isolation threatened by the international community and did not see the creation of a third entity as feasible or desirable, and some openly wondered whether the HDZ was doing this to benefit itself and maintain its profitable businesses.

Thus in its confrontation with the HDZ over the fallout of the 2000 elections, the ongoing constitutive peoples amendment process proved to be a useful resource for the High Representative. It allowed him to criticize the HDZ elite in the very terms of collective representation that the HDZ was using to confront the foreign authorities in Bosnia and Herzegovina and to contest their exclusion from positions of power. It further allowed Petritsch to counter the claims of discrimination against Croats and could be used as evidence to back up his ongoing rhetorical strategy of claiming to be a better representative of the interests of Bosnia's peoples and citizens. In order to justify the removal of a democratically elected member of the Bosnian presidency, the High Representative cast his decision (and the constitutive peoples amendments process) as a matter of fundamental human rights, the inevitability of Europeanization, and democratic values. Perhaps most importantly for the story here, in the process the importance of the constitutive peoples amendments process was heightened and the High Representative's legitimacy became ever more closely wedded to its successful completion.

The *konstitutivnost naroda* principle was, in the meantime, being loaded with new meaning and indexicality: in addition to being an index of the commitment by Bosnia's "peoples" to live together peacefully in a common state (socialist-era meaning), or an index of the separatist right to ethnic self-determination (war/postwar meaning), it was now promoted as an index of Bosnia's peoples' capacity to political maturity, a European future, and "democratically honorable" behavior. This emphasis by the OHR idealized a polity where the relations between individuals were not mediated by labor, or by the bonds of ethnonational fraternity, but rather by the morally legitimate commitment to and desire for "multi-ethnicity."

The Passing of the Election Law and the Poor Functioning of the Commissions

Once contextualized as a matter of democratic and European values, the constitutive peoples amendments process became a metric with which to judge other political developments along these lines. The passage of a new election law is a case in point. According to an earlier agreed upon deadline, statewide elections were set to be held in October of 2002, the first to be completely run by Bosnian authorities. As all previous elections had been run by the OSCE, this was a key test of the commitment by foreign authorities to promote "local ownership" and thus further legitimize the primary ritual of democratic process. It was also a test of their ability to scale down their presence in the country.

Holding this election, however, required that an election law be passed by Bosnia's State House of Peoples. The passing of the election law was not only important in order to actually hold the 2002 elections, but it was also a basic democratic prerequisite for membership in Europe-wide institutions like the Council of Europe. After repeated failures, much delay, and considerable pressure from foreign authorities (who in fact directly oversaw the writing of the draft law), an election law was eventually passed by the Bosnian state parliament in August of 2001. Its legality was immediately called into question by many commentators in the Bosnian press who noted that it seemed to violate the principles of the constitutive peoples decision by continuing to hold certain positions in the Republika Srpska and Federation governments for Serbs and Bosniaks or Croats only.

Despite this, the OSCE, OHR, EU, and US embassy all praised and welcomed the passage of the election law. Since the High Representative and other foreign authorities were providing much of the impetus moving the constitutive peoples decision forward, their optimism regarding the new election law led some to wonder about the fate of the constitutive peoples decision. Writing in the Banja Luka daily *Nezavisne Novine*, one commentator, using stereotypical "Muslim" and "Serb" names, pointed to inconsistencies that the law embodied in the very terms that the international bodies were praising it:

> Why can't Mujo be a candidate for President of the Republika Srpska, and why can't Radoje be President of the Federation? They cannot because that is what is stated in a law which, according to some, was created according to the highest democratic standards. Is this the kind of democracy to which we can *all* feel a real commitment? In fact, the law knowingly violates the decision of the Constitutional Court of BiH about the constitutiveness of all three BiH peoples across the whole territory of BiH. It is thus simply not true that we have built European, much less democratic, standards into the text of the election law. (Živak 2001)

This juxtaposition between domestic and international commentary also appeared on a page of *Oslobodjenje*, where one headline read "The Law Which Does Not Value the Legal Equality of All Peoples in BiH," in contrast to another article where the major representatives of the "international community" were quoted as calling the law "a meaningful step forward for BiH," for democracy, and for Bosnia and Herzegovina's inclusion in European institutions (August 23, 2001).

It was not just the enthusiastic international reception of the election law that appeared to question international commitment to the constitutive peoples amendments process or its contextualization as a sign of equality, democracy, or European standards. The functioning of the constitutional commissions set up by the OHR seemed to violate the spirit of the court's decision. For instance, an article in the Sarajevo weekly *Slobodna Bosna* (Metiljević 2001) reported a regular breakdown between Serb and non-Serb delegates in the Repulika Srpska constitutional commission. Using an ironic tone, the reporter noted that even after fifteen meetings of the constitutional commission, its delegates were engaged in a struggle over the meaning of "constitutive," remarking that it had not yet decided "who is constitutive in this entity and who is (only) equal." He characterized the Serb members of the commission as treating Bosniaks and Croats as tenants or lodgers (*podstanara*) in the Republika Srpska, and as behaving as if their achieving equal status in the republic depended upon the good will of the "more equal" (*ravnopravnije*) Serbs and not on precise constitutional norms and their elaboration in the law.

The notion that the commission's work was a strategic "game" was underlined in the author's description of the disagreement over constitutional language between the commission delegates. The author noted that the Serb delegates wanted the words "equitable representation" (*pravedna zastupljenost*) inserted into the language of the amendments, but without spelling it out further or stating precisely what it meant. Bosniak members were quoted as saying that "equitable representation" should be defined as proportional representation according to the 1991 census. The Serb members counterproposed that it should be defined according to the next election's results, that is, according to the proportion of the ethnic groups voting in the Republika Srpska election, a measure that would represent a drastic drop in the percentage of non-Serbs in government.

Articles like this served less to offer evidence of the progressive promise of the amendments process as a sign of Bosnia and Herzegovina's growing commitment to European standards and democratic values, and more to focus attention precisely on the reordering wrought by the war, and the continued commitment of Republika Srpska governing elites to that reordering. In other words, it presented the amendments process as a continuation of the state-building projects of the war by other means.

The Stakes Are Raised

By the time 2001 drew to a close no visible progress had been made on drawing up, much less adopting, the amendments necessary to bring the entity constitutions into compliance with the court's decision. With the end of his term as High Representative just a half year away, Petritsch came to see the issue as a referendum on his tenure, particularly regarding Bosnia's democratization, Europeanization, and progress in becoming an "ownership" country that did not need the government of the international community. Indeed, two separate deadlines loomed that heightened the stakes for Petritsch. First, he wanted Bosnia's accession to the membership in the Council of Europe to happen on his watch, as it was something that he and his office had vigorously promoted for nearly two years as a major step on the "road to Europe." However, accession was tied to the passage of provisions in the election law that reflected the constitutional court decision and attending amendments; this of course required the amendments be passed. The lack of any progress on an issue that Petritsch had repeatedly argued was an "historic opportunity" and fundamental issue of human rights was potentially embarrassing. The related deadline had to do with the elections slated for the fall of 2002. Because the constitutional amendments were expected to have an effect on the shape and composition of the entity governments, the longer passing the amendments was postponed, the more likely it would be that the changes foreseen in the court's decision would be put off for at least another election cycle—and the longer Bosnia would need an international presence. For these reasons, in his New Year's Message for 2002, Petritsch called the passing of these amendments the "biggest test of the coming year" (2001d).

Imposition and New Elections

Chapter 1 described the ways in which Republika Srpska politicians eventually adopted a set of amendments that appeared to violate the constitutional court's decision, restating their position that the *konstitutivnost naroda* principle was not something shared by Bosnia's peoples but something that divided them. And we know that, in response, Petritsch imposed the Sarajevo Agreement amendments upon the Republika Srpska and the Federation constitutions as well as amendments to the election law to match them. The new constitutional amendments saw the extension of the national key concept already in place in Bosnia and Herzegovina state institutions into all levels of public institutions and courts, amounting to a proportional representation or quota system following the results of the 1991 census.[8] It also elaborated new representative bodies (the Council of Peoples) whose mandate it was to protect the "vital national interests" of the three constituent peoples (and others) by giving them veto power over any new legislation proposed. Finally, it created new entity-level constitutional courts empowered to take up the question of whether new laws violated the constitutive peoples principle now enshrined in the entity constitutions.

In an April 19 press conference (OHR 2002c), Petritsch spent considerable time putting the best face on his decision to impose the amendments upon the entity constitutions. He continued to contextualize the amendments process as evidence of local ownership, and the *konstitutivnost naroda* principle as an index of democratic and European standards.

> The readiness of the leading parties of your country to engage in these discussions has been an important step forward, and I sincerely applaud them for these efforts. This shows to me that the concept of ownership of the local authorities, which I initiated when I took over as the High Representative, is indeed working. BiH's political class is recognizing its responsibilities; it is living up to the requirements of a modern European

> democracy, the rule of law and the multi-ethnic character of this country, this State of BiH.
>
> . . . I am able to issue my Decisions today knowing that the leaders of BiH have taken this country a huge step forwards towards a future based on modern European norms, which include consensus and a sensible compromise. The international community and I myself are exercising our role as a partner for BiH and its leaders, and the Alliance leaders and the RS leadership have shown courage, strength, persistence and commitment. More than this, they have shown responsibility and statesmanship when faced with one of the most complex questions a democracy can confront itself with, and that is, of course, the constitution. (OHR 2002c)

His contextualization of the amendments and the *konstitutivnost naroda* principle as signs of democracy, equality, and progress toward Europe included an argument that the new changes ushered in by the amendments would make it impossible for nationalist parties to survive. At the press conference cited above (OHR 2002c), Petritsch claimed that the constitutional amendments would mean the end of the "nationalistic dinosaurs" of the HDZ and SDA whose "time [was] definitely over." This theme had been repeated in the months leading up to the imposition of the amendments. For example, in an interview in early April, he claimed that "nationalists are not interested in a common state and multiethnic coexistence . . . they will be superseded and we will have a multiethnic structure, and that is an automatic advantage for a multiethnically organized party" (*Nezavisne Novine*, April 4, 2002). Returning to the April 19 press conference, Petritsch pursued the dinosaur metaphor further:

> ASSOCIATED PRESS (ALEKSANDER DRAGICEVIC): Are you going to punish these dinosaurs?
>
> HIGH REPRESENTATIVE: I believe it's the fate of dinosaurs that they die out. I do believe that democracy in this country is by now so well rooted that they will simply not be elected into important offices any longer.
>
> KUNA (YASIN RAWASDEH): Do you want to describe those dinosaurs?
>
> HIGH REPRESENTATIVE: I don't want to describe the dinosaurs. This is just a metaphor, and I wouldn't want to go too far in this comparison. But when you look into the history of our planet, then you realize that they had their time and they've died out. The same, of course, also happens in a dynamic European democratic society. This kind of parties [*sic*] that still exist here don't exist in the rest of Europe any longer. You have different parties, a different concept for a party, and

> so therefore I'm quite confident that this is going to be a thing of the past pretty soon.

The election results of autumn 2002 proved such expectations to be premature. Contrary to Petritsch's assertion that the constitutional changes would spell the end for nationalists, the same three nationalist parties that had won the first multiparty elections in Bosnia (the Muslim SDA, Croat HDZ, and Serb SDS) emerged as the largest vote-getters. The greatest loss was felt by the postcommunist SDP, who as leaders of the State and Federation governments under the Alliance for Change had received the full backing of the international community and were the most closely tied to the amendments. Indeed, the constitutional amendments, with their formalization of the national key principle and quota system in government and public institutions, entrenched ethnic identity in a way that benefited the self-image of monoethnic nationalist political parties as protecting the rights (and resources and jobs) of their group (rights, resource, and jobs both opened up and threatened by the new quota system).

The surprise at the strong showing by these nationalist parties turned to cynicism when these parties, who had constantly made wide-ranging and specific attacks on one another as iconic of the threat of ethnic domination (this was particularly the case between Muslim SDA and Serb SDS), ended up in coalition government at the State and Entity levels. In some ways this was a completely logical reaction to the system the constitutional amendments had put into place. As after the first multiparty elections in 1990, each party sought less to form a common government and more to use their access to government positions to strengthen their party. They had more to fear, in fact, from nonnationalist parties than they did from one another. Indeed, they could even argue that being in coalition with other nationalist parties was the best way to keep those nationalist parties in check.

For those public figures who were strongly critical of the nationalist politics of ethnic difference, the victory of the three parties who "led the country into war" was a sign that any gains since the war were illusory and produced a forlorn sense of déjà vu. For others who were sympathetic to or outright supporters of nationalist politics and Bosnia's separatist state projects—particularly in the Republika Srpska—willingness to enter coalition with "the enemy" appeared as the ultimate betrayal.

In ways eerily reminiscent of 1990, these parties began to divvy up ministries, positions in governmental and other public bodies, and the make-up of the new House of Peoples according to the quota system set in place by the constitutional amendments. Not surprisingly, the Houses of Peoples—the bodies in the entities designed to protect the "vital national interests" of Bosnia's constituent peoples—became sites of considerable maneuvering and devolved into little more than an extension of party politics. In response, a widespread discourse about corruption and self-interest spread rapidly through the public media and in international circuits.

The Recontextualization of *Konstitutivnost Naroda*

Given the role played by the *konstitutivnost naroda* principle in conceptualizing the common, multiethnic sovereign basis of the socialist republic of Bosnia-Herzegovina after the Second World War, it seems clear that any attempt to remake the state would require revisiting and recontextualizing the meaning of that principle. In the early 1990s Serb nationalist politicians in Bosnia did this quite self-consciously, for it helped strengthen their position on the question of Bosnian independence in an increasingly hostile republican parliament, and it helped legitimize and authorize the separatist state project they eventually pursued. The principle came to be partly associated with the ethnic politics of division and the master narrative of the Serb separatist state-building project which claimed that Serbs could not live equally, peacefully, or securely with non-Serbs—precisely the opposite of its former association with the trope of brotherhood and unity that formed the basis for the socialist state. But such claims required evidence, and the violent "unmixing" of the population was in part about producing such evidence and discrediting or rendering irrelevant the previous, socialist-era associations of the *konstitutivnost naroda* principle. And yet their attempts to do this remained partial because they did not go uncontested, and this meant that the principle continued to bear the traces of its former context for large parts of the population. This incompleteness paralleled the incomplete nature of the Bosnian state, and the way that the Dayton Agreement cobbled together contrary state projects—the Republika Srpska as the expression of the self-determining capacity of Serbs, but within a Bosnian state whose constitution recognized Serbs, Croats, Muslims, and others equally as its sovereign peoples.

Petritisch clearly did not set out to use the *konstitutivnost naroda* principle as a vehicle for his goals of political transformation. It was an improvised response to the vagaries of intervention encounters. A constitutional court case brought by Alija Izetbegović; the timetable of regular elections; increasing pressure to scale back the international presence by promoting "local ownership" over state functions, like elections; the need to provide evidence that Bosnia and Herzegovina under international supervision was headed toward a democratic and European future; the demand to create the conditions, such as full political equality and equal rights, for the return of refugees to their prewar homes; and an open rebellion against the international community and the Dayton state structures by the HDZ: all these played a role in how, why, and when the *konstitutivnost naroda* principle was taken up by Petritsch.

Petritsch was able to fold it into the discursive strategies he developed to manage diverse intervention encounters: because it was about a certain kind of equality and part of a process initiated by the constitutional court, Petritsch could align the process and principle with virtues of democracy like rule of law, freedom, and equality. In an example of recombinant democratization, this made it possible to justify the removal of an otherwise democratically elected official from the presidency. Because the principle was about securing collective rights, he could use his oversight of the amendments process as evidence of his claim to represent the interests of the people(s) of Bosnia—and claim that his opponents did not, if the occasion arose. Because of the links between the amendments and the election laws, itself a requirement for admission into pan-European institutions like the Council of Europe, he could align any obstruction of the amendments process as against the supreme value of "European standards." The immediate accession of Bosnia into the Council of Europe after the imposition of the amendments to the constitutions and election law provided further evidence of the "democratic" and "pro-European" nature of the High Representative's decision.

As described here and in chapter 1, this was enough to beat off the HDZ challenge and keep the Dayton political institutional structure intact, and to persuade or compel the reluctant participation of most major political parties in the amendments process even if, in the end, those amendments had to be imposed. And there is little doubt that the conclusion of the amendments process changed the institutional, political, and discursive landscape of postwar Bosnia and Herzegovina. In some ways, it initiated dynamics that the international community would welcome: it changed the monoethnic face of the entity governments and proliferated new legal, institutional, and moral avenues to challenge everything from the ethnicized names of towns and city streets to public holidays and budget apportionment. Some dynamics it would not welcome, such as binding the "international community" to its role as the guarantor of a political situation that it was instrumental in creating, a situation noted by political commentator Nerzuk Ćurak at the opening of this chapter.

For instance, in 2003 in the town of Prijedor, Bosniak politicians in the municipal assembly drew on the constitutive peoples principle to challenge the changes that had been made during the war to the municipal coat of arms and the date chosen to be celebrated as the Day of the Municipality. Identifiably "Serb" symbols had been added to the coat of arms, and the Day of the Municipality had been changed from May 16, the date in 1942 when Prijedor had been liberated by the Partisans in the Second World War, to April 30, when the SDS-controlled "Crisis Committee" had taken control of the government in Prijedor in 1992. When a motion failed to gain enough votes to change the coat of arms (but did succeed in nullifying the date for the Day of the Municipality), the Bosniak speaker of the assembly (a beneficiary himself of the national key) was quoted as saying he would engage the international community and take the issue to the newly created Republika Srpska Constitutional Court because the symbols "do not represent all three constitutive peoples" (*Nezavisne Novine*, April 4, 2003). While Petritsch would probably have been satisfied that a Bosniak who had such a complaint now had an institutional and legal framework to seek justice, he probably would have been less pleased by the implication that international oversight would be required to make sure that it functioned properly.

So did the High Representative's actions change the meaning of the *konstitutivnost naroda* principle—how it was understood and mobilized to make sense of Bosnian politics and society? I would argue that it did. We might think of it this way: I described many of the meaningful associations that the principle had in its socialist-era context as part of a state socialist master narrative. Then Bosnian Serb politicians attempted to shift those meaningful associations, redefining the principle by fitting it into a new master narrative, trying thereby to render the older meanings socially and politically irrelevant. And I have argued that they succeeded, but only partially because the old associations were attached to the memories and experiences of the bulk of the population and thus did not go away. The question then became: Under what conditions would such prewar experiences and memories become socially or politically relevant? Along came the High Representative and attempted less to contest the earlier associations carried by the principle than to load it up with additional meaning in a new context, that of postwar Bosnia and Herzegovina under international supervision. Now it was promoted as a sign of democratic and European values like equality, rule of law, secure rights, freedom from discrimination, and political maturity, as well as a sign of progressive teleology—movement forward on the path to Europe (and membership in the European Union).

But although the meaning of *konstitutivnost naroda* did change through this process, it was not always in ways foreseen or hoped for by the High Representative. The reason for this is twofold. On the one hand, the concept bore the traces of its former contexts, which highlighted for some Bosnians comparisons between past and present that drew attention to changes wrought by the war and this undermined the attempt to define the new amendments either as an historic achievement, as progressive, or as ushering in European standards. Some, for example, recognized the constitutional court's decision as amounting to little more than restoring a basic foundation of Yugoslav sociopolitical order. In an article entitled "Bosnia Returns to Its Senses," Sarajevan political analyst Nerzuk Ćurak observed that the decision brought Bosnia "back to the future," ready to again take its place on the stage of history after the interruption of the war and its effects in denying the multiethnic fact of Bosnia's existence. He noted that the decision could be seen as progressive only in light of the war, and quoted Banja Luka philosophy professor Miodrag Živanović who argued that the court's decision "represents nothing new, rather it only returns to the peoples of Bosnia and Herzegovina [the constitutive status] which the Dayton construction of the state had dispossessed them of [by recognizing the Republika Srpska and Federation as its integral units]" (Ćurak 2000, 18). Indeed, the idea that a status which most Bosnians and Herzegovinians over the age of twenty-five grew up taking for granted needed to be restated or "re-bestowed" at all produced a palpable feeling contrary to the progressive metaphor of "transition"—at moments like these, time itself could appear stuck or even to regress. This was only reinforced by the 2002 election victory and coalition government of the three parties that "led the country into war."

Moreover, the idea that the amendments designed to realize the *konstitutivnost naroda* principle were a critical step toward achieving "European standards" rang hollow given that the principle had been shorn of its socialist-era commitment to socioeconomic equality and a high standard of living (which is what most Bosnians first associate with "European standards"). Still, the amendments did open up a space within which some could challenge the master narrative of the Republika Srpska state project by comparing it with the notion's earlier context, thus making the political task a restorative rather than progressive one. In the April 19, 2003, issue of *Nezavisne Novine*, Prijedor native and former SDP candidate for the Serb member of the Bosnian presidency Mladen Grahovac used the controversy over the changes in the Day of the Municipality and the municipal coat of arms to draw parallels between the kind of Prijedor that was based upon the socialist revolutionary tradition and the kind of Prijedor that was created by the most recent war:

> That period (1942) laid the foundations for coexistence in this area, because the leadership of the Kozara Partisans included the legendary "red" doctor Mladen Stojanović (Serb), Josip Mazar Sosa (Croat), and Osman Karabegović (Muslim). While celebrating that day [in 1942 when Prijedor was liberated] and tradition, our town grew from being a small provincial backwater to a modern economic, cultural and sporting center of the Bosnian Krajina.

After proudly noting the productive capacities of Prijedor's industries, and the notable reputation gained by its artists, theater, and football players in Yugoslavia and the world (all clear signs of the town's "modern," "civilized," and "European" status), he wrote that the people of Prijedor needed to face their past and change the coat of arms and Day back to their prewar forms:

> This task has been given to us by the constitutional changes regarding the constitutiveness of peoples in BiH . . . or as some say: We need to return to being Partisans, because domestic traitors and occupiers are on the scene [referring to the SDS, HDZ, and SDA coalition partners]. The masks have fallen. It is clear by now where the false protection of national interests and mythomania leads . . . Now that the world has changed, the greatest national interest is to live well, at the level that once existed in Prijedor. (2003, 21)

If one limit to the High Representative's ability to resignify the *konstitutivnost naroda* principle was the fact that it bore traces of its former contexts, another lay in the fact that by attempting to turn *konstitutivnost naroda* into a sign of equality, democracy, or European standards, the High Representative introduced new metrics with which to evaluate its use. And here, people more often pointed to the ways in which it fell short. For example, a December 2006 article in *Dani* argued that Serbs in the Federation were "equal citizens of a second class," zeroing in on the lack of work as the most critical problem facing Serbs in the Federation. While noting that Petritsch's amendments required that the ethnic key be applied to employment in public institutions according to the 1991 census, the article pointed to the Una-Sana canton in northwestern Bosnia to which 18,000 Serbs had returned and yet the author could find evidence of only one or two Serbs filling any position within the cantonal assembly, its ministries, or public firms. Moreover, the article noted that in the few months since the fall 2006 elections it had been impossible to fulfill the mandated number of Serb delegates to the Federation House of Peoples—the institutions meant to protect the "vital national interests" of each constitutive people—because none of the parties in the governing coalition had nominated any for those positions. Such evidence was often used in the Republika Srpska to point to the *lack* of equality rather than its achievement, to restate the need for a Serb state and to discourage the return of Serb refugees to their prewar homes in the Federation (*Dani* 2006).

On the other hand, even when the national key was fully applied, some used it to point out how it was undemocratic. For instance, a March 2003 article in *Dani* entitled "We Did Not Choose Them but They Are Governing," presented a withering critique of the first postamendments government of the Sarajevo canton as fundamentally unrepresentative and unprofessional. It argued that because of the national key principle, there were numerous people in the new government who had received hardly any votes. The article began by noting that everything was decided by the parties among themselves, such that the parties forming the cantonal government decided who would be the candidates occupying the tripartite cantonal presidency. This meant that the eventual Serb and Croat vice presidents of the cantonal assembly received less than 3 percent of the potential voting population, even though there were Serb and Croat candidates who received thousands more votes than those who eventually occupied the vice president positions. Moreover, the amendments' requirements of a minimum number from each constituent people in the assembly meant the inclusion of some delegates whose voting population, as the article derisively put it, "you could fit into a single café bar" (*Dani* 2003).

Articles like this only scratch the surface of the range of critiques the *konstitutivnost naroda* principle has been subjected to for being unrepresentative and undemocratic. The best-known of these was a case brought before the European Court of Human Rights (ECHR) in 2006 by a Jewish citizen, Jakob Finci, and Dervo Sejdic, a Roma citizen of Bosnia and Herzegovina (one of the provisions of the Dayton Agreement granted the European Convention on Human Rights priority over all other law in Bosnia and Herzegovina, making the ECHR another international venue in which to make Bosnian politics). In essence, the plaintiffs argued that the inclusion of the *konstitutivnost naroda* principle in the Bosnian constitution, and its application in Bosnian government, in fact discriminated against citizens who did not identify as Bosniak, Croat, or Serb, making it impossible for such citizens to be elected to the tripartite presidency or the State Parliament's House of Peoples. In 2009, the ECHR ruled in their favor, finding that this application of the *konstitutivnost naroda* principle violated the convention protocols regarding free elections and the general ban on discrimination. The ruling stated that Bosnia and Herzegovina needed to change its constitution so as to allow national minorities to run for office. Thus far, Bosnian politicians have resisted this ruling, despite pressure from the Council of Europe and European Commission. Given that ratifying and fulfilling the protocols of the European Convention on Human Rights are a requirement for membership in the EU, this ruling has made the *konstitutivnost naroda* principle one of the greatest obstacles to Bosnia's progress on the "path to Europe."

In this chapter I offered an in-depth analysis of a core instability that shapes the setting and the effects of international intervention: the fact that, in seeking to legitimize their goals and actions, foreigners like Petritsch often have to pursue their goals using cultural forms and historical materials—and according to a timeline—not of their choosing.[9] The way that the High Representative initially used the *konstitutivnost naroda* principle and the amendments process in his encounter with insurrectionary forces was improvisational, but it set in motion efforts to resignify the principle which shifted its meaning and helped to define the postwar political context—but it did so in ways that could not have been foreseen. This was not the socialist-era context of multiethnic common state under Communist Party rule; nor was it the prewar and wartime context of separatist violence designed to make impossible a common life among Serbs and non-Serbs; nor did the amendments aid nonethnic or multiethnic political parties at the expense of nationalist parties, as Petritsch had hoped. In fact, rather than settling the question of the self-determining basis and form of Bosnia's statehood, the constitutive peoples amendments process kept that question open. It did not end Bosniak opposition to the existence of the Republika Srpska by affirming its multiethnic basis; rather, it gave Bosniak parties and politicians an institutional and legal position within the Republika Srpska from which to continue that opposition. It did not bring an end to the monoethnic nature of Republika Srpska government; rather, it provided a forum for Serb elites to restate the logic for and legitimacy of the separatist Serb state project. The amendments furthered the development of an entrenched political party system divided along lines of ethnonational difference and the perpetually open question of the state, in which ethnic veto powers are a recipe for political stalemate and in which parties see the *konstitutivnost naroda* principle as a way to proliferate positions and safeguard their power through patron-client relations. The attempts of Petritsch to turn the principle into an index of democratic values and European standards foundered in the aftermath of the amendments process, precisely because of the changes it ushered in.

The amendments also had implications for more intimate intervention encounters far from the centers of power as foreign officials, aid workers, and refugees engaged one another around the return process. The next section of this book shifts to analyze these face-to-face interactions and explore their distinctive performative requirements, instabilities, and forms of social and cultural production.

INTERLUDE

Field Sites, Field Methods, Field Contexts

The municipalities of Prijedor in the Republika Srpska and Sanski Most in the Federation were an ideal place to investigate intervention encounters because of the intensity of the refugee return process there. The two towns of Sanski Most and Prijedor lie less than 30 km apart, and the main road which connects them runs alongside the Sana River and is bisected by the Inter-Entity Boundary Line separating the Republika Srpska from the Federation. The international community paid special attention to Prijedor because it had been iconic of the tactics of "ethnic cleansing" ever since the summer of 1992, when photographs and film footage of emaciated men herded behind barbed-wire fences circulated throughout the world and caused an international outcry. The violence in the camps was accompanied by systematic efforts throughout the region to eliminate the physical evidence of the presence and culture of its substantial non-Serb population.

It is for this reason that foreigners were initially bewildered by the desire of tens of thousands of Muslim refugees from Prijedor to return to their prewar homes. Though the institutions of the international community were reluctant to do what it would take to make such "minority return" successful, this did not stop those who wanted to return home. In 1998, one group of refugees defied international warnings not to return (ostensibly out of concern for their safety), slipped through roadblocks erected by the Republika Srpska police and set up camp on the ruins of their bombed out homes. They then demanded that the international community provide the security and resources necessary for them to make their return a reality. The leaders of this returnee community were not hesitant to recall what they had suffered in the camps, and crafted their return narrative in ways that fit the international community's vision for a multiethnic democratic Bosnia. It was the initiative by returnees such as these that forced the international community to take refugee return seriously.

Sanski Most was subject to the same "ethnic cleansing" campaign of non-Serbs in 1992 and was ruled as part of the Republika Srpska from 1992 to 1995. In 1995, Sanski Most was captured by the Army of Bosnia and Herzegovina. This triggered a mass exodus of Serbs, many of whom settled in Prijedor as refugees. Serb return to Sanski Most did not start in earnest until 2001 and 2002, prompted in part by the decision of the OSCE to open up a second field office in Sanski Most (in addition to the one in Prijedor) as on-the-ground advocates for returnees.

Prijedor and Sanski Most constituted what the OHR called an "axis of return," meaning it was a promising area in which to invest minority return efforts, because many Bosniaks who were prewar residents of Prijedor lived in Sanski Most (sometimes in the prewar homes of Serbs). At the same time, many Serbs, prewar residents of Sanski Most, lived in Prijedor (often in the prewar homes of non-Serbs). Making refugee return a reality meant allowing people to repossess their prewar homes. As this process got underway, it was hoped that many of the Serbs being evicted from Muslim homes in Prijedor would initiate the repossession of their prewar homes in Sanski Most and start a chain reaction along these lines. Also, because of the proximity of the municipalities, the international resources dedicated to the area would go twice as far. Locating my research along this "axis" enabled me to track the evolution and routinization of the relationship between international organizations and returnees. As will become clear in the following chapters, this axis of return enabled returnees to compare and evaluate the neutrality and impartiality of the international community regarding different ethnically marked returnee populations. For example, a common tactic used by Serb returnees to Sanski Most when demanding various actions on the part of "internationals" was to point out a similar international effort performed on behalf of Muslims in Prijedor. Serb returnees demanded that such actions be matched, lest the international community be seen as favoring one ethnic group over another and thus lose its legitimacy as a neutral arbiter.

As I was interested in the encounters between foreigners and Bosnian returnees as one of the locations where the new international order was being erected and contested, I situated my field research at those sites of interaction. Over the course of nearly twenty months between 2000 and 2004 I attended countless meetings held by returnee representatives in office spaces or public sites, sat in on working group sessions among foreigners, returnees, and municipal officials in the municipalities of Sanski Most and Prijedor, observed consultations in the offices of the OSCE, OHR, or aid organizations, as well as coordination conferences between members of the international community in rented hotel space. Just as often I followed the staff of NGOs, IGOs, donors, and diplomatic missions into "the field" as they investigated incidents of violence, selected beneficiaries of return projects, carried out "needs assessments," unveiled completed development projects, and bore witness to sites of trauma and ethnic cleansing.

Across these sites of encounter, I explored the discursive and institutional practices through which foreigners came to understand Bosnian society and politics, as well as their roles in Bosnia (as mediators, transformers, standard-bearers, protectors)—roles that were organized around the key categorical distinctions I outlined above—international versus local, neutral versus political, universal versus particular, and so on. I was alert to how these distinctions came into play in the discursive strategies of enlistment on the part of returnees as well as foreign actors, as each worked to draw the other into their ongoing projects. In particular, I tracked the appeal to and circulation of dominant representations of the "international community" and aid organizations, of returnees, of ongoing political crises at the centers of political power in Bosnia, as well as of various visions for the Bosnian state, because all of these found expression in the intervention encounters on the ground in Prijedor and Sanski Most.

It cannot be overlooked that my research was made possible by international intervention—both in the obvious sense that it was the object of my investigation, and in the less obvious sense that my research relationships were forged in a postwar context structured by the presence of thousands of NATO troops, by foreign officials supervising government, police and courts, and by hundreds of millions of dollars in foreign aid money and other financial resources. It was also a context of structured inequality between "internationals" and Bosnians and Herzegovinians. Kim Coles describes the geographies of access and privilege which "internationals" occupied while working in Bosnia, such that many lived largely segregated lives—committed to "building a state" without actually having to engage with it (2007: 63–72). "Internationals" working for IGOs were often granted diplomatic status and were not bound by most Bosnian laws or regulatory mechanisms; they enjoyed services like health care provided by the international organizations for which they worked. They were exempt from many Bosnian traffic laws and taxation on their income or on goods like tobacco and alcohol; they were paid in foreign currency, and granted special border-crossing privileges. Their difference was also marked by their white SUVs and Land Rovers, vehicles that no one else in Bosnia and Herzegovina owned or drove.

I benefited by occupying an interstitial position in this context. Returnees and other Bosnians undoubtedly made time for me because they often encountered me for the first time as an "international" from the West, traveling alongside the staff of international NGOs or IGOs whose work I was observing. Although I had no diplomatic status or the privileges that went with it, I spoke fluent English and lived in an apartment previously rented out by someone working for the OSCE. But I was also different from most other *stranci* (foreigners)—even other foreign researchers—in ways that also influenced the formation of research relationships. Rather than the SUVs driven by foreigners, I drove a Zastava 128, a Yugoslav automobile. I had enough linguistic competence to converse directly with Bosnians, and I stuck around. Moreover, I took an active interest in returnee lives, in their experiences and perspectives. Rather quickly I came to see that for vulnerable populations living under the uncertainty and stress of long-term displacement, this attention was valued as a form of recognition parallel to but distinct from that which was so often sought out in other intervention encounters. On the other hand, as I repeatedly made clear, I had no real control or influence over the resources and decision making that were so consequential for Bosnian returnees, although as a foreigner studying other foreigners I was often asked to explain how that decision making worked. Nevertheless, merely by virtue of being categorizable as an "international," I found myself drawn into local projects and goals—sometimes wittingly and willingly, sometimes less so. For example, I spent many long days at the office of an organization that represented returnees to Prijedor and surrounding areas. Occasionally they needed a translation of a text or document into English, or help editing something already translated, which I was happy to do. At other times, the head of the organization would swing by the office with donors visiting from Norway or Austria and introduce me as their "American partner," no doubt hoping that my presence as a researcher would communicate something positive about the seriousness and worthiness of their work.

Research relationships with the staff of IGOs and international NGOs were also enabled because I occupied that intermediary space—I was interested in their work and its effects, but I also had the kinds of "local knowledge" that they often lacked. Given the uncertainties structuring their work, I often found myself used as a sounding board for worries, potential solutions to problems, and complaints about the conditions under which they had to fulfill their mandates. And particularly for foreign staff located away from major urban centers, I was sought out socially as one of the few fluent English speakers who would not compromise their neutrality. And publicly socializing with foreigners undoubtedly shaped how I was seen by other Bosnians, with consequences for my research.

3

DOING THINGS WITH ETHNICITY

> **Years after the war, people's ethnic identity had lost none of its meaning. People no longer die for it, but they continue to live for it. No small number of people live off it.**
>
> —Dušan Kecmanović

It was on a cold day in January 2003 that I received a call from Miguel, a Spanish lawyer and the Human Rights Officer at the OSCE office in Prijedor, the urban center of a municipality in the Republika Srpska to which a large number of Bosniak refugees and a much smaller number of Croats were returning. He said that he had been approached the day before at a café by Dubravka, a self-identified Croat who was a very active member of the main returnee organization in Prijedor. She had tried to discuss something with him, but because his B/C/S language skills were very limited, they did not get very far, and his translator was out of town on vacation. She had suggested that he call me and set up a meeting with the three of us so that I could act as a translator between them. Both of them were long-term interlocutors of mine, and I agreed.

The next day Miguel and I arrived at about the same time at Le Pont, a restaurant as well known for the privacy of its high-backed booths as for its view of the slow-moving currents of the Sana River. Ostensibly the meeting was to talk about the implications of the constitutive peoples amendments on local government in the aftermath of the most recent elections, and how the municipality might employ more returnees. However, as we sat sipping coffee in relative seclusion, Dubravka brought up her distrust of one of the local staff at the OSCE office, Gojko. In particular, she questioned his discretion when he translated in meetings between her and the foreign staff like Miguel. She offered an example of how a critique of Prijedor's mayor made by a returnee had gotten back to the mayor, apparently through this translator (who happened to be a Serb, like most of the domestic staff in the OSCE Prijedor field office). Miguel took this accusation very seriously. His very reason for being in Bosnia was to monitor the human rights situation and advocate for returnees and other vulnerable populations who might be facing official discrimination. He worried that mistrust of Gojko might prevent Dubravka or other returnees from coming to him when they had information or concerns that they wanted to share, sensitive or otherwise. He assured her that *his* assistant, Svetibor, was very discrete and could be trusted, but that if this was unacceptable, he knew someone who worked as a translator at the UN International Police Task Force (IPTF) unit in town whom she could use. Before translating this for Dubravka, I asked him what was special about the IPTF translator—was Miguel suggesting this person because he did not work for the OSCE? He replied, no, it was the fact that the translator is not a Serb but a Bosniak. When I translated this for Dubravka she replied that she did not care whether the translator was a Serb or Bosniak or Croat. Instead, she said, the question of trust turned on the professionalism of the translator.

For me, the interesting thing here is that Miguel had actively interpreted Dubravka's complaint to be about ethnic difference, when in fact nothing she had said indicated that the problem for her lay in the translator being a Serb. Given what you have read in this book about postwar Bosnia and Herzegovina thus far, you may also not find Miguel's assumption unusual. And indeed, this kind of interpretive leap was not at all uncommon. In fact, the likelihood that a discourse about ethnic difference would be used in intervention encounters between officials like Miguel and returnees might even seem overdetermined. In the aftermath of a war fought in the name of ethnic groups, the return of refugees to territories where they would be an ethnic minority had been regularly obstructed. We have already seen how assumptions about hostility to returning refugees motivated the constitutional court's decision that initiated the constitutive peoples amendments process. Those very amendments seemed to write the expectation of ethnic antagonism into the highest levels of Bosnian government, creating the internationally supported state and entity-level chambers called the House of Peoples, which contained seats for ethnic representatives whose explicit goal was to protect "vital national interests." The logic entailed here was that only Serbs can be entrusted to truly represent and protect Serb interests, only Muslims can be entrusted with representing (or translating for foreigners) Muslim interests and aims, and so on.

And yet such a logic did not motivate Dubravka's complaint about Gojko. Miguel's assumption that it did points to the broader role played by ideologies about ethnic difference in structuring the field of encounters between foreign officials and returnees. In this chapter, I describe and analyze this role, particularly how these ideologies helped intervention agents make sense of postwar Bosnian politics and society—and their own part in it. Understanding this broader role helps explain the inventive ways in which returnees engaged foreign officials and tried to persuade and animate them to act on their behalf—and the ways in which foreign officials responded.

A starting point of my analysis is that ethnic groups are not naturally existing things in the world, even if many people experience the world in such "groupist" terms. As Rogers Brubaker (2002) has argued, if we want to avoid the mistake that Miguel made—assuming that ethnic identity played a role where it did not—we need to avoid the ideology of groupism, the tendency to "take discrete, sharply differentiated internally homogeneous and externally bounded groups as basic constituents of social life, chief protagonists of social conflicts, and fundamental units of social analysis . . . as substantial entities to which interests and agency can be attributed" (2002, 164). Instead of assuming the objective existence of ethnic groups, we ought to explain how people come to experience "groupness," that is, we need to identify the ideologies and practices which make seeing and experiencing the world in terms or categories of ethnic groups appear logical, even natural. This means being alert to those settings where—and moments when—the experience of "groupness" happens, and where and when it does not. Brubaker observes that group categories need "ecological niches in which to survive and flourish" (2002, 185). Intervention encounters between foreign officials and returning refugees made up just such an ecological niche within which the ethnic categories of Serb, Croat, and Bosniak flourished. Let me recount my own introduction into how and why this was the case.

When I first visited the country at the turn of the century, I arrived wary of using groupist terms to make sense of Bosnian politics and society, knowing as I did that ethnic antagonism was not the cause of the war but its product. I felt that using groupist terms would make me complicit with separatist state-building projects that had destroyed so many lives. Yet I quickly came under pressure to interpret social and political life through an ethnonational lens: international NGO staff talked in this idiom; the foreign and domestic officials of the OSCE and the various UN bodies did; I read it in newspapers and encountered it unsolicited in informal conversation with a wide range of interlocutors in the most ordinary settings. On later trips to Bosnia, academics, activists, and returning refugees alike bemoaned the "triumph" of ethnonationalism and the political entrepreneurs that appeared so skilled at exploiting this discourse for their own benefit. Still, this did not prevent people from regularly making judgments about others by virtue of their ethnic identification, from regularly talking about "Serb," "Croat," or "Bosniak" sides and characteristics—and in ways that were usually uncontroversial for the speakers or their audience. In postwar Bosnia across a wide range of contexts people were under constant pressure to experience themselves and others as members of these groups, and to categorize and identify themselves and others with the positions articulated by powerful, often self-appointed, ethnic spokespersons. Given this context, the ability to recognize, identify, or display "ethnicity" was all the more urgent for foreigners because ethnic identity was not necessarily discernible from physical appearance or linguistic practice alone.

Indeed, the very ubiquity and apparent inescapability of the discourse of ethnic identity for my foreign interlocutors—the way in which it appeared to totalize and reduce all social life to its terms—made its terms both seductive and necessary when trying to navigate a social context they knew relatively little about. Thus many foreign-Bosnian interactions—including those that took place in the context of refugee return—were mediated by what I call here *identity ideologies of ethnonationality*. These are systematic sets of ideas about individual/group sameness and difference that become meaningful in purposive action. In Bosnia, these identity ideologies constituted a ready-made model of sociality, a persuasive heuristic for international actors to understand, govern, and, perhaps most importantly, *legitimize* their state-building interventions in Bosnia, including the refugee return process. What is more, intervention encounters provided foreign officials with ongoing evidence of the relevance and salience of interpreting and acting upon Bosnian politics and society in these ideological terms.

In the next section I describe and defamiliarize what might seem to be commonsense, even banal ideas about ethnonational identity in order to show the kinds of interpretations and actions they made possible, and thus account for when, where, how, and why "groupness" happened and with what consequences. My aim here is to develop an analytic framework that militates against essentializing and reifying categories of ethnonational identification by pointing to their strategic, performative, and nonessential nature, while still recognizing that the purported essential, natural, and ineluctable character of such identifications is a key to their social force and their phenomenology.

The subsequent section describes the relationship of these ideologies to how foreigners made sense of Bosnian politics and society, and how they understood and legitimized their roles as mediators and civilizing missionaries in Bosnia and Herzegovina. I also show how they were socialized into the performative requirements of fulfilling those roles, particularly the requirement that they be neutral. I then analyze the creative ways returnees sought to engage foreign officials, and how foreigners responded to those attempts while navigating a tension created by fulfilling two roles. Throughout this chapter I demonstrate how everyday intervention encounters in the context of refugee return reproduced the political and social salience of ethnicity and ethnic difference, and also how foreign officials were able to disavow any part in this process.

Identity Ideology

The concept of "identity ideologies of ethnonationality" foregrounds the interpretive and interactional activities that ideas about identity make possible, and is based upon an action-oriented rather than referential theory of meaning. It points our analysis toward interactions, understood as made up of defining and conceptualizing activities, which often organize individuals, institutions, and their relationships. Using the term "ideology" is a reminder that the cultural conceptions we study are partial, interest-laden, contestable, and contested.

I now outline the ideological premises of ethnonational identity that formed the basis of political communication and social action in many foreign-Bosnian interactions I observed. I supplement my field observations with those of various scholars of nationalism and ethnic identity (Blommaert and Verschueren 1998; Brubaker 2002; Calhoun 1997; Comaroff and Comaroff 1992; Handler 1988; Herzfeld 1987, 2005; Malkki 1992). What follows is a distillation of these premises and their affordances.

Individual/Group Indistinguishability

As Dumont (1986) among others has noted, Western notions of collectivity are grounded in individualist metaphors, with ethnic groups or nations seen as individuals writ large—both in the sense of being indivisible and metaphorically as "singular beings that move through history as ordinary people move through their biographical life courses" (Calhoun 1997, 44). Thus qualities attributed to human individuals, such as agency, will, and purposive action, are also attributed to nations as individuals. In Bosnia, because the meaning of ethnonational identity was discursively represented as fixed and collectively held, it could be viewed as a means of assessing any individual style or statement against the background of the imagined whole.

The ideological premise of individual/group indistinguishability is key to the kinds of generalizations made about ethnonational groups, and leads to the conflation of an individual's interests and the national whole of which they are a member—and vice versa. It constitutes a social epistemology and makes possible the claim that once you know a person's ethnonational "identity," you know their position or desires in a given social situation. This allowed interlocutors of mine to generalize from the statement or claims of one ethnonational person or persons to an aggregate collective stance or position. Take one unremarkable example, an analysis of the "security situation" in Prijedor that was written up in an interoffice memo by the OSCE Human Rights Officer in the Prijedor field office in December 2002. Based on limited and translated discussions with a handful of (Bosniak) returnees and other (Serb) townspeople regarding a few recent acts of violence, he felt confident enough to claim and generalize that perceptions of security "break down radically along ethnic lines," what he called an "ethnic imbalance," and which he outlined in a few sentences under the headings "the view from the Bosniak side" and the "view from the Serbian side."

Furthermore, a corollary of individual/group indistinguishability is the premise that nations exist across historical time and geographical space, making possible the claim that acts that happened hundreds of miles away or hundreds of years in the past are directly and personally relevant (to the degree that they can be ethnonationally characterized). Thus in the same memo the OSCE officer described the "deterioration of the security situation in Prijedor," connecting a recent explosion at a Prijedor imam's house with two explosions in Doboj—a town located over 100 miles away—as evidence. Instances of this are so commonplace as to be banal. When Zoran Đinđic, the prime minister of Serbia, was assassinated in Belgrade, Serbia in 2003, a man on the streets of Banja Luka in Bosnia commented for television "This was an attack on the Serb nation. What can I say? We are killing each other." Muslim religious leaders in Sarajevo could also claim when, upon hearing of the desecration of a 400-year old Muslim graveyard in Banja Luka (five hours distant from Sarajevo by train or bus) that "the attack on these tombstones" represented "an attack on every Muslim." As we will see below, this practice—the collapsing of time and space and the aggregation of a single act or statement to collective meaning and categorical applicability—was entailed in numerous claims of general discrimination through which returnees attempted to mobilize international authorities to act in specific cases.

Universal, Essential, Ineluctable

Many have pointed to the pervasiveness of the ideological premise that the world is divided into nations as its most basic and natural units, and that individuals always participate in the broader world system as part of a national group (Calhoun 1997; Duara 1995). Thus being "national" is (or ought to be) a universal characteristic of each individual. At the same time, a world of nations is a world of difference. This premise, and the global legal and institutional frameworks that organize human and other rights, result in a continuing pressure to identify oneself and others as national and with a national group. In a postwar context in which how you identified yourself ethnonationally could make the difference in accessing housing, jobs, and other state-provided resources, this pressure was only heightened.

Connected to the premise that the world is divided into nations, and that everyone is a member of a national group, is the tacit assumption that people are normally members of *one and only one* nation, and that this membership describes neatly and concretely some *essential* aspect of their being. Membership in an ethnonational collective is purported to be based upon and proceed from the supposed unique and essential qualities that unites its members as a whole. By extension, individual members of an ethnonational group are the same in the most important ways, and by corollary, they are different in equally essential ways from members of other groups so defined. This ideological premise is both metonymical (each member is a microcosm of the encompassing whole) and metaphorical (each member is a version of the national character or mentality).

A final ideological premise that flows from individual/group indistinguishability and the essentialism of national being is the idea that ethnonational membership is *ineluctable*, usually something you are born into and about which you have little say. This is a particularly strong notion in Europe, but it contrasts with official policy in Bosnia and Herzegovina. Continuing a practice begun during the socialist Yugoslav period, citizens choose their national affiliation, or choose a nonnational affiliation (like Yugoslav), or no affiliation. Such a practice was and is anathema to nationalists, who denied that national being was something that could be chosen. And here internationals may have unwittingly colluded with these nationalists because, as we shall see, the premise of the ineluctable, irreducible, and thus fixed nature of ethnonational identity promised a stability to knowledge of a social situation once it could be rendered in ethnonational terms.

Categorical, Boundary-Producing, Homogenizing

Scholars have long recognized that the purported discreteness and universality of ethnonational groups generates powerful regimes of classification and categorical orders, what Malkki (1992) has called the "national order of things." In this light, the ideological premises of ethnonationality act as a dichotomizing principle, which, when brought to bear upon a social setting, sets in motion a partitioning process of individuals into groups. This partitioning process is also a homogenizing and essentializing process, and productive of boundaries. The emphasis on group sameness and difference homogenizes people identified as members of the same group, downplaying or erasing intragroup difference, and focuses attention on maximal difference between people identified as members of different groups.

In research on newspaper reporting across Europe, Blommaert and Verschueren 1998 noted the ways in which descent, history, culture, religion, and language are treated as a "feature cluster" according to which one can identify "nations" in the world. They show how the existence of any one feature tends to be predictive of the others, with a specific language perhaps most powerfully predictive of a distinct history and culture. By extension, the absence of a feature, like "distinct language," tends to cast doubts on the existence of the other features and thus also on the legitimacy of claims to nationhood.

In Bosnia and Herzegovina, "feature clustering" was apparent in the ways in which various actors attempted to discredit the nation-based claims of others. I came across this, for instance, when interlocutors questioned the existence of a distinct Bosnian or Bosniak language to underscore the artificiality of the Bosniak nation and thus also claims made in the name of that nation. Alternatively, foreign authorities often took the existence of what was previously called the Serbo-Croatian language and the mutual intelligibility of Slavic speakers from Croatia, Serbia, Montenegro, and Bosnia, as evidence of the artificiality, self-interested, and thus "political" nature of actors making demands in Bosnia and Herzegovina regarding the Serbian, Croatian, and Bosnian languages.

Constituting Social Subjects and Spokespersons

It follows from the ideological premises outlined above that individual membership in an ethnonational collective makes it possible for any single "member" to claim to speak on behalf of and represent that collective, endowing individuals with an agentive capacity—what Bourdieu called "spokespersonship" (1991)—by virtue of that membership. Bourdieu has shown how in interactions, particularly effective spokespersons performatively create the group that creates them, and upon whose behalf they are endowed to speak and act. It also allows individuals to claim that their ethnonational concerns carry the categorical weight of the group as a whole.

International Authority and Bosnia's Categorical Imperative

Ethnonational ideology not only played a crucial sense-making role for foreign actors in Bosnia. As I already observed, it was also built into the definition of Bosnia and Herzegovina as an object of international intervention: as a place riven by ethnic conflict that required impartial foreign supervision and mediation. In order to understand this link, it is worth recalling what kind of situation most new arrivals found themselves in upon landing in Sarajevo. They were expected to navigate a social field most knew nothing about, and to work within the context of a language they did not know (and which at times uses an alphabet, Cyrillic, most could not read). At the same time, their very presence in the country was predicated on the assumption that they were there to supervise and/or transform it. And part of what they were there to transform was the culturally defined backwardness of sectarianism. Thus not only were the ideological premises of ethnonational identity already familiar to these new arrivals, but their utility was heightened because they promised to bring clarity and order to what could otherwise be uncertain everyday interactions. Over the course of my fieldwork, every foreign member of an NGO or intergovernmental organization (IGO) I met revealed him- or herself to be a seasoned ethnonational interpreter. This was even more the case for refugee return, which was by definition a problem of ethnic difference. On more than a few occasions, I shared a story with a staff member of the OSCE or foreign NGO about a conversation I had had with someone in the field. One of their first questions was always "is he Bosniak? Is she a Serb?" Ethnonational identification appeared to be such a powerful cognitive mechanism that any understanding of a given situation was premised on knowledge of this sort.

Being able to make these distinctions came with particular urgency, an imperative to categorize, insofar as the definition of Bosnia as an object for international intervention and the legitimacy of international actors to promote, mediate, and represent refugee return were based upon this social ontology—the assumption that individual/group identity and alterity were the primary sources of cooperation and conflict in most if not all social interactions, and that they almost always defined individual interests, desires, and ways of understanding the world. In foreigners' role as mediators, then, their knowledge of Bosnia depended upon ethnonational ideology.

Their role as mediators, however, might seem to be in tension with their role as educators or civilizing missionaries; the former required the active use of ethnonational interpretive frameworks, while the latter was based upon their ability to transcend ethnic premises in favor of nonethnic, voluntary, and rational bonds of social and political solidarity. Both roles, however, relied upon the self-definition of foreigners as neutral and "even-handed" regarding Bosnia's ethnic "sides": being "neutral" as a mediator meant not picking "sides" and neutrality as educator meant modeling the nonsectarian ideal of civic government that was promoted as the solution to Bosnia's problems. This in turned hinged on the ability to maintain a broader distinction between foreigners and Bosnians, as well as the promise of its eventual subversion. Thus while foreign actors were not at all external to or disinterested in the politics of Bosnia, their authority to supervise or mediate in a context defined by antagonistic ethnic difference came in part from claiming to be so.

To anticipate a discussion later in this chapter, there was another tension between the roles of mediator and educator, and it reflected a tension inherent in ethnonational ideology. Occupying the mediator role—claiming to be neutral and external to Bosnian politics and society—was based upon the idea that one was simply observing reality: the immutable fact of ethnicity, ethnic groups, and ethnic conflict. As already discussed, there are plenty of examples of how internationals came to experience this as a social fact. But the supposed stable existence of ethnic groups did not translate into stability of meaning. And indeed, in their roles as educators or civilizing missionaries, they were supposed to transform the reality of ethnic conflict. This was based upon the idea that how, where, when, and why "groupness" mattered was fluid, contingent, and malleable. Foreign officials often tacked between these two roles, depending upon the particulars of the encounter. For example, occupying the mediator role made it possible for "internationals" to routinely ignore their part in structuring the contexts within which ethnicity "mattered," and to elide their power to impose legitimate principles of defining and dividing the social world.

Thus each foreigner who came to Bosnia to work in an NGO or for an IGO entered a sociopolitical field already organized around the "problem" of ethnic difference and structured by the expectation that they could (and should) mediate that difference. Experience often quickly educated them to take up this role and socialized them into the performative requirement that they be neutral.

For instance, in April of 2002, I attended the second meeting of a Sanski Most "working group" created to discuss and resolve Serb returnee-related problems. It was initiated by the Italian head of the local UNHCR office because she was getting inundated with so many of the same complaints of discrimination regarding basic municipal services and issues like employment. Rather than ignore them or take up each individually, she decided that the situation required direct collective mediation. The authority she wielded was evident in that she could initiate such a working group and bring Serb returnee representatives and Muslim municipal officials to the same table. By the time the second meeting rolled around, however, she was no longer working in Bosnia. Instead, her replacement, a young American who had arrived only weeks earlier, presided over the meeting together with an Italian coworker and a Swiss immigration lawyer serving as the human rights officer for the OSCE office in Sanski Most (also brand new to Bosnia).

When I arrived a little early to the meeting in a basement room of Sanski Most's city hall, I found the four Serb returnee representatives already there, sitting on one side of a long table. Most of the municipal officials were also there, sitting directly across from them. Clustered at one head of the table were the representatives of the three IGOs and their translators/assistants. Sitting at the other end of the table were invited representatives of various international NGOs which were active in the return process, and one anthropologist. The physical and performative arrangement of the meeting turned out to be an almost literal instantiation of mediation: the returnee representatives directed their complaints and problems to the foreigners at the head of the table. These were then translated into English, and then, in English, one or another of the foreign staff would restate or redirect the complaint to the municipal officials, and it was then translated back into BCS for them. As one can easily imagine, this setup could not be sustained throughout the entire meeting. When disagreements arose or possible solutions were proposed, often there were direct interactions between the returnees and municipal officials that the IGO staff never fully understood and of which they ever got only cursory translations. Indeed, they had to insert themselves more than a few times in order to maintain their authority and to keep the meeting from degenerating into arguments between returnees and municipal staff. I later asked a translator who worked for the UNHCR, a self-identified Serb from Banja Luka, whether the *foreign* staff needed to be there at all given the cumbersome arrangement. She replied that when the topics to be discussed were of a political nature (like ethnic discrimination), the foreign staff was needed in order to preserve the UNHCR's image of neutrality, to make sure that no one could say that any decisions taken and legitimized by an international authority favored one ethnic group over another (see Coles 2007: 96–108 for a similar discussion of the role played by the "mere presence" of foreigners in legitimizing foreign-run elections in BiH).

It was in settings like this that foreign staff came to understand and instantiate their role as mediators and to connect their authority with their ability to occupy a neutral position and with their lack of "ethnic bias," which was automatically projected onto the two "sides" between which they were there to mediate. It was also moments like this that trained foreigners to make the interpretive leaps like the one made by Miguel described above, particularly when it came to claims made by returnees.

The structure of international authority described here entails a few important effects. The first is that I found, at least in public settings, individual and collective claims, disagreements, and conflicts gained more attention and traction with international authorities if they found expression within the idiom of ethnonational identity—that is, if they fit into the dominant definition of the problem that foreigners were in Bosnia to mediate. This in turn provided internationals with consistent and ongoing evidence that interpreting Bosnia in ethnonational ideological terms was legitimate and constituted a restatement of the need for their presence. Of course, recognition that foreigners were complicit in eliciting this idiom was elided by the binary distinction which posited them as outsider observers, external to the problems of postwar Bosnia.

Let me now describe how ethnonational identity ideology featured in the creative and pragmatic strategies used by returnees to initiate encounters with foreign officials, attract foreign interest in returnee issues, and animate a response.

Identity Ideology and the Moral Metric of Equality

The commitment to neutrality and "evenhandedness" on the part of foreign actors translated in the Bosnian context to the widespread use of what I call the *moral metric of equality*. This was a standard of categorical equivalence against which returnees and foreigners alike evaluated events and circumstances, personal or otherwise. Any difference, particularly in personal experience, that could be tied to ethnonational difference of a categorical nature enabled a moral critique of international actors whose legitimacy was based upon their ability to demonstrate neutrality and equivalence in their encounters with ethnonational populations—and thus ensure a multiethnic social and political field free from discrimination. Thus accusations of active bias or passive tolerance of discrimination became a common way to initiate interaction with foreign authorities, and attempt to enlist their intervention in any number of projects and contexts. Recall, for example, the interaction with Miroslav Pantić that Marcus complained about in one of the opening vignettes of this book.

Let me offer an extended example. On a bright sunny morning in May of 2003, I attended a *svesrpski sabor* (pan-Serb parliament) in a drab municipal annex building in Sanski Most. It was staged as a public event, attended mostly by Serb returnees to the municipality, but also by a representative of the OSCE, members of the news media from Banja Luka, as well as members of the Party for Democratic Progress (a "moderate" Serb political party) working in various ministries in the government of the Republika Srpska. It was an event whose very form—*svesrpski* (pan-Serb)—underlined an ethnonational basis of collective organization and representation, and projected the image of a united, common will. As a few organizers told me, it was largely conceived of as a way to put pressure on international authorities to force municipal officials in Sanski Most to respond to a number of demands made by Serb returnees.

Before the meeting began, the organizers admitted to being a little disappointed with the turnout of about forty people, most of whom were middle-aged men or older pensioners. Some carried notebooks and wrote in them, but most sat passively with their arms folded. At times, it was hard not to be distracted by the sounds drifting in through the windows of children playing in the river. As the meeting began, a television cameraman from Радио-Телевизија Републике Српске (Radio-Television Republika Srpska) slowly swept across the rows of seats as audience members did their best to look concentrated on what the speakers were saying. After he had enough footage, a few of the more prominent members of the audience ducked out of the meeting to make brief statements in time for the crew to return to Banja Luka for the afternoon television program *Српска Данас* (Srpska today).

The first speaker, Nebojša, an officer in the Republika Srpska military originally from Sanski Most, but now living in temporary housing in Prijedor, welcomed everyone and read the minutes and report on the "condition of the Serb population in Sanski Most" from the last meeting, about six months prior. It was a type-written document filled with claims and demands made by the "Serb people." (Typical lines read "The Serb people seek an investigation into the responsibility of all individuals and organs of government for the destruction of around 1,200 Serb monuments, fifteen churches . . . ," and "The Serb people in Sanski Most are not satisfied with the security situation in the municipality.")

He paused when he got to a section of the report having to do with a book circulating in Sanski Most and Prijedor entitled *Zločin je zaboraviti zločin!* (It Is Criminal to Forget Evil!). The book detailed acts of violence against non-Serb populations in the area in the early 1990s and was considered particularly controversial because it named alleged perpetrators. The section of the report Nebojša was reading began, "The Municipality of Sanski Most published the book *It Is Criminal to Forget Evil!* about Sanski Most during the war of 1992–1995 and in which 293 members of the Serb nation from Sanski Most were declared to be war criminals without a trial." He then looked up from the minutes and remarked

> The next question is about the responsibility of the publisher of . . . those so-called books. I read one from A to Z. What disturbs me—me personally—besides all of the stupidity . . . actually, the crimes against the Bosniak people between 1992 and 1995 which were carried out by individual members of the Serb people—unfortunately in our name . . . what I am missing is the fact that there is not a single sentence, not one positive example when perhaps—not perhaps, certainly there are numerous such cases—when Serb neighbors helped Muslims when it was truly very difficult here for Bosniaks in Sanski Most. One only reads the worst and most terrible things about the Serb people.

He quickly added that so much attention was devoted to finding the bodily remains of Muslim civilians and so little on Serb civilians. He then returned to reading the report and soon paused again to complain about statements made by municipal officials that were circulating in the media and in which Serbs were referred to as "Četniks" (recall that for many, this was a derogatory term that roughly meant "murderous Serb fascist"),

> . . . the speaker for the municipal government said after the last sabor literally that we are all Četniks. That we are not Serbs, but Četniks.

> [Pauses and looks around] Never were there any sanctions. We informed the OSCE office in Sanski Most, the OHR office in Banja Luka, the OHR office in Bihać . . . however, no sanctions . . . now if I or if any of us were to go, as spokespersons, and say that a Bosniak or Croat gentleman are Ustaše, I think that that person would be dismissed, sanctioned, and fined. I bring this up only to show that this municipal government can treat us however they want to, call us Četniks and there will be no sanctions.

He then returned to reading the minutes and upon concluding brought up the issue of Serbs, like himself, whose land had been "usurped" by the municipality after the war. He remarked that now they were having trouble repossessing this land or getting fairly compensated. "We who lost our land in Sanski Most are having a very hard time reclaiming it. Why? In Kotorsko, they forced illegal builders to begin tearing down their illegal homes, and look at Stari Grad in Prijedor. Why do we have such a hard time?"

Finally, as he began to open up the discussion, to "analyze" what had been done in the time between the last meeting and the current one regarding the problems and demands they made of the international community, he returned again to the theme of how Serbs are portrayed in the media, the "propaganda against us" and offered his own commentary.

> I am not a Četnik. No one here is a Četnik. I think we are bigger democrats than all the members of the Sanski Most municipal assembly. No one *here* has the goal of provoking international tensions. This sabor does not have that kind of goal. The goals of this meeting are only to analyze the problems and figure out solutions to those problems—not nationalism, not revanchism, not any kind of tension!

After Nebojša finished, a much older gentleman, Veso, got up and continued on the subject of land "usurpation." He was clearly upset, and underlined that the goal of the usurpation of land was to prevent Serbs from returning, and he wanted the international community to acknowledge this intent behind it. He echoed what Nebojša had said about the resolution of such land issues in Kotorsko and Prijedor and then reposed the question: Why not in Sanski Most? He later answered his own question after making numerous comparisons between Prijedor and Sanski Most, stating baldly that the international community has two ways to deal with things: one for Serbs and another for Bosniaks.

The meeting continued for another two hours, with eleven other speakers. Although the subjects of their commentary shifted, the "international community" almost always figured as addressee, usually in the form of complaint about how little they respond to the threats, corruption, and general problems that Serbs faced in Sanski Most. Much of the preceding description is unremarkable, a common example of complaints regarding discrimination by returnees. Yet it is worth dwelling upon the ideological premises that lie behind the characterizations and representations used by speakers like Nebojša to comment upon and mobilize international action, because they are shared by foreign authorities, if not always in ways that they would like.

Categorical Comparability

A significant amount of interpretation and commentary is made possible by tacking back and forth between the individual and the categorical/collective, and not only for ethnonational persons. Foreign members of the "international community" were also subject to the same kinds of interpellation as individual parts of an ill-defined whole, as we shall see below when we unpack the kinds of arguments being made in the above-described meeting.

The name and form of this meeting—*svesrpski sabor* (pan-Serb parliament)—was designed to provide the image of a collective will, and the collective representation reflected in the report acted to erase individual authorship. Moreover, such a representational form homogenized those attending by eliding intragroup differences and invested speakers like Nebojša with spokespersonship. Drawing upon the premise of individual/group indistinguishability, he elevated his complaints (on property repossession, for example) to a general, categorical level—thus adding heft by arguing that his troubles were not an individual or capricious act, but an intentional policy against Serbs. Once this categorical level was achieved, a number of things became comparable across time and space, and claims about Serbs in Sanski Most could be legitimized on the basis of this comparison. These included the events in Kotorsko and Prijedor that Nebojša and Veso alluded to in their comments.

Kotorsko selo is a village located near Doboj in the Republika Srpska, about 125 miles from Sanski Most, where the municipality had given land that had belonged to Muslims before the war to Serb refugees to build houses upon. This had elicited accusations by Muslim returnee representatives in Doboj that it was illegal and was being used as a way to prevent Muslims from returning. In early 2002 the OHR brought pressure on the local government to put a moratorium on building until the question of legality could be resolved; the moratorium was defied and building continued. At this point, a show of force was organized and all of the building that had taken place since the moratorium was taken down, with local police providing protection to the construction workers doing this work. It was this show of force that brought the case to the attention of the news media, which is how I, and presumably the returnees in Sanski Most, heard about it.

The other comparison was made with the Stari Grad neighborhood in the town of Prijedor (also in the Republika Srpska). It was the oldest settlement in the town, and before the war it had contained 130 houses belonging almost entirely to Muslim families. In mid-1992 the houses were looted and razed, the plumbing and electric cables were dug up, and a flea market was built on top of it. Under considerable pressure brought by the OHR, OSCE, and the US embassy, the Prijedor municipality closed the flea market in late 2002 so that land could be repossessed by its prewar Muslim owners (I return to this case in chapter 4).

It is not only the question of land that made Sanski Most, Kotorsko, and Stari Grad comparable. It is a comparison made possible by the premise of categorical equivalence: Kotorsko and Stari Grad were issues of *Muslim* land being usurped by *Serb* authorities and given to Serbs to build upon, or, stated differently, it was a question of an ethnic group made vulnerable by minority status being abused by an ethnic majority that held the reins of government. Thus Serbs in Sanski Most in the Federation saw themselves as categorically equivalent to Muslims in Kotorsko or Stari Grad in the Republika Srpska.

Once categorical equivalence was asserted, contrasts could then be made between the two, and questions posed about those contrasts, particularly about the role of the international community in each case. Nebojša, Veso, and others claimed that a categorical difference existed in the way the international community behaved toward Serbs and Muslims. Of course, given how deeply international legitimacy and authority relied upon maintaining a convincing image of neutrality and equivalence, and given how deeply invested it was in "minority return" and the vision of a multiethnic Bosnia behind it, this was a potentially damaging accusation. This is also why Veso insisted that the "international community" recognize that the reasoning that had impelled them to act in Kotorsko and Stari Grad—that Municipal authorities were obstructing "minority return"—held true for Sanski Most. This would compel international actors to articulate why they had acted differently in each case.

Ethnonational ideology not only facilitated these kinds of categorical comparisons. It also imbued them with a moral force linked to the purported ineluctability of ethnonational identification. Nebojša had little choice as to whether to be a Serb. Thus when he claimed that he was targeted not because of what he did (and was thus accountable for), but of what he was, this was a powerful form of injustice and bestowed moral capital on those who claimed this sort of victimhood.

This is what I mean by moral metric of equality: the formal categorical equivalence of ethnonational individuals/groups in Bosnia, the grounding in and commitment to neutrality as the basis of international authority, and the ineluctability of ethnonational identification invited returnees to compare and interpret their experience first within terms of ethnonational sameness and difference, particularly in the presence of international authorities. This was clearly exhibited in the thinly veiled accusation regarding the differential treatment of Serb and Muslim returnees regarding property. It was also, however, part of the accusation of how the international community had allowed municipal officials to defame Serbs by calling them Četniks. This complaint had multiple audiences and was part of a chain of complex claims and counterclaims.

The complaint that there were no consequences for Muslims who called Serbs Četniks refers, of course, to the period before the 1990s war when such speech would have been grounds for sanctions against the speaker. This contrast is unlikely to have meant as much to a foreign audience as it did to a domestic one, particularly the officials present who were part of the RS government and had a vested interest in being able to claim they represented Serbs regardless of what part of Bosnia they were in. This complaint, and the double-standard implied ("if I say that a Bosniak or Croat gentleman are Ustaše, I . . . would be dismissed, sanctioned, and fined") was thus partially aimed to get Serbs not immediately involved in the affairs of returnees to Sanski Most to align themselves with their plight. Broadcasting these claims on Republika Srpska television was also designed to amplify them and bring pressure on the international community to prove themselves to be unbiased.

However, the form of this complaint was also part of another common strategy, the protest at unfair generalization. Indeed, the categorical nature of ethnonational ideology worked in multiple ways: statements or claims made about ethnonational groups could simultaneously be claims about each individual "member," and acts carried out in the name of a collective potentially attribute responsibility for those acts to each "member." Such statements and acts were thus excellent ways to implicate and recruit vast numbers into aligning their senses of self to definitions (of citizenship), projects (like state-building), and conflicts (over resources) that were articulated in the ideological terms of ethnonational groupness. The use of Četnik by Muslim municipal officials was itself part of collective moral argument meant in fact to legitimize ignoring the complaints of Serb returnees by suggesting that they were in fact being targeted for "what they had done." This was clear in Nebojša's discussion of the book *It Is Criminal to Forget Evil!*, which illustrated still another discursive possibility enabled by ethnonational ideology—differentiating oneself from the whole.

A Good Serb

The premise of individual/group indistinguishability allowed any single "member" of an ethnic group to turn their individual experience into a categorical claim regarding an ethnonational collective. But "members" are not the only ones who carry out this "inflating" work; others can as well. This gives individual "members" countless opportunities to set themselves apart from unfair or poorly fitting collective representations. In the preceding section, this was most clearly done by Nebojša when he sought to present himself as moral, as "a good Serb," in a field of collective representations that held "Serbs" as guilty for the majority of war crimes in the 1990s war. As I described in chapter 2, assertions of collective guilt and innocence were common and regularly touched off mutual incriminations, particularly for those who were implicated by virtue of membership in one of those collectives. Assertions of genocide against Serbs in the Second World War competed with assertions of genocide against Muslims in the most recent war, with speakers claiming to represent either group downplaying or denying the claims of the others.

Thus Nebojša's commentary on the book was something of a novelty. While he was wary about the way the book names alleged perpetrators, he in no way denied the crimes of which the book speaks; in fact, he went so far as to recognize them and to recognize that they were done by "individual members of the Serb people—unfortunately in our name." In his comments regarding the book, he thus presented himself as "reasonable" and "fair" by acknowledging the crimes committed against non-Serbs.

This tacking between collective and individual is critical: by virtue of reading the sabor's report, with its demands articulated in terms of the collective "Serb people in Sanski Most," he took on the legitimacy of ethnonational spokesperson without taking personal responsibility for authoring the report. He then commented on the book in a way that promoted himself as moral, and by virtue of his being a Serb spokesperson, heightened the sense of injustice that lay behind his critique of how Serbs were being treated in Sanski Most. The form of his performance offered an excellent way to differentiate himself from the collective, tacking between reading from the report and pulling away and offering his own commentary (recall how he qualified his comments on the book: "what bothers me, *me personally*"). He could then protest the collective representation of Serb guilt by critiquing the book for being unbalanced, for its "one-sidedness," and lack of inclusion of any positive examples where Serbs acted honorably regarding their Muslims neighbors. This unfair one-sidedness was then quickly extended to characterize the search for the bodily remains of civilian victims of wartime violence, with public attention almost exclusively focused on Muslim victims. Together with his complaints about being labeled a Četnik, he presented himself as moral and not the "kind of person" who dismissed Serb crimes out of hand, thus making the anti-Serb prejudices appear all the more unfair. He then extended his reasonable self-presentation to characterize the goals of the meeting, making it more difficult for others, including foreign addressees of the international community, to dismiss his complaints and the group's concerns as extreme or exclusively Serb-oriented. It worked, in other words, to heighten the stakes of his demand for the intervention of foreign and domestic authorities.

In the preceding section I have tried to show the kinds of interpretive action and political communication that the identity ideology of ethnonationality made possible. International authority, based upon neutrality in a sociopolitical field defined by antagonistic ethnic difference, the commitment of the international community to "minority return," as well as the substantive prewar commitment to freedom from ethnic discrimination for all Yugoslavs, combined to create the conditions of possibility for (and may have even elicited) these kinds of calculations. The ideological premises of ethnonationality offered a wide range of interpretive possibilities: the premise of individual/group indistinguishability and of homogeneity and the categorical equivalence that follows from these premises made events in Doboj and Prijedor comparable and relevant to Sanski Most. They invested the position of an individual like Nebojša with the weight of a collective spokesperson, and at the same time they allowed for the differentiation of any single individual from ill-fitting and thus unjust stereotyping of a collective nature. They made possible the combination and inflation of disparate events and individual acts to a categorical level and, together with the premise of ineluctability, enabled a moral critique of international actors as ignoring or treating differently innocent people whose only crime was to be saddled with an ethnonational identity about which they had no control.

Were such accusations regarding the international community successful at mobilizing foreign actors? At times, they clearly were; note the meeting called for by the UNHCR to respond to complaints of discrimination, or the interpretive leap made by a staff member of the OSCE. This suggests that foreign authorities were sympathetic and ready to respond to such claims (real or imagined). At other times, however, they were not successful. In these cases, foreign actors justified their lack of response in any number of ways, often by employing many of the ideological premises described above: they would resist the attempt to invest individual experience with collective weight by questioning the representivity of the speaker. For instance, an official at the OSCE office in Sanski Most once told me that he wished that Nebojša would stop claiming his property case was a typical example of discrimination, because it was not. At other times, foreigners would argue against the comparability of disparate events and people and deny the categorical characterization of difference implied in such comparisons. For instance, regarding the comparison with Kotorsko and Sanski Most, the same OSCE official routinely argued that he did not have the authority to order the removal of illegal building in Sanski Most. Rather, he argued that only the OHR had that power, thus blocking their attempt to get him to acknowledge a relation of obligation as a member of the "international community." And a member of the OHR in Banja Luka foregrounded all the specific details about Kotorsko selo to argue that it was a "special case," and thus not comparable to other situations. Finally, there were times when the agentive nature of the speaker, revealed in the overly strategic use of ethnonational ideology, was identified by foreign officials as problematic. They argued that such speakers were being "political," a term that connoted self-interest and a morally dubious character, to legitimize acting against or simply ignoring critiques aimed at animating foreigners. This too was based upon the ideological premises of ethnonational identity, but in a different way than I have previously discussed.

Ethnonational Ideology and Politics—Ethnonational Ideology as Politics

One day in May of 2002, I sat down to talk with an Italian woman, Carmela, from Trento, who ran an international NGO in town, the Local Democracy Agency (LDA, loosely affiliated with the Council of Europe). We met in the organization's office, located in the Hotel Balkan opposite Prijedor's main square. I had heard from many of my returnee interlocutors about her and was now finally getting around to meeting her and finding out more about what the LDA did. After a long monologue about the LDA and its funding and partner organizations, she told me that one of the main projects for the LDA was entitled *Prijedor: Grad Suživota* (Prijedor: city of coexistence), with the explicit goal to "create connections and relations between ethnicities."

Our conversation over the next hour touched on many aspects of refugee return and international intervention, and then turned to a particularly well-known Bosniak politician, Muharem Murselović, with a prominent role in the Prijedor municipal assembly. Her opinion of him was decidedly mixed, and in a disparaging remark, she called him a "true Muslim politician," meaning that she found his political style objectionable. As evidence, she recalled a recent encounter with him where he, using the moral metric of equality, complained about how much aid her organization gave to Serbs in Prijedor, when it was in fact the Bosniaks who really needed help there. Feeling compelled to respond, she told him that the LDA was planning to give aid to a Bosniak returnee women's association through an economic regeneration project. His response was that Bosniak returnees would be better served if the LDA would support Serbs to return to Sanski Most than aid Bosniak women in Prijedor. She found this response both baffling and a rather crude expression of demographic politics.

This puts another twist on the discussion of ethnonational ideology: on the one hand, the ideological premises of ethnonational difference clearly lay at the heart of the work her organization does. The very name of the project, "Prijedor: City of Coexistence," problematized social relations in the essentializing, homogenizing, and collective terms of ethnonational ideology: "our goal is to create connections and relations between ethnicities"—not people. On the other hand, there were times when making arguments that rely upon those same ideological premises are objectionable, or "political."

This interaction with Carmela was emblematic of an apparent contradiction that I encountered repeatedly during fieldwork. On the one hand, the foreign staff of IGOs took the ideological premises of ethnonational ideology to be unproblematic, in part because the argument legitimizing their presence as mediators was dependent upon it. On the other hand, they disparaged the use of the very same ideological premises by local actors in particular contexts as "political"—evidence of the "primitive sectarianism" that distinguished them from the Bosnians they were there to transform. This apparent tension emerged from a contradiction built into the premises of ethnonational identity ideology itself: on the one hand, individual/group sameness and difference is presented as essential, fixed, and totalizing, while on the other, in practice, the meaning of group categories is socially intersubjective, performative, and context-dependent. I suggest that the strategic use or deployment of ethnonational ideological premises by particular speakers exposed the variable, shifting, and context-dependent meaning of "ethnic identity," the fact that just as "groupness" happens in some contexts, it may not in others. This may have been unsettling to foreign actors because it suggested that their presence might actually be eliciting such discourse, that they were in fact participating in the reification of an ethnonational model of sociality which was supposedly responsible for the conflict they were in Bosnia to mediate and overcome. It thus threatened to collapse the binary distinction between "international" and local that legitimized their presence in Bosnia.

This led to a discernable distinction I came across repeatedly. On the one hand, abstract representations such as opinion polls that controlled for ethnicity and asked questions like "Do you believe Bosnia is your state?," or election results that favored nationalist parties, were taken as unproblematic evidence of the social facticity of ethnic groups. On the other hand, any individual argument or use of ethnonational ideology, where the agency of the speaker became apparent (thus revealing the strategic rather than supposed essential nature of "identity"), could be judged "political." This latter designation justified a whole set of possible actions, such as removing elected officials from office or ignoring the demands for resources or action like those made by Nebojša.

This parallels what Keith Brown, in his historical study of various political and territorial claims to Macedonia, called the "double standard" of nationalist thought. In analyzing narratives that reflected competing claims to Macedonia as Bulgarian or Greek, he found that each sought to portray opposing national claims as the product of human agents with their own agendas, and as thus going against an underlying (natural) reality or order of things. He writes that the underlying argument being made in these narratives was that "genuine collectivities are given by history, products of processes beyond human agency. False collectivities are those held together by fear, coercion, or manipulation" (2003, 91).

I would argue that foreign actors in Bosnia operated with a very similar notion, and would pivot to their role as civilizing missionaries who needed to model the right (European) kind of nationalism, which celebrated the freedom of identity, while at the same time disavowing or condemning its "strategic" uses. Of course, they reserved for themselves the power and capacity to make these distinctions, and when they did they implicitly restated the need for an international presence. Perhaps the most common instance was when foreigners pointed to the demands made by Bosnian Croat and Serb politicians to have separate interpreters during common interactions with foreigners—completely unnecessary from a strict translation point of view. For them, this justified condemning or ignoring their claims as immoral. In another example, Coles (2007) writes about how foreign OSCE election workers strove to embody the distinction between themselves and the supposed sectarianism of their Bosnian interlocutors: "internationals often attempted to nullify ethnicity as a salient category. Some purposely avoided learning the ethnicity of Bosnian colleagues; others referred to the now distinct languages as the 'local language' or ridiculed (along with many Bosnians) the cultural politics that distinguished coffee into three ethnicized drinks—Serb kafa, Croat kava, and Bosniac kahva" (2007, 46).

This link between the use of nationalist discourse and "politics" was shared by many Bosnians. Marking strategic uses of ethnonational discourse as "politics" or *politika* was a way for Bosnians, particularly those not in officially sanctioned positions of power, to negatively comment on the interpellations that they were subject to but about which they had little say. As a category of immoral action, *politika* was used to identify and stigmatize the pursuit of power for its own sake, corruption, and self-interest, and was often but not always applied to politicians. Kolind (2007) describes how a Muslim returnee to Stolac, a Croat-majority town in Herzegovina, described the link between ethnic politics and *politika*:

> *Politika* is something that is above you, something ordinary people do not understand or have any influence over. *Politika* is something being done by people far away, those who do not have to live with the consequences of their actions; it is cynical and egoistic acts. For instance, our people [Muslims politicians] in Sarajevo are requesting people to return to Stolac, so when a year has passed they can say: "Look, now a thousand Muslims are living in Stolac, now the Croats can no longer say that this is Croat territory." But none of them ever come down here to see how we live, or just to talk to us. They do not care about common people, what we think or feel. We have a saying: "*politika je kurva*" [politics is a whore]—they are only doing it for themselves, like a whore is only doing it for money. (2007, 126)

Later Kolind shows how the category of *politika* was employed by Muslim returnees to explain the war and to make space for a multiethnic life in sites of return—by blaming the war not on their old/new Croat or Serb neighbors, but on self-interested politicians who placed normal, *pošteni* (decent) people "in situations beyond their control, in situations without choices" (2007, 127). In fact, for many foreigners and Bosnians alike, the mere use of ethnonational discourse in certain contexts by a Bosnian interlocutor set off alarm bells as a possible index of self-interest and "politics," and was thus to be viewed with suspicion.

In another example, Azra Hromadžić (2015) provides an excellent ethnographic account of how schooling in postwar Bosnia and Herzegovina, a site of significant international investment in overcoming ethnic division, became an ecological niche where ethnonational ways of viewing and experiencing the world flourished. She found a similar use of the term *politika* when students and staff wanted to resist being reduced to ethnic labels and manipulated as mere categorical beings. She found that people used the term *narod* (meaning people or nation) to refer to each other as ordinary people beyond ethnic labels, united in being exploited and abused by more powerful politicians. And chapter 2 provided some examples of the scorn and cynicism with which the *politika* of ethnic difference—in the form of the "national key"—was viewed by some Bosnian commentators. So when foreign officials also denigrated the use of ethnonational ideology in these ways, they may have found local support. At the same time, in no way did any of this critical or evasive commentary upset the basic precepts of ethnonational ideology or the possibilities of its strategic use in other encounters.

Conclusion

I have shown in this chapter why and how intervention encounters around refugee return became an interactional space where ethnonational ideology and discourse flourished, and why it was so hard to escape, even for those who may have wanted to. First, the apparent ubiquity of ethnonational discourse created the illusion that people—from international authorities and aid organization staff to domestic politicians and returning refugees—were all talking about the same thing. Over time, individual interactions or single events combined to provide foreigners with consistent and ongoing evidence that interpreting Bosnian social and political life in ethnonational terms was legitimate. It thus acted as a de facto argument for the enduring salience, if not fixed reality, attributed to such ideologies and attached to the people and places of the former Yugoslavia. It also constituted a restatement of the need for a foreign mediating presence. Of course, any recognition by foreigners that they may be complicit in eliciting this idiom—the feedback effect of the terms of their intervention—was routinely elided by the binary distinction that posited them as external to postwar Bosnian life. Their commitment to a self-definition as neutral required that they (1) call the strategic use of ethnic identity discourse "politics," (2) restate the distinction between themselves and such Bosnian "manipulators," and (3) delegitimize the latter's claims. Each such instance restated the need for their mediating and civilizing presence. Studying the broader role of ethnonational identity ideology in intervention encounters also brings to light the ways in which both foreign officials and returnees acted, and justified their actions, "in terms of the perceived (and misperceived) cultural premises of their interlocutors" (Faier and Rofel 2014, 366).

In each of the examples given in this chapter—the face-to-face interaction between Miguel and Dubravka; the meeting between and among Serb returnees, Muslim municipal officials, the staff of IGOs, international aid organizations and their translators; the recounted conversation between Carmela and Muharem Murselović; or the speeches by Serb returnees aimed at animating foreign interest in their plight—we see the hallmarks of intervention encounters. These were interactions across difference and inequality by people from differently positioned groups, in which the nature, meaning, and legitimacy of that difference and inequality were defined and contested. We saw hierarchies being asserted and subverted, and uncertainties emerge and submerge, demonstrating "the ongoing negotiations of cultural practices within unequal, but also unstable, relations of power" (Faier and Rofel 2014, 366). In these interactions the roles, relationships, obligations, responsibilities, and goals of intervention were being worked out, coconstituted through performances of "neutrality" by international officials and their evaluation by returnees.

It was not, however, only foreigners whose self-definition and self-authorization required a robust and regular performance and demonstration of "neutrality." The staff of aid organizations also came to rely upon ethnic identity ideology to fill the placeholder for "politics" against which they structured the humanitarian contexts of their interventions. As we will see in the next chapter, this had major consequences in depoliticizing the refugee return process and was a major factor in shaping its outcome.

4

FROM HUMANITARIANISM TO HUMANITARIANIZATION

Managing the Instabilities of International Aid

Only if you're politically savvy can you be politically neutral.

—Staff member of the Red Cross

Much of contemporary international intervention takes places under the sign of humanitarianism, and we can trace the post–Cold War expansion of transnational humanitarianism to the Bosnian war. The vast organizational system dedicated to caring for refugees and displaced persons both during and after the war meant that many Bosnians' main relationship with international intervention was through an encounter with aid organizations. The enormous resources involved meant that being a humanitarian in postwar Bosnia and Herzegovina was not easy; it required navigating a complex and volatile field of political and economic forces, expectations, and encounters.

For example, in the spring of 2002, I joined a group of Muslims and Serbs assembled in a classroom in an otherwise empty school building, located at the village center of Budimlić Japra, in northwestern Bosnia and Herzegovina. There I found myself witness to a contest over the terms and relations of a housing reconstruction project, part of a massive effort by the European Union and the United States to move refugees back to their prewar homes and reverse the effects of ethnic cleansing. This was the oft-described goal of refugee return, a process the international community hoped would work against those forces that sought to keep postwar Bosnia's political-territorial units ethnically homogenous.

Everyone in the room watched as the mayor of the municipality pressed Jasmina, a Bosnian aid worker with an international NGO, about the amount of aid and how it was going to be distributed. The mayor claimed that she heard that it would be thirty houses, and suggested that it could break down fifteen houses for Serbs, fifteen for Muslims, or even thirteen for Serbs and seventeen for Muslims.

"I'm not interested in your *politika*!" retorted Jasmina with a force that seemed disproportionate to the mayor's simple suggestion. Jasmina added that because she worked for a *humanitarian* organization, such decisions would not be made according to some sort of ethnic calculus. As I show in more detail below, Jasmina effectively silenced and sidelined the mayor for the rest of the meeting by stating that the mayor's reference to ethnic difference was motivated by "political" reasoning. She then turned to instruct the assembled group how they should represent themselves as the kind of humanitarian subjects that would facilitate the flow of aid resources to their village.

A few months later in the neighboring town of Prijedor, a similarly unruly scene was unfolding. A group of Muslim returnees was assembled in the office of an organization that represented refugees and displaced persons to hear who would be included as beneficiaries of a foreign-funded housing reconstruction project. The project was to be located in Stari Grad, the oldest settlement in town and once almost entirely populated by Muslims. It had been razed in the 1990s war as part of the effort to drive non-Serbs from the area.

As the list of selected beneficiaries was read out, I could see that one woman was clearly upset that she had not been included. She began to sharply criticize some of the selections, possibly for my benefit, mistakenly assuming that I worked for the organization overseeing the project. She questioned the inclusion of at least three women, claiming that one woman on the list had a house somewhere else (and thus did not need housing), that another was living full-time in Holland (thus not likely to return), and that a third woman was not even the woman she claimed to be, but her sister. She questioned whether the international humanitarian organization running the project was following its own need-based criteria for selecting beneficiaries and openly wondered whether there were other interests or *politika* involved. Others who were not selected murmured their agreement. She then presented herself as a more deserving subject for humanitarian aid. Rather than focus on herself as needy, she highlighted the large number of family members lost in the war, and mentioned that the Muslim speaker of the local municipal assembly had promised that she would get a house because of all that she had suffered.

Jasmina was compelled to investigate this woman's very public complaints, and she and her coworkers reviewed the information they had received and interviewed other returnees in the area. Through this process they satisfied themselves that all the claims were true, and the three suspect women were excluded from the aid project. Yet the organization did not feel that anyone else from Stari Grad fit their need-based criteria, including the woman who had complained, and added no one else to the project. Jasmina told me that the woman's aggressive communicative style, reference to her suffering, and the promises of a local politician made it difficult to categorize her as the kind of subject that Jasmina's NGO sought to aid.[1]

That was not the conclusion of this episode, however. Further complaints were made about the remaining project beneficiaries, some claiming that those selected had sold their homes to the Prijedor municipality before the war as part of longstanding urban development plans to build a sports complex in Stari Grad. Although the sports complex was never built, to "rebuild" these homes would be to give these returnees something they had no right to. Unlike the previous complaints about beneficiary selection, Jasmina and her colleagues could neither prove nor disprove these new claims. The techniques and procedures they relied on to prevent these moments of dissent about aid distribution had failed, creating a situation that threatened the NGO's legitimacy as a humanitarian organization. The situation had become, as Jasmina told me, "too political." The aid project was suspended.

These two episodes illustrate the social and cultural work that Jasmina and other aid workers had to engage in to stabilize the categorical distinction between things humanitarian and things political, and thus establish and maintain a humanitarian field of action and encounter—a process I call humanitarianization. To explore this process is to reveal the complex social entanglements that have a decisive influence on shaping the effects of intervention encounters focused upon the question of aid. In this chapter I do this by following the social life, technical imperatives, performative demands, and ethical consequences of the humanitarian-political distinction, and by focusing on the many bureaucratic procedures that aid workers relied on to maintain that distinction in an environment that constantly threatened to collapse it.

Sorting out the nature of the political in humanitarian discourse and action has long preoccupied anthropologists and others working on international responses to suffering and need. This is in part because international humanitarian organizations have sought to distinguish themselves as morally good, as guided by neutrality, impartiality, and independence—that is, by a studied avoidance of "politics." It is now commonplace in critical scholarship on humanitarianism to reject the humanitarian-politics dichotomy and point out that humanitarianism is not apolitical or neutral (Barnett 2011; Redfield 2010; Terry 2002); to argue that humanitarianism constitutes an antipolitics that depoliticizes by transforming contentious issues—from dispossession to armed conflict—into "humanitarian problems" amendable to "humanitarian solutions" (de Waal 1997; Pandolfi 2008); or to claim that humanitarian logics or reason have become a part of contemporary forms of politics (Fassin 2011; Ticktin 2006).

I share the skepticism about the utility of the humanitarian-politics dichotomy in the analysis of aid projects, but am wary of rejecting it wholesale. The collective point of the critical scholarship on humanitarianism is that we cannot assume the apolitical, political, or antipolitical nature or effects of humanitarian action. Instead, we need to disentangle, on the one hand, how this distinction operates as a crucial category of practice in the contexts of aid intervention and, on the other, what effect the use of this distinction has on relations of power (what is often meant by the term "politics" or "political") at various scales (local, national, international). In Bosnia and Herzegovina, to declare oneself or a project to be "humanitarian" is precisely to pose the question of politics. Such declarations initiate boundary-making and categorizing activity, such as attempts to define what counts as politics, what counts as humanitarian, and what are the criteria used to make these distinctions.

Placing the social and cultural work necessary to establish and maintain a humanitarian field of action—humanitarianization—at the center of analysis reveals a set of key parameters shaping the everyday interactions and consequences of aid projects. First, a focus on humanitarianization demonstrates that we can never take the humanitarian status of aid projects as ever more than provisionally settled, constituting a key instability with which aid workers (and those studying them) must contend. Indeed, humanitarianism and the establishment of "politics" are social *achievements*—and as the second episode described above shows, they are at times fragile achievements.

Second, attention to humanitarianization highlights processes of contextualization. Every episode of humanitarian action must be made to fit into a context already filled with culturally and historically specific ideas about what constitutes "politics" and how aid and other resources are to be distributed. It also highlights the contingency of the politics-humanitarian distinction and thus of the nature of the political in humanitarian practice itself. What I advocate in this chapter is less a new theory of humanitarianism than a shift in analytic emphasis, and I suggest that the relationship between politics and humanitarian action that so much scholarship focuses on is influenced, if not constituted, by the requirements of humanitarianization.

A focus on humanitarianization has much to offer those interested in the position of researchers in the aid encounter and how the stakes of research on humanitarian aid gets framed—subjects of some debate within anthropology. Miriam Ticktin (2014) has noted how the post–Cold War study of humanitarianism coincided with a transformation in anthropology's privileged object of analysis, which as Joel Robbins argued, shifted from a focus on "the Other" to humanity "united in its shared vulnerability towards suffering" (2013, 450). As a consequence, anthropology changed "its relation to those it studied from one of analytic distance and critical comparison focused on difference to one of empathic connection and moral witnessing based on human unity" (453). According to

Ticktin, this generated a new role for the anthropologist and a new moral mission for anthropology, namely, to intervene and try and improve the world. Put another way, in the ethnographic encounter of the researcher with needy or suffering subjects and those attempting to aid them, research practice became reimagined as a form of care.

For Robbins, however, there are important drawbacks to writing about (and siding with) suffering subjects (like refugees). He argues, for example, that violence and suffering are portrayed as "realities beyond culture . . . that do not require cultural interpretation to render them sensible" (Robbins 2013, 454), and thus the anthropological study of suffering elides the cultural context when it offers its lessons in universal humanity. His broader concern is that with the tendency to emphasize ethnographic intimacy and empathy with interlocutors over cultural context, we lose the comparative and critical potential that comes from the notion of difference.

My own insights into the merits and drawbacks of analytic distance and the possibilities of empathy emerged from fieldwork encounters. I did not set out to study humanitarianism or even to work with refugees. My focus was on the politics of intervention encounters that brought together foreign agencies and diverse populations in postwar Bosnia and Herzegovina around assorted projects of transformation. It was because the refugee return process was the single most intensive site of such encounters that it came to be a focus of my field research.

By moving with aid organizations and international institutions across sites and populations of refugee return, I often first met returnees while alongside the agents of intervention and was confronted with the challenges of forging a research relationship as a foreigner in a postwar political economy structured by international aid. This movement across sites and populations also raised questions about the nature of humanitarianism when the requirements of aid work made empathetic relations with refugees difficult to create or sustain. Answering these questions led me to consider how intimacy and estrangement are both analytic stances and—like humanitarianization—pragmatic achievements which cannot be understood outside of their sociocultural and political-economic contexts.

This consideration dovetails with a trend in the anthropological study of transnational humanitarianism to move beyond moral sympathy with humanitarianism *and* beyond the task of denunciation (Ticktin 2014, 283). This latter observation refers to the fact that much critique of the political in transnational humanitarianism has focused on interventions that blend humanitarian ethos with coercive force (Agier 2010; Fassin and Pandolfi 2010). Such critiques might lead one to believe that any organization or actor operating under the sign of humanitarianism had free rein to impose its will on vulnerable populations by virtue of the moral discourse, financial resources, or coercive force at their disposal.

Some pushback against this narrow view of humanitarianism was probably inevitable as the interest in humanitarianism expanded, and anthropologists and others discovered concrete scenarios of humanitarianism that complicated its sometimes benevolent, sometimes sinister image (Dunn 2012; Robins 2009). This shift has been driven in part by a broadening of the object of analysis: whereas earlier ethnographic or historical accounts tended to focus on the agents of intervention and their discourse, the ethnographic focus has now broadened to include the populations who are the targets of these interventions (Dunn 2014; McKay 2012) and to the encounters that aid projects bring into being (Feldman 2007; Hilhorst and Jansen 2010). The result has been a more empirically robust and differentiated understanding of the possibilities and limits of humanitarianism in practice. As Michael Barnett puts it, we live in a world of humanitarianisms, not humanitarianism (2011, 10); not all forms of transnational humanitarian action and intervention are the same.

My study of humanitarianization thus takes an emic approach to the production of the political in aid interventions. Because what counts as "politics" in Bosnia is produced through a contrast with things "humanitarian," I use the term operating in my field site—politics as *politika*. This has the added benefit of responding to the sometimes vexing fact that "politics" is a labile and often undefined term, shorthand for a broad range of practices, conditions, and relationships. An ethnographic orientation to politics in humanitarianization offers empirical and analytic clarity that might otherwise be missing.

That said, such an approach to politics gets us only part of the way toward understanding the stakes of humanitarianization processes. It does not fully account for the relations of power created in and around aid projects like postconflict housing reconstruction. For example, it does not capture how defining what is and is not *politika* itself creates a relationship of power, or how and why humanitarianization might limit action in particular ways, or how refugee return relates to larger state-building struggles. Here Hannah Arendt's ([1958] 1998) conceptualization of the qualities and human capacities that distinguish action, power, and politics help clarify the stakes of humanitarianization.

For Arendt, "action" is a form of activity that is defined both by its plurality—to act is always to act in concert with others—and by the ability to initiate or create anew; every act is a fresh beginning.[2] Power is the potential created when people act and speak together, and the main effect of this power is to preserve the "space of appearance" that makes acting and speaking collectively possible.[3] For Arendt, power does not rest upon force or compulsion, but on the consent and support of those speaking and acting together. Politics, then, can be thought of as the action of gathering in public for common purpose, and as the persuasion and judgment ([1954] 2006, 221) that takes place to shape collective action as well as to produce or maintain consent—and thus sustain the power that preserves the space that makes speaking and acting collectively possible.

Arendt argues that because power is the potential that lies in the relationships between people, those relationships must be constantly recreated in action for power to factually exist. Any given collective endeavor is thus inherently unpredictable and fragile: it requires the ongoing, nonautomatic, noncoercive consent and support of its coparticipants, continually manifested through deeds and words. Because this action takes place within and through a plurality of human relationships, no actor can control its final outcome.

Finally, although power "springs up whenever people get together and act in concert," it "derives its legitimacy from the initial getting together rather than from any action that then may follow" (Arendt 1972, 151). In other words, power is legitimized by appealing to the past and is subject to ongoing evaluation and judgment.

Conceiving of humanitarianization in these terms thus offers unique insights into the distribution of agency and power in encounters over aid projects like housing reconstruction. It foregrounds the importance of foundational moments, when people initially come together around an aid project to bring it into being; it is here that the legitimacy of that collective endeavor *as humanitarian*, and thus its ethical parameters and requirements, is established. This perspective suggests that if that collective endeavor is to endure, those necessary to bring it into being—from donors and aid workers to beneficiaries and their neighbors—must be persuaded to support it.

The Arendtian perspective also underscores the performative nature of humanitarianization. Because of the fraught history of humanitarianism during the 1990s war in Bosnia, it was not enough to simply declare oneself humanitarian to be accepted as such in the postwar context. This placed a special burden upon aid organizations and their staff to continuously display or enact the qualities and commitments that made their projects humanitarian. In other words, the inherent instability in the humanitarianization of aid projects made it necessary to establish and *maintain* support for them. The two opening scenes of unruly returnees, accusations of "politics," failed procedures, and suspended aid projects illustrate this instability and demonstrate how it can limit what aid workers like Jasmina can accomplish, regardless of the resources at their disposal.

Humanitarianism, Refugees, and the State-Building War of the 1990s

The returnees I spent time with had long been the objects of "humanitarian intervention," from their initial displacement, their stays in camps, and their placement abroad to their forcible return to Bosnia after the war. Yet that war radically transformed the field and scope of humanitarian action, both in the Balkans and beyond.[4] The war in Bosnia and Herzegovina was the first major conflict to be dubbed a "humanitarian crisis" rather than war, with international efforts dedicated to delivering humanitarian aid to the victims of conflict rather than to negotiating a peace settlement. Although the Bosnian war initially held out the promise of a new moment for humanitarianism as moral action "above politics . . . [and as a] critique of the inhumanity of the rigidities of the Cold War and of its suffocating political etiquette" (Duffield 2001, 77), it very quickly laid bare the limits of humanitarianism as a just or effective response to violent conflict.

During the war, aid workers on the ground faced dilemmas that directly challenged the neutrality, impartiality, and independence that they promoted as setting themselves apart from other actors in the war zone. For instance, Fiona Terry (2002), former research director of Doctors Without Borders, points out that although formal neutrality was viewed as an operational tool to gain access to populations in need, "negotiations with faction leaders and local commanders that aid organizations undertake to gain access and security guarantees implicitly recognize those groups' authority over a territory or population" (44). What is more, aid resources were often stolen, diverted to sustain warring factions, and fed into a thriving black market (Andreas 2008)—not at all a neutral presence.

Indeed, neutrality tended to favor the strongest party in any given war, thus nullifying the claim to neutrality even as it was being made. Terry recalled how Bosnian Muslims criticized humanitarian organizations, complaining, "We have no need of you, we need arms to defend ourselves, your food aid and medicines only allow us to die in good health" (2002, 22). International humanitarian organizations found themselves instrumentalized by various Bosnian factions in struggles to claim political and moral legitimacy, to persuade international opinion to pick sides (labeling certain populations "victims" in need of humanitarian care simultaneously created "perpetrators"), and to provoke foreign military intervention. And at times international humanitarian organizations faced an impossible moral choice that left the claim to neutrality in tatters: abet ethnic cleansing by removing refugees from war zones or leave them to suffer and die.

Once the war was concluded, it was the interstitial, liminal position of the hundreds of thousands of refugees in Bosnia and abroad—by definition unsettled and out of place in the "national order of things" (Malkki 1992)—that kept the question of state form open. Although the Dayton Agreement recognized Bosnia and Herzegovina as an independent state, it also legitimized the main separatist state-building projects of the war by identifying the "ethnically cleansed" territories of the Republika Srpska and (Muslim-Croat) Federation of Bosnia and Herzegovina as the state's constituent political units. At the same time, the Dayton Agreement provided for mechanisms meant to undo the ethnically divided postwar status quo, most prominently the right of refugees to return to their prewar homes.

Where one came down on the question of refugee return was a predictor for one's political vision of Bosnia's future state(s). Bosnian Serb politicians in the Republika Srpska saw their political survival linked to the monoethnic logic of the Republika Srpska project, and thus actively prevented the return of non-Serbs to Republika Srpska territory and hindered the return of Serbs to Federation territory. This began with the policing of the Inter-Entity Boundary Line and physical intimidation, extended into a denial of rights to housing, social and municipal services, and political representation, and found expression in an overall official policy of hostility toward the idea of minority return, particularly to the urban areas that functioned as centers of administrative power. This was the evidence used by the constitutional court to justify its decision that inaugurated the constitutive peoples amendments process.

Hostility in the Republika Srpska to "minority return" also included efforts to root and integrate Serb refugees from elsewhere in Bosnia as well as Croatia, and to "resolve" their status from refugees into that of citizens (of the Republika Srpska). They enlisted this Serb refugee population in the policy of exclusion by giving them jobs and housing that had belonged to non-Serbs. With official support, this policy gained the appearance of a popular movement, and resulted in parts of the Serb refugee population in the Republika Srpska forming local chapters of an NGO network called *Ostanak* (meaning "to stay or remain") in order to advocate for their right *not* to return to their prewar homes (a right also included in Annex 7 of the Dayton Agreement).

In order to keep *their* vision of a territorially and politically undivided Bosnia alive, Bosniak nationalist politicians worked to maintain the unsettled and unresolved status of Bosniaks as refugees, thus extending the claim that their rightful place was in their former homes. In a place with a wartime history like Sanski Most's, however, this did not necessarily extend to welcoming the return of Serb refugees, who were often categorized as collective perpetrators of ethnic cleansing. More often the policy of large Bosniak parties like the SDA and SBiH was to passively discourage the return of ethnic Others. At the same time, they pushed for the return of Bosniaks to their former homes in the Republika Srpska by maintaining large populations in shelters and other temporary accommodations.

Western governments were initially reluctant to confront the barriers to making refugee return a reality, particularly to areas where refugees would be an ethnic minority. The first barrier was bureaucratic: repossessing homes meant initiating a complex process of determining ownership or residence rights, a process rife with possibilities for manipulation. A second barrier was financial: there were no local resources to rebuild or repair housing on the scale necessary to make return a reality. The third barrier was the opposition of local governmental officials. Insofar as they were committed to an ethnically pure state project, they resisted the return of refugees and the (re)creation of a multiethnic polity that would undermine that project. Return also threatened a key resource for political parties to create and maintain patron-client relations, namely the power to allocate housing. Furthermore, it promised to create new demands on municipal government: return meant repossessing property and evicting hundreds or even thousands of residents who themselves were often displaced from elsewhere in Bosnia. It also meant reconstructing individual houses or even whole villages. Thus, in addition to having to accommodate a newly evicted population, municipal officials would face fresh demands on already strained infrastructure and budgets for road maintenance, schooling, health care, and transportation.

It was refugees themselves that provided the impetus for so-called minority return. They evaded organized attempts to keep them away, camped on the ruins of their former homes, and demanded that the international community care for them, ensure their safety, and make possible their return. This forced the hand of the international community, which eventually came to see minority return as a way to break the hold of nationalist forces on government and to substantiate the international commitment to "multiethnic" communities, routinely touted as a supreme "European" and "democratic" value. Morally, there was a sentiment among foreign actors that the violence and effects of the war were as much a sign of Europe's failure as of "Balkan barbarism." "Reversing the effects of ethnic cleansing" took on the cast of a moral obligation for the EU and individual countries like the Netherlands.

The refugee return process was not only a site of postwar reconstruction, but also of postsocialist transformation. It was taken by the international community as a vehicle through which to promote elements of the post–Cold War order of democracy and market capitalism. For example, the privatization of socially owned housing and state firms was promoted "in the name of return." Abolishing the institution of socially owned property created new anxieties for returning refugees: with housing no longer the responsibility of socially owned companies or the state, neither employment nor party membership could stand as reliable pathways to future accommodation. Reconstructing or repossessing homes was thus a final foreseeable moment to gain access to secure housing for many returnees.

Given the financial[5] and political stakes of refugee return, foreign donors and international authorities were wary that domestic officials would obstruct return. Indeed, early attempts to partner with local authorities to promote "minority return" utterly failed (Heimerl 2005: 379–380). There was also good reason to fear that resources devoted to this process would be diverted into the channels of political-party patronage. For these reasons, the refugee return process, and particularly internationally financed projects to rebuild homes, were routed outside of existing institutions of Bosnian government, with dozens of international NGOs competing for housing reconstruction contracts.

The ability of aid organizations to successfully humanitarianize their projects thus had a lot to offer international donors seeking to make return possible. Humanitarian organizations could keep resources from being used to support local party patron-client relations. Moreover, by turning the placement of refugees into a humanitarian problem, aid organizations could foreground refugees as subjects of need rather than ethnic subjects, thus skirting around the forces seeking to maintain the postwar status quo of ethnically homogenous political-territorial units. But humanitarianization was not a straightforward process because Bosnia was home to multiple and overlapping ideas about who deserved aid and why. In other contexts, people could and did claim resources based upon wartime suffering and loss, on the basis of general impoverishment, and on the basis of their ethnic identity. Humanitarianization could also be tricky because of the role that politics played in humanitarian self-definition.

Humanitarianization and *Politika*

To declare oneself or a project to be "humanitarian" was the first step to humanitarianize a field of action; the second step was usually to define what counted as politics and what did not. For international and domestic humanitarian actors in Bosnia, "politics" constituted a placeholder against which they defined "humanitarian" interventions as morally good. To be persuasive, what filled this placeholder had to reflect locally meaningful understandings of the political. The challenge to humanitarianize aid was not insignificant, because in postwar Bosnia most people expected to see "politics" any time significant resources were at stake.

Filling the placeholder for politics often meant foregrounding the humanitarian injunction to care for those in need while discursively aligning any alternative basis of decision making or action with the morally tainted category of *politika*. As described in chapter 3, the moral discourse of *politika* in Bosnia shares many of the same negative connotations of politics elsewhere, but its semantic associations were shaped by the specific experience of the war and the end of state socialism. *Politika* evokes corruption, self-interest, and the pursuit and cynical manipulation of power for its own sake. The common phrase *politika je kurva* (politics is a whore) is a gendered and sexualized stereotype which illustrates the immorality of political deal-making (Helms 2007). The moral murkiness and suspicion implied by discourses of *politika* are commonly associated with bureaucratic practice, and they were attached to those people operating in the field of party politics and government who often used their positions for private gain or personal ends. In ethical terms, *politika* also described people whose position, status, or connections made them unaccountable for the consequences of their actions.

The stakes of the humanitarianization process could clearly be seen in the foundational moments of housing reconstruction projects, usually at meetings at the outset of a project. Given that postwar Bosnian party politics was structured around ethnic difference, the local basis for decision making that aid workers often encountered was one in which people had learned to claim resources or other rights as ethnic subjects (i.e., as Croats, Serbs, or Bosniaks), or as victims of wartime suffering or postwar discrimination (at the hands of ethnic Others). As we saw in chapter 3, complaints made in these ethnic terms featured regularly in encounters with foreign officials. And it was this discourse of ethnic difference from which humanitarian actors most often had to distinguish themselves. Let me illustrate by returning to the first episode I described at the beginning of the chapter.

It was an overcast day in the early spring of 2002, when I accompanied Jasmina to a meeting in Budimlić Japra. Before we arrived, Jasmina told me that the village we were visiting was unique because it was a site to which both Serbs *and* Muslims were returning; usually refugees returning to a village like this one belonged to a single ethnic group.

Like many initial meetings, the purpose of the meeting was to solicit a list of potential beneficiaries for housing reconstruction aid. She added that she also expected the mayor of Srpski Sanski Most, a middle-aged woman, to be there. I asked why, and Jasmina replied that the mayor was probably going to insert herself into the process for political gain. The prospect of this clearly irritated Jasmina. She outlined the way she thought the conversation would go: "The returnees and the mayor will probably ask how many houses each side is going to get. I will tell them that I do not care about ethnicity: I only care about need and return."

Soon we were inside the school building, sitting down with the mayor and the members of what we learned was the village's *srpska mjesna zajednica* (Serb village council), a group of mostly middle-aged men. After a few pleasantries, the mayor presented Jasmina with a list of names. Immediately seeing that all the names on the list appeared to be Serb, Jasmina asked where the Bosniak names were. She was told that there was a *bošnjačka mjesna zajednica* (Bosniak village council) that probably had those names. Sensing that their absence might be intentional, Jasmina refused to let the meeting go any further without Bosniak representatives present, saying, "I do not deal with separate groups—I only deal with returnees." As Jasmina had anticipated, the mayor pressed on, asking "But how many houses will each side get?" Jasmina refused to even answer that question, and instead stated that she needed a unified, common list agreed upon by members of both councils.

After the Bosniak representatives were summoned, the mayor continued to focus on the number of houses each "side" would get. Jasmina refused to engage these parameters for the distribution of resources, but the mayor initially misunderstood her objection. Perhaps believing that Jasmina's protestation had something to do with my presence as a foreigner observing her work, the mayor spoke earnestly about how all representatives present wanted a multiethnic Bosnia, that everyone in that village was tolerant, treated equally, good neighbors, and so on. A little cross, Jasmina retorted "Mene ne zanima vaša politika" (I'm not interested in your politics) and repeated that she worked for a *humanitarian* organization and did not make decisions according to some sort of ethnic calculus. While the mayor seemed unfazed by this, the village council members appeared a bit distressed. Having acted under the assumption that their role at the meeting was to negotiate resources as representatives of an ethnic group, they were uncertain about how to proceed.

Here was humanitarianization in action: As a representative of a self-proclaimed humanitarian organization, Jasmina was entering a new but familiar context, already made wary by the presence of the mayor. She was also in a position of lesser social status as a young "urban" woman in a mostly rural, male space, with those present being at least thirty years her senior. What occurred was a clear struggle to define the principles and boundaries of legitimate negotiation that would take place, and the role and status of the participants—including her own—in that negotiation. She was confronted with a setting already marked by ethnic division: *separate* groups of *ethnic* representatives armed with *separate* lists of *ethnically marked* potential beneficiaries. What seemed a fairly innocent question—"How many houses does each side get?"—was interpreted as anything but, especially coming from the mayor.

The stakes were significant. Had Jasmina acknowledged the logic of ethnic division, she would also have entered into a discussion in which the priorities guiding her organization (to care for and settle refugees) would have been subordinated to the principle of ethnic calculation. Moreover, it would have signaled a shift in the balance of power between her and those in the room: acknowledging the legitimacy of the principle of ethnic division would at the same time have empowered these actors as legitimate negotiators on the question of beneficiary selection. Furthermore, it would have given the mayor some standing, and possibly associated the project with the moral taint of ideas about ethnic difference, which were linked with the war and nationalist political parties. Jasmina was thus also compelled to humanitarianize the social situation to prevent anyone (including myself) from making an issue of Jasmina's ethnic identity, and from levelling accusations (or encouraging solicitations) of ethnic favoritism when beneficiaries were selected.

As she indicated during our conversation on the drive to the village, Jasmina had anticipated the boundary work she would have to do. In acting to humanitarianize the context, she worked to disparage the logic of ethnic difference as *politika* in order to simultaneously claim that she and her organization were not motivated by morally dubious private agendas and deal making—and that her interlocutors, by contrast, were. In this case, ethnonational discourse filled the placeholder for politics, or *politika*, against which Jasmina defined and shaped the "humanitarian" context of her project and the interactions within it. This excluded any principles other than "need" to guide the decision-making process.

And at least in this meeting, she was successful: the mayor was sidelined, leaving Jasmina to more easily work with the members of the village councils. She could retrain these members in their new roles not as ethnic representatives but as *returnee* representatives, a social role with new capacities and expected behavior in which she would instruct them. Jasmina succeeded in shifting the interaction to a discussion of the procedures involved in carrying out the aid project, giving her a clear advantage in setting up the parameters of future action and interaction within the context of the project.

And yet, having set out the parameters for what legitimately counted as humanitarian action and project relations, her commitment to its terms was constantly tested. More precisely, maintaining the housing project as humanitarian required the ongoing support and agreement of a range of actors—both Bosnian and foreign—that the project and the aid staff were indeed operating according to "need" and were free from *politika*. In other words, initial interactions like those in Budimlić Japra were foundational acts shot through with ethical implications.

Beyond this single episode, I found that aid workers were often effective in aligning ethnicity discourse with *politika* because most Bosnians agreed that projects designed around "need" ought to be free from the moral murkiness of self-interest or the machinations of political elites. In such cases, depoliticization need not be sinister. Although these foundational moments often established the terms of interaction in ways that empowered aid workers, a project was able to proceed only because it was based upon a moral claim about how aid ought to work that had gained at least tentative consent. Because suffering (like ethnic difference) had been manipulated in postwar Bosnia to serve the ends of political party elites, it could arouse the suspicion of *politika* when it was invoked. Perhaps this is why "need," defined in material terms, seemed less compromised as a basis for distributing resources, less susceptible to manipulation because it was a condition that most people felt they could evaluate themselves.

Yet even as the foundational event of humanitarianization empowered Jasmina to proceed with the aid project according to parameters she had argued for, it was conditional—it did not give her free rein to do as she pleased. Indeed, the humanitarianization of this project would not hold unless a second assertion was met, namely, the claim that "need" could be measured objectively. To substantiate this claim, aid staff pointed to selection procedures that would accurately measure relative need; and they claimed that every moment of the selection process would be transparent and contestable. This was not, however, the only role that routinized assessment and selection procedures played for aid organizations. In fact, my argument about the vulnerability and stakes of the humanitarianization process requires first demonstrating some of the ways in which aid workers relied upon such procedures to manage relations and obligations in the wider social fields they navigated.

The Social and Ethical Management of Humanitarian Action

The role played by technical procedures in managing social relations and ethical obligations in aid projects was brought home to me when I accompanied Jasmina as she performed the relatively tedious work of preselecting beneficiaries for housing reconstruction projects. During one of my first such trips, I was somewhat taken aback by Jasmina's curt, just-the-facts style of interaction at each site we visited. We would pull up in her NGO's white SUV, and Jasmina, clipboard in hand, would look around, take a few photos of the site, ask the returnee a few questions, look at a few documents they had, fill out a questionnaire, and then we would move on. Such visits might last only five minutes. I was most surprised by the fact that she usually did not even look returnees in the face when speaking with them, often cutting them off and reducing their interactions to the minimum exchange of information. This seemed so inconsistent with my ideas about humanitarian aid that I asked her about it later that day.

She surprised me again by replying that this was more or less deliberate, to protect herself from the emotional stress of having to reject so many deserving people. She told me about the previous year's housing project cycle (her first as an aid worker), when she spent lots of time with returnees in the course of her work, learning about their lives, accepting their meager gestures of hospitality, and conducting interviews over coffee. This made it all the more difficult when she had to later tell them that they were not included in the project. She recalled crying with many of them, and said that she could simply not handle that anymore.

There was another reason why she cut such interactions down to a minimum. The year before, someone from another aid organization had seen a coworker of Jasmina's having coffee in a local café with a returnee. Sharing coffee with someone in Bosnia denotes a specific kind of social intimacy, and when the matter was brought up in a meeting between aid organizations and foreign donors, it raised questions about the neutrality of Jasmina's NGO. Such questions could have an impact on her NGO's ability to win future contracts; there were at least nine other international organizations working in the area on housing reconstruction for returnees. Consequently, all the staff of Jasmina's organization had been forbidden to share drinks or spend time with returnees, or take anything from them that might suggest an "improper relationship" and thus place her or her organization on the wrong side of the *politika*-humanitarian divide. Jasmina's production and maintenance of social distance was thus as much a matter of professional ethics as it was a matter of emotional management.

Jasmina's accounting for her brusque interactional style thus points to a tension that aid workers the world over have had to confront, particularly self-defined humanitarians. On the one hand, being humanitarian is often conceptualized as a commitment to action on the basis of common humanity and equality, motivated by compassion and a dedication to care for those suffering or in need merely by their being human. On the other hand, the aid relationship is one of structural inequality: there are donors and recipients, and as many have pointed out, charity constitutes a relationship of dependence, not equivalence. More importantly, there are always finite resources, which necessarily limits the capacity to care for those in need, leading in some cases to practices akin to triage (Redfield 2008). Such limits require a rationalization of aid distribution that can work against humanitarian self-definition: it backgrounds relations of empathy, stigmatizes social intimacy, and opens aid workers up to accusations of indifference—the rejection of common humanity.

As Jasmina told me, her first year as an aid worker was a rude introduction to this tension, with emotional and ethical consequences. In carrying out her organization's aid project through relations of interpersonal empathy and practices of reciprocity and social intimacy, Jasmina cocreated with refugees the parameters and expectations of future action and interaction. According to Jasmina's account, beginning her project work on this foundational basis made living with the consequences of her acts and those of her organization—rejecting "so many deserving cases"—unbearable. It was unbearable emotionally, because the social intimacy created through empathetic relations opened her up to the disappointment and despair of her interlocutors and put her in a position of partial responsibility for it. Moreover, it was also untenable *ethically*, because for reasons beyond her control, Jasmina was unable to successfully withstand an evaluation of her actions as *humanitarian* according to the criteria she had coestablished with these returning refugees.

Yet this experience did not make her quit her job, nor did she stop calling herself or her actions "humanitarian." In fact, she was quite proud of the aid work that she and her organization accomplished. Rather, what emerged was a humanitarianism that operated largely through bureaucratic procedures and documents, to manage this core tension of aid and remain free of *politika*. This is not surprising, given the transformative capacity of documents and documentation—for example, they can erase individual agency from decision making, depersonalize and abstract information from social contexts and individual biographies, create social distance, and produce the appearance of commensurability between diverse objects or relations (Hull 2012).

I observed many occasions when Jasmina or other aid workers would employ documentation procedures to avoid social entanglements of exchange and obligation, particularly when approached spontaneously by people and asked for help.[6] These interactions often began with pleas or demands and could include a range of emotions, from tears and stories of suffering, loss, and discrimination, to angry harangues about the unfairness of aid distribution. All were attempts to solicit a response, initiate a relationship of some kind, and get aid workers to accept a role of responsibility; all reflected reasoning that had currency elsewhere in Bosnia about who deserved aid or other resources. In almost all these interactions I observed with Jasmina, she would more or less sympathetically brush off these attempts by saying there was nothing she could do by herself. Instead, she suggested that they visit her NGO's office, and explained the procedures that had to be followed and forms to be filled out.

Foreclosing interactions or producing social distance through standardized procedures and paperwork not only secured the appearance of neutrality and impartiality so instrumental to humanitarian action but also ended up reducing the scope and range of the ethical obligations, evaluations, and expectations to which aid workers like Jasmina were subject. This, in turn, meant that their self-definition as humanitarian would be rendered less vulnerable to accusations of *politika* or indifference.

The Social Life of Procedures and the Provisional Achievement of Humanitarianization

To operate outside of *politika*, aid workers needed to substantiate their claim to make decisions primarily according to need.[7] Yet *need* was not an innocent or unambiguous term. By defining and assessing economic need as part of housing reconstruction projects, humanitarian actors participated in larger processes shaping new forms of postwar (and postsocialist) subjectivity.

The socioeconomic status of returning refugees was highly variable and depended in part upon their social location before the war (urban versus rural), as well as the path of their displacement. Many refugees went to western Europe, and some had the opportunity to work there during the war. When the war ended, hundreds of thousands lost their residency rights and were forcibly returned to Bosnia. Others were able to secure foreign passports before returning of their own volition. In the area of northwestern Bosnia where Jasmina's aid organization was active, it was the Muslim population who had largely been displaced to western Europe. For this reason, returning Muslims who had spent time abroad were often seen as wealthier, and as having more life opportunities than Serbs and Muslims who never left Bosnia during the war. Moreover, when such Muslim returnees sought to repossess their homes, even while still living abroad, this generated resentments around economic inequality.

For their part, returnees pointed out that while return might involve repossessing or rebuilding a home, it did not involve returning to the job that many had been dispossessed of during ethnic cleansing. That said, with unemployment at epidemic proportions, many Serbs were also out of work. Whereas the distribution of resources and employment during the socialist period was guided by a scrupulous policy of multiethnic equality, the distribution of aid in the postwar period was often targeted to only one ethnic group as part of refugee return, and this could not help but solidify the social distinctions around ethnic difference created by ethnic cleansing in the first place. Thus while socioeconomic status did not correlate strongly with ethnicity, housing reconstruction projects and their selection criteria intersected with these complex histories and proliferated lines of potential conflict and contestation among and between those who identified as Muslim and Serb.

In postwar Bosnia and Herzegovina, then, defining need was a complex issue when so many—returnees and nonreturnees alike—could be said to be "in need." Moreover, need, however defined, competed with wartime suffering and sacrifice (as well as party membership, patron-client relations, and ethnic identity) as conditions motivating the distribution of resources. To substantiate their claims to keep *politika* out of their selection procedures, aid organizations usually defined "need" narrowly in material terms which, they argued, could be measured transparently and objectively through a series of uniform procedures. As a consequence, aid workers sought out attributes of their interlocutors that could be quantified. The selection procedures thus flattened and even erased the history and experience of returnees and reduced their existence to a set of objective, decontextualized, largely technical elements amenable to a calculus of relative material poverty: Did anyone in the household have a job, a car, claims on an occupied apartment, or land? How many people were in the house, and were any of them disabled or did they require care? They also focused on procedural matters: Were the questionnaires filled out properly? Did they have documents to back up their claims?

In following these protocols, aid workers like Jasmina endeavored to preclude other evidentiary bases for calculating who deserved aid, such as stories of suffering, sacrifice, or ethnic discrimination. Yet even as these procedures were indispensable in producing social distance and reducing obligations for aid workers, aid workers depended on potential beneficiaries for such procedures to function as designed. This was because much of the information that aid organizations required to measure the need of returnees came from the returnees themselves. Aid workers thus spent much time and energy on making sure that returnees gave full and truthful accountings of their material circumstances.

To this end, aid workers intervened directly into neighborly relations and attempted to use the intimate knowledge neighbors have of one another to create consensus among project participants that the neediest were being selected for housing aid. As I often witnessed, one of Jasmina's procedures was to interview potential beneficiaries in front of one another and explicitly ask neighbors to speak up if they were not being truthful. The idea was that potential beneficiaries would have an interest in exposing the lies of others because it might increase their chance at being included in a project.

Not surprisingly, this was fraught social terrain for returnees to navigate. The reality that they were placed in relations of competition over limited resources butted up against the expectations, duties, and ties of reciprocity of *komšiluk*, a term that denotes both the physical environment of a neighborhood and the moral relations of neighborliness that take place within it (Bringa 1995; Helms 2010; Henig 2012; Sorabji 2008). In Bosnia, particularly in the rural or village areas to which most refugee return occurred, neighbors are a source of aid, company, collective labor, and protection. Among Bosniaks, *komšiluk* relations have the overtones of religious duty, where there is a moral imperative to control negative emotions, to forbear, endure, and tolerate the actions of one's neighbors. I would argue that this applied to lying neighbors vis-à-vis a third party, particularly outsiders whose presence and role in the community was of a very limited duration.

Interestingly, I found that such procedures both failed and succeeded in their goal. They failed because *komšiluk* injunctions ensured that returnees would resist upsetting longstanding neighborly relations, and thus they did not contradict one another at any moment of the selection process, even when they might have reason to. And yet the procedures inadvertently succeeded because they allowed the projects to proceed by ensuring the absence of dissent regarding beneficiary selection.

The second episode described at the outset of this chapter, however, illustrates the vulnerability of humanitarianization when rationalized procedures fail to work as designed, making it nearly impossible for Jasmina and her organization to occupy a position free of *politika*. Recall how one woman complained about the selections and suggested Jasmina's organization was not following their own need-based criteria. This compelled Jasmina to investigate and to remove three beneficiaries. But she did not add anyone new to the project; instead she shifted resources from Stari Grad in Prijedor to another reconstruction project in the region, where there was less *politika* and more people who fit their category of need.

Thus far, the procedures had worked as designed: they had exposed deception and prevented the distribution of resources to people who did not fit the project criteria of need. Yet this did not settle the issue. Jasmina and other staff from the aid organization were subjected to even more complaints about the fairness and objectivity of their selections.

Stari Grad was a symbolically significant site—it was the oldest settlement of the town, once the site of an Ottoman fort, and it had been razed during the war. Bosniak returnee activists and politicians, and their foreign allies, saw Stari Grad as a key symbolic site of "urban" minority return to the Republika Srpska. When I first visited Prijedor in 2000 for a Reconstruction and Return Task Force meeting chaired by the OHR, it was to the tent encampments at Stari Grad that they took us for a "field visit" to illustrate the needs to donors as well as to show the international community's commitment to supporting return (Figures 4.1 and 4.2). Every subsequent visit by a foreign dignitary to Prijedor (from various ambassadors and High Representative to the head of the UN Mission to Bosnia) included a tour of sites of wartime trauma, beginning with the camp at Omarska and ending at Stari Grad, the latter presented as a sign of hope for the future and

FIGURE 4.1. A refugee return site in the town of Prijedor prior to the reconstruction of houses.

Photo by author.

FIGURE 4.2. A refugee return site in the town of Prijedor after housing reconstruction had begun.

Photo by author.

the possibility of reconstituted lives—if only the resources were made available and the right political pressure applied.

After the neighborhood had been razed, part of it became an outdoor flea market where many Prijedor residents made a living. In the postwar period this flea market had to be removed for housing reconstruction to proceed, an unpopular move in an era of widespread unemployment. Municipal officials stalled this removal, arguing in part that the flea market occupied space that the municipality had bought before the war in order to develop a sports complex. Despite what appeared to be some truth to this claim, foreign authorities saw it as part of an overall strategy to prevent minority return; eventually, the US embassy combined financial incentives with political pressure on local authorities, and the market was removed.

As mentioned above, the question of which residents of Stari Grad had sold their houses to the Prijedor municipality was raised as part of the beneficiary-selection process. Apparently, although people had been compensated for their property, the war began before any new building could begin, and the houses that had been sold were destroyed in the violence that leveled the neighborhood. Complaints came into the aid organization that some of the people who had sold their houses before the war were now trying to get those homes rebuilt.

Unlike the previous accusations, this one proved impossible for aid workers to verify. Municipal officials were uncooperative. They would confirm only that a development plan had existed, and that some people had been compensated, but would not say who; aid workers had no leverage to make officials be more forthcoming. Moreover, the recent history of the flea market, in which the municipal claims on Stari Grad land were ignored, together with the state-building goals and resource burden of the return process itself, did not incline municipal authorities to see the challenges facing international housing reconstruction projects as much of a priority.

Interviews with neighbors resulted in conflicting responses about who had been compensated and where exactly the sports complex was to have been built. Faced with the inability to satisfy themselves, let alone others, that their selection criteria could be verified, and probably tired of finding themselves in the middle of a tug-of-war that did not match their own self-image to "do good," the organization decided to suspend the reconstruction project in Stari Grad altogether.

Unreliable information from returnees and a failure of *komšiluk* injunctions made it impossible for the selection procedures to work as designed. Some of those people whose support was necessary to maintain the aid project as a collective endeavor no longer agreed that beneficiary selection was operating according to the project's terms. This posed dilemmas for Jasmina. She could proceed with the project despite this uncertainty, but doing so would risk collapsing the *politika*-humanitarian dichotomy that underwrote the ethical parameters of her project. In such an instance she would not be accused of corruption or self-interest. Instead, she would be entering the space of *politika* inhabited by people (like bureaucrats and politicians) whose positions made them unaccountable. In this case, she could be—and was—accused of disregarding her commitment to select those most "in need." Her humanitarian status was vulnerable to complaints, from those affected, that she refused to live with the consequences of her actions.

Halting a reconstruction project like this was rare, because it did nobody any good. The aid organization would have to explain to their donors and others why there was such a problem and why they could not resolve it. This could threaten their humanitarian credentials in the community, as well as their reputations with donors as a partner that was able to effectively (and morally) fulfill their contracts. The returnee population in Stari Grad would lose, as would those with a stake in seeing refugee return happen.

Therefore it was not surprising when the situation was eventually resolved, and in a creative way that repaired the damage caused by the unverifiable accusations made about some Stari Grad residents. A regional returnee representative devised a special document that he had all Stari Grad returnees sign. In effect, it pledged the signatories to agree to the final selection of beneficiaries made by the neighborhood council according to the humanitarian organization's regulations. In other words, despite the distinct possibility that people who did not objectively meet the criteria of need would get their houses built, all parties agreed not to make this an issue. This restored the appearance of consensus and allowed the humanitarian organization to implement the project unhindered by accusations of *politika*.

Conclusion: Politics, the Human Condition, and the Effects of Humanitarianism

Hannah Arendt's influence on the humanitarianism scholarship has mostly been through her writing on refugees, rights, and the nation-state form ([1951] 2004), and via Giorgio Agamben's (1998) theorization of bare life. I have drawn on a less referenced aspect of her conceptualization of the human condition, for it helps illuminate important elements of intervention encounters around questions of aid, what I have called here humanitarianization. This includes the significance of foundational moments, of the persuasion and consent necessary to preserve the possibility of acting together for common purpose, and the performative nature of speech and action which seeks to persuade others and withstand their evaluation.

I have demonstrated the importance of beginnings, wherein the parameters and performative requirements for legitimate humanitarian action are established. There are many such moments in the course of humanitarian practice, such as when a government crafts an intervention plan, or when people begin to collect money for the care of others (Brković 2014). There are also ways of humanitarianizing a social field of action other than relying upon the humanitarian-politics distinction (see Brada 2016). And within that distinction, one might imagine discourses other than ethnic division or *politika* filling the placeholder for politics when defining what counts as humanitarian.

Any of these instances, however, will undoubtedly introduce a set of performative demands, be subjected to the evaluation of a diverse set of actors, and thus include a set of potential instabilities that need to be managed. In this way Arendt's conceptualization of power, as the potential which springs up between people speaking and acting together, draws our attention to what is productive and limiting about humanitarian action. Humanitarianization generates ethical chains that link people and projects in relationships of mutual evaluation, and these, in turn, bind how aid workers and their interlocutors act and what they say.

The subject of stakes and limits brings us to the issue of what constitutes the political in humanitarian action. An emic approach to politics in humanitarianization revealed that culturally and historically specific materials, such as the moral discourse of *politika*, contained a range of associations and meanings that complicated and shaped the ability of aid workers to deploy them for specific purposes. By working through the meaning of *politika* in Bosnia, I was able to identify the larger historical forces with which any aid project is confronted, in this case allowing me to situate the microinteractions of housing reconstruction aid within ongoing postconflict and postsocialist transformations. It also disclosed how aid projects are shaped by the contexts of their realization and thus how we might measure their effects, both individual and collective.

While not necessarily sinister, depoliticization—a shift in power relations related to locally salient notions of politics—does have diverse and sometimes unpredictable consequences. For example, in northwestern Bosnia the successful humanitarianization of housing reconstruction facilitated refugee return and resettled thousands of Muslims in what had become Serb territory, and vice versa. Living villages began to spring up where empty ruins once lay, and other villages or areas saw a dramatic shift in the ethnic makeup of their population. At the same time, temporarily sidelining the ethnic calculus as a logic of resource distribution did not erase or undo the ethnic and socioeconomic divisions wrought by the war. As chapter 3 demonstrated, there were just as many intervention encounters in the refugee return process that featured a discourse of ethnic difference as those that did not. Even today in Bosnia and Herzegovina "returnee" remains a durable social category that marks, in different contexts, either economic or ethnic difference.

Finally, to focus on processes of humanitarianization means acknowledging that there is much we cannot take for granted about intervention encounters. To analyze them and understand their stakes and their effects means confronting history and the plurality of actors involved, and requires attention to cultural and political context. Indeed, rather than universal humanity united by its shared vulnerability toward suffering, in my fieldwork I found difference and inequality, along with a struggle to define what constitutes suffering (as well as victimhood and need); suffering can both divide and unite. Rather than a view of humanitarianism as “unquestionably good” or “morally untouchable” (Fassin 2011, 244), I found that the goodness of a self-described humanitarian organization was constantly questioned. In Bosnia and Herzegovina, making something humanitarian and free of *politika* was not merely to preserve it as “good,” but to produce the terms on which its goodness depended.

5

ENTEXTUALIZATION AND THE MAKING OF INTERNATIONAL AUTHORITY

> **Legally, everything is fine. There is simply no will on the part of the authorities to do anything. What we need is influence from the internationals, for we have none.**
>
> —Serb returnee to Sanski Most

The problem of employment was one of the most frequent topics that Serb returnee representatives in Sanski Most brought up in their interactions with foreign officials of the local OSCE field office, particularly the lack of Serbs in the public institutions of municipal administration. The recently imposed constitutional amendments provided additional grounds for existing returnee strategies to prod and persuade foreign officials to do something about the situation, strategies which sought to align returnee goals with the OSCE's stated commitment to promote refugee return and the (re)creation of a multiethnic Bosnia. Not only, they argued, was the exclusion of Serbs a violation of their right as a constitutive people of the Bosnian state to see themselves reflected in all levels of government, this exclusion also made possible the anti-Serb discrimination and corruption they felt was a constant threat in their dealings with municipal officials. More Serbs in public administration would mitigate the possibilities for discrimination, provide returnees with access to stable jobs, extend the social networks of Serb returnees into local government, allow them to secure access to public resources for other returnees, and thus stabilize what was agreed to be a fairly precarious existence.

In many of my observations of OSCE/returnee encounters like these, I often got the feeling that the constitutive peoples amendments, and their championing by influential members of the international community like the High Representative, created more problems than solutions for the foreign officials who regularly interacted with returnees. Indeed, for many returnees, the amendments created the promise of new access to government resources and jobs, and the expectation that "internationals" could be enlisted to help realize that promise.

Whenever these concerns about employment were raised, OSCE officials responded in the same way: if there was a specific complaint about discrimination, they asked for the details and offered to investigate. Otherwise, they said that it was not within their power or mandate to force an ethnic quota upon the municipality. Moreover, doing so would contradict their self-authorizing definition as neutral actors in a context characterized by ethnic antagonism. What they did offer, repeatedly, was to get the municipality to sign on to OSCE-generated transparent fair hiring practices for all *new* public administrative positions, which the OSCE would then monitor for compliance. Not only, they argued, would this eventually add some Serbs to new municipal positions, but even more in line with OSCE goals in Bosnia, institutionalizing concrete and open procedures promised to dispel the murkiness and hidden practices that made nepotism, corruption, and discrimination possible.

For reasons I will describe in more detail later in the chapter, the offer to promote and monitor fair hiring practices was regularly brushed aside by returnees, and most declined to give specific details of complaints about discrimination. I bring up these examples of misalignment between returnee desires and OSCE responses because they exemplify several important features of intervention encounters between foreign officials and Bosnian returnees. For example, they reveal an ignorance of Bosnian history and politics. The OSCE could present fair hiring practices as something novel and transformative for Bosnia only by overlooking the commitment to fair hiring principles that already existed, a holdover from the prewar socialist regime. Indeed, in his book on Yugoslav workers courts, Robert Hayden showed that a significant percentage of the cases that he observed in the country's capital in the 1980s dealt with just this issue. He describes how such cases were common because recruitment for employees in most Yugoslav firms had to follow detailed procedures designed to ensure impartial selection. He writes that "this is not an unreasonable concern in a society in which the importance of 'connections' . . . is acknowledged by all and well represented in folk aphorisms. Not infrequently, a disappointed applicant sues to have a hiring decision reversed; also not infrequently, such a plaintiff wins" (1990, 91). In other words, not only was the problem of "connections" and nepotism recognized under socialism, but there were bureaucratic procedures and legal mechanisms set up to deal with it—to make the hiring decision "transparent" and fair—and which offered individuals the real possibility of redress.

The OSCE's response to returnee concerns also points to something beyond the issue of "fair hiring"—the confidence in the transformative power of rationalized, technical procedures, even in bureaucratized contexts already saturated with them. This chapter identifies the roots of this confidence, despite the OSCE's ignorance of local conditions. It also aims to explain what influence this confidence had on the mismatch between the concerns of returnees and the responses offered by the OSCE (like new fair hiring practices). In doing so, I look to open up a broad field of international practice and encounter. I do this by focusing on the role played by *entextualization*—putting information into a text artifact form—in helping foreign officials stabilize their knowledge of Bosnian society in order to act upon it, and by analyzing how this process fit into a broader self-authorizing distinction made between internationals and Bosnians that problematized the latter as in need of transformation by the former.

I have already discussed how one of the major tensions structuring intervention encounters was between the expectation that foreign officials did not need to know much about Bosnia in order to transform it and the reality that their ability to fulfill their roles was limited precisely by their lack of this knowledge and their limited ability to engage in and navigate the social networks of Bosnian politics and society. As I will show, these networks were a site for the generation and circulation of knowledge relevant to their intervention mandates, and thus a source of epistemic uncertainty and anxiety for foreigners precisely because their linguistic and cultural competence was so limited.

A dominant way for foreigners to manage this uncertainty was through the production and circulation of English-language text artifacts. Such entextualized knowledge not only rendered Bosnian politics and society visible, knowable, and thus open to intervention for foreign officials, it also played a symbolic role within the hierarchical binaries that organized how OSCE officials made sense of and legitimized their role in Bosnian society: (foreign) text-based forms of knowledge and action were seen as superior to (Bosnian) forms of knowledge and action which were not text-based.

This became clear to me when OSCE officials criticized, variously, returnees' lack of interest in the procedures and methodologies they promoted, returnees' refusal to submit their complaints to foreign documentation, and the returnee desire for more direct forms of intervention—that is, not mediated by texts—as all rooted in forms of "traditional" "Balkan" or "backward" sociality that allowed corruption and nepotism to flourish. The process of entextualization has long been seen as part of a disenchanting process, fixing knowledge in text artifacts which enable a modern rationality that dispels irrational, superstitious, and fetishistic beliefs. This unspoken assumption allowed OSCE officials to argue that their text-based forms of knowing and acting in Bosnia could accomplish their transformative mission to liberate Bosnians from the traditional and unmodern beliefs, practices, and relationships responsible for the problems which plagued them. In a circular fashion, the indifference of returnees, or their refusal to accept what the OSCE had to offer, was taken as evidence of the need for just such a foreign presence, rather than a moment for them to question the limits of their intervention approach.

Intervention encounters, of course, have more than just international participants. In order to understand why returnees largely rejected the OSCE's solutions to their problems we must go beyond the actions and interpretive frameworks of foreign officials; we must also account for the actions and interpretive frameworks of returnees. As I will show, returnees often found the OSCE's focus on procedure, technique, and textual form to be overly cumbersome, to reflect a naïve understanding of how power worked in Bosnia, and to be a curious misrecognition of the OSCE's own influence and authority. These breakdowns of communication were often thus part of larger struggles to gain mastery over the terms—the means and ends—of intervention itself, with OSCE officials and returning refugees attempting to draw one another into their own organization of things.

Of course, entextualization was a common practice across all bureaucratized international organizations in postwar Bosnia, not just the OSCE. We have seen how procedures in the form of documents and questionnaires could be used to rationalize and limit interactions between aid staff and returnees, so we should not be surprised to find a similar role for texts and procedures in OSCE actions and interactions with the same population. And the uncertainties about knowledge that entextualization was designed to mitigate were experienced by the foreign staff of many such organizations, not just the OSCE. But to study the role played by entextualization in the interactions between the OSCE and returning refugees, and in relation to how the OSCE understood and legitimized its role in postwar Bosnia, offers unique insights into the dilemmas and limits of intervention encounters, and this has largely to do with the relationship between entextualization and transparency.

Entextualization and the Promise of Transparency

"Transparency" is a key value and virtue of global democracy and a key concern in intervention encounters across cultural difference. Given the links between the idea of modernity, Enlightenment ideologies about transparent knowledge and communication, and European colonial and imperial interventions (cf. Bauman and Briggs 2003; Comaroff and Comaroff 1991, 1997; Sanders and West 2003), it is not surprising that we find concerns about transparency entangled with foreign intervention and its goal of transforming cultural Others. As Sanders and West remind us, "transparency" is a notion "born of the self-reflexivity of . . . modernity. Transparency is invoked by those who think of themselves as modern as they talk about their vision of a modern society, and it is frequently juxtaposed, not only with conspiratorial ideas, but also . . . with the "ignorance" of "tradition" (2003, 7). Enlightenment thinkers, they observe, believed that "human actions could be rationalized and the workings of society could, thus, be rendered sensible to its members, one and all" (7). More contemporary claims about transparency link knowledge and modernity in ways that underwrite ideas about human freedom and democratic government: "A social world whose workings are transparent is a social world amenable to the dictates of reason, arrived at openly through the public exercise of irrefutable logic exercised by society's sovereign subjects themselves" (7).

Importantly, they also note that these ideas about modernity arose during western Europe's "age of discovery," a "moment of encounter with cultural Others provoking a search for self-identity as well as a quest for means of asserting power vis-à-vis cultural Others" (2003, 9). If international intervention in the Balkans at the turn of the twenty-first century did not constitute quite the same encounter as the "age of discovery," and if the question of Bosnia's Otherness was more ambivalent, the legitimacy of the foreign presence in Bosnia and its concerns about promoting transformation in the Balkans were nevertheless constituted in these same terms of self versus Other, and modern versus traditional.

For foreigners working for the OSCE, however, the reliance upon entextualization practices was more than just a matter of making cultural Others transparent to them, and thus having a secure foundation upon which to base their neutrality while also transforming these Others from "backward" subjects into modern and rational agents. As suggested above, modernity also entailed a particular moral vision of selfhood (Taylor 1989) that gave a salient place to freedom. Such freedom was located in the self-mastery made possible in an age of "disenchantment," to use Max Weber's formulation for the falling away of superstition, irrationality, and tradition with the coming of modern science. Thus both the stigmatization of Bosnian practices and the promise of text-based "transparency-oriented" transformation were couched in what Webb Keane has called the "moral narrative of modernity," manifested in "a widespread set of intuitions about historical progress . . . [that] center on the idea that modernity is, or ought to be, the story of human liberation from a host of false beliefs and fetishisms that undermine freedom" (2007, 5). Many of the proceduralized and "transparency-oriented" practices promoted by the OSCE carried implicitly or explicitly the moral argument that they would free Bosnian politics and society from the opacity, "clan thinking," and fetishistic orientation to personal connections that allowed political oppression and corruption to flourish. As we will see below, in more ways than one the foreign officials of the OSCE cast the stakes of transparency in their encounters with their Bosnian interlocutors in moral terms.

In what follows, I will show that it was because of this ideologized relationship between transparency and entextualized forms of knowledge that those forms became involved in mitigating the epistemological anxieties and uncertainties experienced by the foreign staff of the OSCE in encounters with returnees, conditions created by general ignorance of Bosnian culture, language, and history. I will also show how and why entextualized forms were involved in marking a distinction between foreign officials and their Bosnian interlocutors, and in promising to liberate those Bosnians from the backwardness and traditions that bound them. In order to do this, I remind readers of the reason for the general disregard for "local knowledge" and "local relations" among "internationals," OSCE staff included. I then show how and why transparency lay at the heart of OSCE practices by outlining the origins of its main medium of intervention: surveillance. I round off this section by describing the institutional and sociological context of the OSCE's presence in my field site in northwestern Bosnia.

In the subsequent section, I draw upon extensive fieldwork to illustrate the vulnerability felt by foreign actors and rooted in the fact that their work was highly mediated and dependent upon others in a context of linguistic and cultural difference. I show how they interpreted that difference and sought to manage the vulnerability they felt while fulfilling their mandates and their commitment to neutrality. The next section gets more specific about the role played by notions of transparency, text-based and non-text-based forms of mediation, and the "moral narrative of modernity" in the interactions between OSCE actors and their Bosnian interlocutors. Finally, I explore returnee interpretations of the role and power of the OSCE to explain their frustrations and dissatisfactions with intervention encounters.

The Structural Contradictions of International Intervention

Ignorance of Bosnian history or society was a fundamental starting point when democratization and Europeanization projects were imagined by foreign actors and agencies. Foreigners were hired as experts in those areas in which Bosnia was presumed to be lacking (democracy, European standards, rule of law), rather than for their knowledge of the country's politics, history, cultural logics, or social norms. In part, this approach to intervention was grounded in the prevalent notion that democratization and Europeanization were largely technical (as opposed to social or cultural) matters, transferable and communicable through legal elaboration, institutional reform, public information campaigns and training sessions, and the occasional ritual performance of elections. This notion of transferability assumed transparent communication, a largely referentialist understanding of language, and an easy correspondence and commensurability between languages: if the key words and concepts of democracy and democratization (such as civil society, nongovernmental organization, empowerment, capacity-building, or transparency) have no preexisting analogues in the language of the country being transformed, you just coin new ones—or, often, simply adapt the English terms to local phonology and morphology—and define them accordingly. It is precisely when language and communication do not work "transparently" in these contexts and reveal the profoundly socially and culturally mediated—and not "technical" or "neutral"—nature of these processes, that local practices and perspectives are problematized.

With intervention goals like democratization or refugee return defined as largely technical exercises pursued by disinterested foreign experts, knowledge of the "local situation," whether of its politics, history, or even language(s), was undervalued; moreover, such knowledge might have indicated a potential bias that could compromise the ability of an international organization to retain its image of neutrality and impartiality (and thus legitimacy).

As already discussed, being unbiased and neutral meant being impartial when conflicts arose between Serbs, Muslims, and Croats, and working on the same basis with all people of Bosnia and Herzegovina. But such interactions had to be highly circumscribed because of the belief that social intimacy would damage their objectivity. For example, anthropologist Kim Coles tells about a research participant, Paul, who worked for the OSCE in Bosnia and was "chastised for being too friendly with the locals, which according to the international who reprimanded him, threatened Paul's ability to be neutral and certainly the perception of his neutrality" (2007: 61). She goes on to generalize that "Those willing to search beyond the international community for genuine friendship were few and far between and popularly viewed as brave, unusual, and often biased. Bias and the preservation of neutrality were key concerns in the international community. . . . Neutrality and unbiasedness were associated with lack of involvement" (67). Such evidence suggests that for the foreign staff of these agencies, it was their very ignorance of the "local" that indexed their neutrality and helped maintain their "outsider" status (see also Friedman 1996).[1] This studied ignorance of foreign officials working for the OSCE was curious given that surveillance lay at the heart of how the OSCE exercised its power.

Transparency, Surveillance, and the OSCE

The OSCE's predecessor, the Conference for Security and Co-operation in Europe (CSCE), was founded in 1975 as a forum for ongoing high-level security negotiations between states across the east-west divide in Cold War Europe. One logic of the conference was that confidence- and security-building measures and more "openness" would defuse tension and prevent conflict between NATO and Warsaw Pact countries. Such measures often comprised "monitoring" activities that would allow members of other countries and opposing military alliances to assure themselves of one another's compliance with negotiated arms reduction settlements or of the nonbelligerent nature of military maneuvers. While the conference was mostly focused on matters of security, its members also confirmed the inviolability of human rights (although there was no monitoring regarding these issues during the Cold War).

With the end of the Cold War and the crisis brewing in Yugoslavia, the CSCE drew on its previous commitments to human rights to make a conceptual connection that would become a crucial component of post–Cold War European order and international intervention: that respect for human rights was a "a vital basis for [European] comprehensive security" and, more importantly, that these were "matters of direct and legitimate concerns to all participating States" and belonged not exclusively to "the internal affairs of the State concerned" (OSCE 1992). Membership obliged individual states to open themselves up to the scrutiny of the CSCE, which sought in the early 1990s to expand and institutionalize the surveillance of situations in which human rights violations might occur. It was under this pretext that the CSCE sent its first human rights monitoring mission to Yugoslavia, and called for improving such instruments as fact-finding and monitoring missions with the idea that they would help identify emerging crises and prevent them from developing further.

By the end of the war in Bosnia, the "forum" of the CSCE had become the "organization" of the OSCE, and its first institutionalized mission was in postwar Bosnia, where its mandates centered on its "monitoring" or surveillance capacity. It began by focusing on monitoring the withdrawal of armed forces and overall demilitarization of Bosnia, and continued with the direct supervision of the first six elections in the postwar period. A crucial shift took place in the move from CSCE to OSCE: whereas during the Cold War the CSCE provided a context within which member states would open up certain activities to the surveillance of one another as a way to gain confidence and establish trust, now it was to the OSCE itself that processes had to be opened up and made "transparent." Trust and confidence were now located in the presence of the OSCE—hence the importance of neutrality, secured by defining the objects and processes of surveillance as apolitical technical and expert matters (electoral procedures, rule of law, violations of human rights conventions, etc.).

In her ethnographic study of the OSCE-run elections in Bosnia, Kim Coles describes how the "transparent" and "free and fair" nature of the elections—and by extension the international legitimacy of Bosnia's democratization—was at first predicated on the surveilling presence of foreign observers and supervisors as embodiments of impartiality and neutrality. This was only made possible by a belief that the "transparency" of the election could be achieved through a set of specific documentary practices and procedures, regardless of the politics or history of Bosnia, or the fact that their "observation" of the entire electoral process was mediated by interpreters, the vast majority of whom, according to Coles, "were not skilled enough to provide simultaneous interpretation services [or] to interpret the general, ambient conversation in the polling station" (2007, 207). While anyone could be trained to make sure electoral procedures were being followed, it was in fact the foreignness of the observers and their ignorance of the stakes in the Bosnian election that guaranteed their neutrality and thus the transparency of the process:

> [Foreign] supervisors were taught almost nothing about the political situation in Bosnia-Herzegovina, despite their desire for such information. Some electoral staff believed that such knowledge (both of the political situation in Bosnia-Herzegovina and of the politics behind electoral administration) threatened supervisors' ability to see clearly. Like juries told to disregard information and knowledge learned outside the courtroom, supervisors with independent knowledge were suspected of having clouded vision. Many long-term international electoral officials espoused a "need to know" mentality and commented that too much political knowledge threatened supervisors' neutrality as well as their representation as neutral. Their job, an official told me, was to supervise technical procedures, not to engage in politics or political discussions. Effectively watching the polling and counting procedures, these officials believed, did not depend on knowing the political situation in Bosnia-Herzegovina—in the worst case, such knowledge might have limited a supervisor's effectiveness. (2007, 204)

Coles goes on to argue that the foreign election supervisors and observers usually felt like they were not *doing* anything, and others felt poorly equipped to understand and judge what was actually happening in the polling stations on election day. Still, supervising and observing elections was a far cry from what was expected of the longer-term OSCE staff in the field offices, whose bewilderment at the contradictions of international intervention began first and foremost with their limited social, cultural, and linguistic capacities. It would not be an overstatement to say that foreigners' everyday interactions with Bosnians were often structured by uncertainty and anxiety regarding the reliability and trustworthiness of the information they possessed, how it was interpreted, and where it circulated. This was related, in part, to the encounters set in motion by their wide-ranging mandate.

The OSCE in Sanski Most and Prijedor

By the time I began my fieldwork on the refugee return process in the municipalities of Prijedor and Sanski Most, the OSCE's mandate had expanded to include monitoring human rights (particularly those of vulnerable populations like returnees) and the rule of law (particularly the return of property to its prewar owners), as well as promoting educational reform and a whole host of changes designed to aid in Bosnia's democratization. As the OSCE mission in Bosnia and Herzegovina website put it in 2004, its mandate was to "prevent and address human rights violations, build local capacity and transfer knowledge and expertise to BiH authorities and citizens in human rights and the rule of law," and to assist "the authorities of BiH to develop democratic structures that are . . . open and responsive to the needs of citizens."

When I first visited the neighboring municipalities of Sanski Most and Prijedor in the summers of 2000 and 2001, they were collectively home to field offices of every major international institution in Bosnia, a sign of the importance that the international community put on promoting refugee return to this area. This included the OHR's Reconstruction and Return Task Force (RRTF), UNHCR, the UN's International Police Task Force (IPTF), the Civilian-Military Cooperation (CIMIC) office of local NATO Stabilization Force units, and the OSCE. By the time I arrived to carry out fieldwork in early 2002, however, some of these offices had closed, although these institutions continued to be active from regional offices in Banja Luka and Bihać. By the end of that year, the OSCE field offices in Prijedor and Sanski Most found themselves the only representatives of the "international community" on the ground.

The staff of the field offices changed as the OSCE's tasks changed; when I arrived, each had two foreign staff positions, a democratization officer (DO) and a human rights officer (HRO). Each field office also had a series of positions for domestic staff, all of whom lived in the immediate vicinity. These included the administrative assistant/translators for the foreign staff, an education officer, an office secretary, drivers for the two or three white SUVs maintained by each office, and cleaning staff. English was the working language of the OSCE mission, and all but the cleaning staff had some degree of fluency. The national or ethnic background of the domestic staff tended to reflect the majority population for each town, with the staff in the Sanski Most office predominantly Muslim, and the staff in the Prijedor office predominantly Serb.

The foreign staff positions were filled by personnel drawn from OSCE member states and served according to six-month renewable contracts. Turnover could be fairly rapid. For instance, over a sixteen-month period spanning 2002 and 2003, in Sanski Most there were three HROs (from Holland, Switzerland, and Germany) and four DOs (from France, Poland, Holland, and Germany). In Prijedor, there were also three different DOs (from Canada, Romania, and Japan) over the same time period, and contrary to this trend, only one HRO, from Spain, who had served in that position for over two years when he finally departed. Sometimes a field office would be left without one or both members of its foreign staff for weeks or even months at a time as the mission recruited new personnel. Most of the foreign staff were between their late twenties and early forties; all HROs had law degrees and all DOs had advanced university educations. Some had served with the OSCE elsewhere in Bosnia, others had diplomatic or NGO experience outside of their home countries, but for many, this was their first experience living and working abroad.

The tasks for the HROs and DOs shifted according to decisions made in Sarajevo, but the overriding concern with supporting refugee return in Prijedor and Sanski Most meant that most projects had something to do with this process. Much of what they did could be categorized as some sort of "monitoring" or surveillance, with a focus on local media as well as governmental processes. During my fieldwork, the HROs spent considerable time overseeing the implementation of property law, whereby people who had fled their homes during the war could repossess them. They also examined the work of municipal courts and coordinated with the local SFOR and IPTF units to monitor "the security situation." This could include trips to the "field" to gather information about incidents such as suspected human trafficking, the attempted firebombing of mosques or property damage to churches, grenades thrown into the homes of religious officials, mafia-related violence to commercial property, or the fallout of a particularly contentious eviction from occupied property. They held "client hours" with individual returnees or their representatives as part of their mandate to "prevent and address human rights violations." They also generated weekly "situation reports" and memoranda regarding any local politics that had some bearing on issues of human rights and the rule of law.

DOs had more flexibility as well as a budget, and spent their time promoting democratization by sponsoring training sessions for "local stakeholders" on everything from the proper way to organize an NGO and voter education to how to understand the new Freedom of Information Act (FOIA). They also sponsored youth activism campaigns. Yet much of their time during my fieldwork was spent working with local authorities to reform municipal government and make it more "transparent" and "accountable" to citizens through the nationwide MIFI campaign (Municipal Infrastructure and Finance Implementation). This was part of a general dissatisfaction on the part of the "international community" with national and entity-level politics, and resulted in a concentration on the municipality as the institutional scale that held out the most promise for foreign-mediated democratization.

As the only on-the-ground representatives of the "international community" and its core commitment to support refugee return, DOs often found themselves being called upon by returnees to intervene in a vast range of mundane and extraordinary activities. Negotiating how or whether to respond took up a fair amount of their time. On some occasions, this led to the creation of informal "working groups" that were chaired by members of the international community and brought together municipal official and returnee representatives to solve problems that existed between public institutions and returnee populations, such as timely hookups to the phone grid for rebuilt homes. At other times, it meant going to the mayor or the courts to investigate specific accusations of ethnic discrimination. In one extraordinary example, the HRO of Prijedor even took up the cause of local Muslim returnees to personally lobby Serb members of the municipal assembly regarding how they would vote on a particularly contentious measure. It should go without saying that every meeting with returnees or local officials, every training session, and nearly every other interaction outside of the office required the presence of an interpreter/translator.

Epistemological and Other Uncertainties

In fulfilling their various mandates, OSCE officers faced numerous dilemmas related to the availability and quality of the information at their disposal. At times the tasks at hand centered on the need to manage the interpretation of events—and raised questions about the officers' access to information and their ability to understand how their Bosnian interlocutors might interpret it. At other times, their work was endangered by actions that raised questions about their ability to maintain the trust of their interlocutors. Questions about trust often revolved around whether they could secure the setting and boundaries of communication with returnees, thus controlling the circulation of potentially sensitive information.

One of the most common frustrations for OSCE HROs lay in reconciling the demands of their job to monitor the security situation and feelings of responsibility to advocate for vulnerable returnee populations, with their inherently limited cultural, social, and linguistic resources. Moreover, returnees regularly presented OSCE staff with various scenarios of abuse and discrimination in which they were called upon to intervene. The staff often felt caught between the urgency of these claims and the suspicion that they were being used for ends that they did not fully understand. Recall the vignette in the Introduction where Markus was unsure how to react to the provocations of a Serb returnee over the circulation of a book that accused prominent Serbs in Sanski Most of war crimes.

At other times, the issue at hand was access to information. For instance, on one evening early in December 2002, I was sitting in a café in the center of Prijedor with Markus and Miguel, the HROs from Sanski Most and Prijedor. I had been out of town for about four days and was catching up. Miguel asked if I had heard that a grenade had been tossed onto the balcony of a local imam's house. No one had been hurt, and as far as he knew, no one had a clue as to who was responsible.

Not for the first time, Miguel voiced frustration about how to interpret this act of violence, the latest event in a recent string of incidents that targeted people or infrastructure identifiably "Muslim." It fell within his area of responsibility to monitor the security situation in Prijedor and prevent the human rights abuses of its Muslim returnee population. He feared that without any action taken—a public condemnation by the authorities, a visible investigation by the police—there could be a ratcheting up of ethnic tensions and a deterioration of safety for returnees. I asked what the response of the mayor or police had been. He said that as far as he knew, there had been none.

In considering what, if anything, he might do, he remarked that in the past, the UN's IPTF had brought pressure to bear upon the mayor to condemn such acts, and they also monitored the police to make sure they were "doing their job" to investigate such incidents. However, the UN mission in Bosnia, including the IPTF field office in Prijedor, had just closed its doors, not only leaving Miguel without his usual conduit for information about police and other official action, but also leaving him feeling responsible to take on its role. The speech and action of the mayor and police were of special concern to him because he believed that in the absence of evidence about who had targeted the imam, it was the perception of returnees about incidents like this that needed managing. Getting officials to publicly condemn such acts, he believed, would provide a counterweight to the indifference he saw on the part of the town's majority Serb population. It would also mitigate the fear and hostility on the part of Muslims who would be apt to see these as acts of terror that—if not officially sanctioned, then at least tolerated—were designed to again drive them from their homes. As one of the only members of the "international community" to be stationed in the town of Prijedor, he was already regularly called upon by returnees to "do something" in situations like this. He confessed to feeling as though he had little to offer them except to report the incident to his own superiors in Banja Luka or Sarajevo. He showed me a copy of the memo he was writing to send to his boss in the hopes that someone could try and bring pressure on Prijedor's officials.

The next day I discovered that the mayor's office *had* made a public statement condemning the bombing, and the police *had* made a statement about investigating this to its conclusion—precisely the two things that Miguel had suggested. When I told him about this later that day, he expressed embarrassment about having written his memo and voiced a familiar complaint made by more than a few of my foreign interlocutors: "no one tells me anything unless they want something from me."

In my many conversations with Markus and Miguel, both anxiety and suspicion were never far from their minds: anxiety that they were being left out of critical circuits of information and suspicion that, when information did come their way, it seemed motivated, raising questions about its reliability. In fact, over time I got the distinct impression that part of the reason they talked with me so often was that they saw me as a trusted source for information they might not otherwise get, as well as for a perspective on that information that their limited cultural and linguistic skills did not allow for. It was for that reason that I was called upon to translate in meetings like the one between Miguel and Dubravka which I touched upon in chapter 3 when discussing the interpretive leaps foreigners make to categorize returnee problems in terms of ethnic difference. I return now to describe this encounter more fully because it illustrates the stakes of information and communication in the work of the OSCE.

Miguel and I arrived separately to our meeting. Dubravka was already there and had staked out a booth in the corner, away from the other customers. As we waited for our coffees to arrive, Dubravka and Miguel worked to establish some rapport. She offered Miguel a cigarette and they bantered jokingly—through my translation—about her going to work in a café his mother owned in Spain, and developing a menu of Spanish-Bosnian fusion dishes. The ostensible reason for the meeting was that Dubravka wanted to brainstorm on the implications for Muslim and Croat returnees of the new constitutional changes that many believed would require ethnic quotas for positions in the nearly all-Serb municipal administration. The conversation began, however, with the issue of one of the OSCE's translators.

After our drinks arrived and the waiter had departed, Dubravka lowered her voice a bit and began talking about something she had wanted to tell Miguel some time ago, but felt she could tell him only now, with me as the translator. She recalled a meeting she had attended at the OSCE with another member of the returnee organization, Senad, and the OSCE DO, an American named Caroline. They were meeting as part of a session meant to construct a working group on transparency in municipal administration. Senad had spoken plainly that he thought that the mayor, Nada Ševo, would try and obstruct any attempt at municipal reform. As was always the case, Caroline's assistant Gojko was translating. Dubravka mentioned that later on the day of the meeting she had run into the mayor on the street, noting that she had had a relationship with her before the war when the mayor was a high school teacher. The mayor asked her, "What did Senad say about me at the OSCE today?," and Dubravka, playing dumb, said she did not know what she was talking about. The mayor replied "I am not stupid, I talked to Gojko and he told me the whole thing."

Dubravka related how this led her to start asking questions of people she knew about who this Gojko was, where he was from, and who his parents were. According to one person, she said, Gojko's father was one of the best-known generals in the Yugoslav National Army. This information, apparently, was enough to persuade her that he had connections with Serb political elites, and on the basis of past experience with the unreliability of translators, she said that she was convinced Gojko was a spy working for the mayor and perhaps also for some of the parties in power, mentioning the SDS.

I translated this all for Miguel, and he took it very seriously. Upon seeing his reaction, Dubravka elaborated by saying that not only is an untrustworthy employee a bad thing for him as a boss (at the time he was acting head of office), but it also hurt the reputation of the OSCE in general. Miguel reacted by saying he would like to do something about this but needed to know more; he could not simply act on the basis of her accusation. He asked Dubravka whether she knew of this happening more than once, whether it would be possible to get the mayor to admit this, and so on. He remarked that it was unclear to him whether the mayor had been told this in passing while Gojko and she were talking about other things, or whether it was more intentional than that. He also noted that, in his eyes, Gojko was extremely competent at what he did, and he did not have any other reason to question him. Dubravka said that the mayor would in no way admit to anything, and spoke with conviction that this was not an accidental or onetime occurrence.

Dubravka continued to drive her point home. She said that she was mentioning this as much for his sake as her own, implicitly suggesting that Miguel might face obstacles in his work because neither he nor his returnee interlocutors could trust the discretion of the OSCE's translators.

Miguel responded by again saying that he was taking her seriously. Moreover, he assured her that Svetibor, his new assistant and translator, had his full confidence and could be trusted with no problem as to his discretion. When I translated this for her, she said that it did not matter who the interpreter was, that there would still be things that she would not ever convey through a local translator because, as she said, "you will all leave one day, but I have to live here and what I say may reflect badly on me in the eyes of the translator, and I don't know whether or not he is a professional in his job, and who knows what may get out once the circumstances have changed [i.e., once the OSCE is gone]." This portion of the conversation ended with Miguel telling her he was going to take up the issue with his boss in Banja Luka later that day.

From there the discussion shifted to what was to have been the main topic of the meeting. This amounted to Dubravka arguing that the constitutional amendments would require the Prijedor municipality to hire dozens of Muslim returnees, and that the returnee organization she represented had a proposal to carry out a census of qualified individuals among the returnee population. Senad had already enlisted a member of the OHR to persuade the mayor to fund this survey, but the mayor rebuffed this attempt to have the municipality pay for a "Muslim" organization to insinuate itself into the highly politicized issue of employment in public institutions. The mayor argued that if anyone should carry out this research it should be the municipality. Nevertheless, Dubravka sought to enlist Miguel's participation in this process by giving him sample census sheets that the returnee organization had drawn up and had translated into English, saying that this survey would be a good place to start because it would provide evidence to counteract any attempt by the mayor to obstruct the implementation of the amendments by arguing that there were no non-Serbs qualified for municipal jobs. She also suggested to Miguel that he raise the issue of the constitutional amendments in his upcoming meetings with the mayor as a way of laying the groundwork for the process and forcing municipal officials to "make space in their heads" to think about it.

Later that day, I accompanied Miguel on a trip to speak to his boss at the OSCE regional headquarters in Banja Luka about Dubravka's accusation. I did not sit in on the meeting, but afterward Miguel told me that they decided that there were three possible ways to proceed. One would be to fire the employee straight out. A second option would be to make a general statement to all the staff that they had heard a number of accusations and that they took them seriously, and let that be a warning to all. A third option would be to have Miguel's boss talk to Gojko one-on-one about it. Miguel worried that his boss would decide to act without telling or consulting him, and that this would make things worse rather than better. In the end, Miguel was unsure whether he should have told his boss about the accusation at all.

This episode comprised many of the dilemmas facing foreigners as well as their Bosnian interlocutors, dilemmas rooted in the socially and culturally mediated nature of the OSCE's work. Dubravka's accusation raised troubling questions for Miguel about his ability to act as an advocate for vulnerable returnee populations: if returnees could not trust their communication with him, they would not come to him with the kind of sensitive issues he needed to know about. Moreover, returnees might be unwilling to collaborate on OSCE projects, like the working group on municipal reform that required their participation in order to include "all important stakeholders." Moreover, given the Serb ethnic identity of most of his staff, the problems with the translators could be cast in terms of ethnic discrimination and undermine the image of the OSCE as a neutral and impartial actor for the Muslim returnee population he was there to serve.

It also drew attention to just how much his work—his own agentive capacities and reputation—depended upon his translators, and forced him to consider and question their motives and interests, as well as the veracity of their translation. Indeed, Markus, the HRO in Sanski Most, had a rocky relationship with his assistant/translator precisely because his translator had refused on more than one occasion to translate what Markus was saying on the grounds that it was offensive and would put the translator in an intolerable social position.

Dubravka's narrative also testified to a real vulnerability that came with appealing to powerful foreigners whose presence was only temporary, particularly when returnees could not trust that their words were being properly translated or that foreigners would have the requisite knowledge to understand them even if they were. This vulnerability was only heightened if there was no assurance that the circulation of what returnees said was controlled and might be used against them at a time when there was no longer any OSCE around. Interestingly, as evidence of the seriousness and truth of her accusation, Dubravka offered Miguel information that he would find hard to verify because he could not participate in the personal networks through which she determined that Gojko was not to be trusted—networks that provided information about his family, their connections to politics, and so on. How could he know it was trustworthy knowledge at all, and not rumor, politically filtered "information," or some combination thereof?

Equally important to the "evidence" she offered about Gojko and the logic according to which she interpreted it, was the setting in which she offered it. This meeting—over coffee and cigarettes and in a more social space—seemed designed specifically to create some sort of interpersonal relations of trust and intimacy (despite the language barrier). Meeting outside of the office, as well as having me, someone who was not "local," act as translator, not only signaled the seriousness of her claim but also underscored the notion that is was not *him* she had a problem with, only his translators. Moreover, by presenting this information to him not only as a problem that she had, but also as a potential problem for him and the reputation of the OSCE, she suggested that she cared about him, and was almost doing him a favor by taking him into her confidence. In fact, creating interpersonal relations of intimacy and trust may have been why she brought up the problem with Gojko in the first place. Recall that this discussion was a prelude to the "real" reason this meeting was being held—to enlist Miguel as part of a discussion with the authorities over the highly politicized issue of new ethnic quotas for positions in the municipal administration, quotas that would have to be filled by Muslim and Croat returnees. Whether it was her aim or not, Dubravka gained Miguel's confidence through the conversation about Gojko, and he was afterward open to a wide-ranging discussion of possible strategies to prod the municipal authorities to take up the constitutional changes—and on terms set largely by Dubravka.

Yet the meeting that Miguel later had with his boss in Banja Luka underscored the limited options available for him to act on the basis of Dubravka's claims about Gojko. If Gojko were fired, Miguel would have to find a new translator and train her or him on the ins and outs of OSCE work, and qualified translators with Gojko's experience were not easy to come by in Prijedor. If this firing were unfounded—if Dubravka had been wrong or lying—it would create bad blood and an atmosphere of suspicion among the other Bosnian employees. If a general warning were made, it could raise the tension at work. If a one-on-one warning were made to Gojko—particularly by Miguel's boss—it could damage Miguel's relationship with Gojko, and if what Dubravka said was true, such a warning would not ameliorate the problem she pinpointed but might exacerbate it. It would certainly create mutual distrust between them.

It has been my aim in the preceding pages to paint a picture of the kinds of dilemmas, uncertainties, and frustrations that OSCE officials faced in their interactions with the vulnerable, politicized populations they were in Bosnia to serve. Many of these dilemmas were rooted in a structuring contradiction of their presence in Bosnia. On the one hand, foreigners were not expected or required to have any specific knowledge of Bosnian language, history, or social practices, and their legitimacy lay in the very ignorance of the "local" and in the outsider status that indexed their neutrality. And yet, on the other hand, in seeking to fulfill their mandate they were required to navigate and negotiate a social and political terrain that required precisely that knowledge. They discovered quickly that their outsider status and a lack of Bosnian language skills shut them out of critical circuits of information. They found their attention drawn to the socially mediated nature of the information they *did* possess, to how it was communicated and circulated in ways that raised questions about the reliability, trust, and intentions of their interlocutors—and also their interlocutors' ability to trust them. They learned that, in practice, representing the international community and its goal of promoting refugee return threatened constantly to entangle them in projects not of their choosing.

Understanding these dilemmas sets us up to explore the role that entextualization played in OSCE intervention encounters. For this, we return to Markus in Sanski Most and an extended ethnographic vignette that explores how he navigated this murky, interest-filled terrain. Just how did he respond to the "monitoring" and democratization mandates of his job, the requirement to remain—or at least appear to remain—impartial and neutral, and the constant demands to intervene and stop the purported abuse of Serb returnees by Muslim municipal bureaucrats or otherwise help meet their needs, like employment? And what role did ideologized distinctions between international and local, or between traditional and modern, play in how he interpreted returnee perspectives and actions, including their disinterest in or critique of what the OSCE had to offer them?

Managing Relations

As I described above, the relationship between Serb returnees and the OSCE in Sanski Most was a vexing one for both sides. As the sole on-the-ground representative of the "international community" and its commitment to minority return in Sanski Most, the OSCE was presented by returnees with many scenarios of hardship, abuse, and discrimination, in which they were asked to intervene. This often presented a problem for the foreign staff of the OSCE who had a hard time deciding how to respond to these claims. They found them suspiciously vague or overly "personal," and they had to contend with the possibility that they were being prodded toward ends they did not fully comprehend and that might threaten their self-image as neutral actors or sidetrack their democratization goals.

The commitment to neutrality made Markus and others often wary around those who claimed to "represent" Serb returnees in Sanski Most. Were the issues and complaints they raised about municipal authorities of an individual or, as was usually claimed, of a categorical/collective nature? Would an OSCE response help to create better conditions for all returnees, or would it become harnessed for the benefit of a few, helping them extend their influence, and possibly even exacerbate ethnic tensions? How could you know? What should be the basis of the relationship between the OSCE and the returnee community?

Such questions plagued Markus and the other foreign staff at the OSCE office in Sanski Most. In mid-April 2003, after nearly a year of dissatisfying and frustrating interactions with returnees, Markus and Bernard, the office's French DO, were making another attempt to structure the relationship between the OSCE and the self-styled representatives of the rather fractious returnee community. They had met with fourteen Serb community leaders, including those representing NGOs, political parties, and an Orthodox priest. They described finding a chaotic, incoherent, undisciplined social and political landscape that needed to be ordered. They told me that none of the Serbs they met with (except perhaps the priest) had a clear sense of what their role and responsibility were, none communicated a clear mandate, and they concluded that there was no real difference between any of them. As Markus saw, they all sought one thing: "to be an influential person, to be the one to negotiate with the mayor on behalf of Serbs in Sanski Most."

Aside from imputing to returnee representatives a desire for power, Markus and Bernard zeroed in on the question of their constituency. As far as Markus and Bernard were concerned, none seemed to have been elected in any way, and thus they could not be said to represent anyone besides themselves. They pointed out that even one of the few Serb councilors in the municipal assembly appeared to have no relationship with the president or general membership of the political party that she ostensibly represented. They attributed this to infighting within this party, and emphasized how she was reduced to receiving some people in her home and thus really only acted as an individual, not a party member, municipal legislator, or even a "Serb" representative. They both saw her case as indicative of the infighting among individuals that took up large parts of their meetings with self-styled returnee representatives, and criticized in particular the fact that these representatives had no "clear agenda," did not work according to a "problem-solving manner" or with "goal-oriented tasks." The sense that personal interest was at stake was only heightened when Markus asked for examples of the various claims brought to him and the representatives tended to use their own experience as typical of the problems facing returnees. In Bernard's and Markus's observations we can discern a few basic concerns: Did these returnees occupy delimitable roles, recognizable by certain practices and motivations? Were their relations of representation and accountability to other returnees visible and identifiable?

Having recently completed their survey of Serb "community leaders," Markus and Bernard called them all to a meeting. Beforehand, they told me that they had decided to tell these leaders that in the future they would not be dealing with political parties over returnee issues because they were always too busy fighting each other over the meager spoils of power. They also said that they would not deal with the "NGOs" because they don't do anything. Rather, they had decided to take seriously the organization that claimed to represent all returnees, the *Udruženje povratnike sanskog mosta* (UPSM or Association of Returnees of Sanski Most). Despite what they called the "questionable legitimacy" of the organization, they said that at the very least it had the "vocation" of an association that represented the common demands of returnees. When I brought up the fact that the present leader of the UPSM was also a prominent member of a Serb political party, they said they would not deal with him on that basis. Anticipating that the people they invited might not understand their decision, they stated that they would work to educate these people as to their roles: NGOs had to leave the political scene and define themselves as issue-based organizations; the political parties needed to concentrate on developing a platform and orient themselves towards building their voter base; and the UPSM would be educated as the place for common ground. The idea was to force the fractious group of would-be representatives to fight it out amongst themselves behind closed doors before coming to the OSCE—"we will crown him [the leader of the UPSM] but the honor will also be a burden."

According to Markus and Bernard, the confusion over roles was part of what plagued Bosnia. Markus clarified this by resorting to historical explanation: conditions in the Ottoman Empire and under the communist regime led to the development of patron-client relations and a corresponding fetishistic orientation among the general population toward people with powerful offices. Those in such positions did not think in modern democratic terms about "who I represent," but rather "who do I know and whom can I trust." Even today, Bernard told me, in Bosnia and Herzegovina, "people do not belong to a political party because of its concrete platform but for emotional reasons, like you belong to a church. Leaders do not develop ideas, but extend their relations and are judged on whether they can deliver material goods to those within their network. Political parties here do not fight over ideas but according to the distribution of favors." Markus called it "clan thinking."

The conversation then veered off onto the question of what the OSCE's role was. Bernard said that they could not force politicians to do anything, and any moralizing advice was likely to be ignored. Using the example of the youth who were routinely ignored by the municipality, he said that rather than telling the political parties that they needed to pay attention to the youth, the OSCE worked to train the youth in how to bring pressure on local political parties, how to make politicians nervous and thus accountable and responsive. But even as he suggested that the problem for the youth (and returnees) was a lack of knowledge on how to organize themselves properly, he wondered whether what the OSCE had to offer was that useful. He said that the OSCE was always and only training, but the problems were political: rather than a lack of knowledge or organizational capacity, it was a lack of will that mattered. And, frustrated, he said that the issue of political will was not in their mandate and something that training could do little about.

As the conversation drew to a close, I asked them whether their disciplining action would have much of an effect, particularly given that Bernard was to leave his post in a few days, and Markus a few weeks after that. Markus said it depended upon his replacement but was not optimistic because it was not really a part of their mandate and besides, the OSCE never really did anything in-depth. They told me that while their bosses within the OSCE were not against their attempts to structure a regular working relationship with returnee representatives, they were also skeptical—and rightfully so, according to Markus: when you deal with a large group of people, you will not get any concrete action done. Still, the upcoming meeting did have at least one important role to play: shoring up the reputation of the international community in general and the OSCE in particular by protecting them from accusations of doing nothing. This meeting with returnees and the relationship they hoped to forge through it was at the very least to be taken as evidence of the OSCE's commitment to returnee issues.

At the meeting a few days later, the Serb returnee community leaders assembled at the OSCE office in Sanski Most. All of those invited came, with the exception of the one who worked for the municipality. Markus began by recounting the interviews he had had with all of them over the past weeks, which had had the goals of identifying common ground between the OSCE and returnees, identifying partners for the OSCE to work with, and setting up a "task-related" agenda to begin "concrete" work. After tallying up the list of problems the returnees had mentioned in the interviews, he remarked that all of them had agreed that cooperation between the OSCE and returnees was poor. However, he reminded them that cooperation between these "community leaders" was also poor and pointed out the consequence of this: that the Serbs "in the field" (*na terenu*) were not getting the advocacy they needed.

He then said that the OSCE could not solve all the problems brought to their attention, but that they could work on some of them. Regarding employment, particularly the low number of Serbs working in the public sector, he said, "We are willing to help in the recruitment procedures and make them more transparent, and to stop discrimination. Of course it's not for us to decide [who gets work] that's up to the municipality. Still, we will monitor this process, work on the advertisement of positions in a proper way." Regarding the recent constitutional amendments that would seem to require a quota for Serbs in municipal government, he said, "I can do nothing without guidelines from OHR." As far as Article 143 in Bosnia's Labor Law, which states that everyone is entitled to get their prewar jobs back or be otherwise compensated, he said, "we are ready to collect information from the field through you, but we have to admit that this process is stuck in Bosnia and we cannot promise that the collection of this information will fix anything." For social welfare issues, he offered to monitor cases of discrimination and follow them up if they could be proved.

One member of a political party interrupted and asked what the point of this meeting was if no member of the municipal government was there, arguing that it was likely to go nowhere. He wondered whether he should just leave Sanski Most because there is no real coordination between the municipal government and returnees, and with the current mayor they were not likely to get anywhere on the problems they faced.

Markus countered that although this meeting was not about "solving" anything, previous meetings with the mayor and all the important people in the municipality had met with little success or results, which is why a different approach was necessary: returnees, he said, needed to be prepared about how to approach the government to solve problems and that this meeting was part of that preparation. "We need meetings with fewer people who are willing to work, rather than a meeting with 100 people giving their opinions but not working at all and with few conclusions."

He then continued with his prepared remarks, stating that success on resolving returnee problems required better knowledge of what returnees "in the field" were actually facing—"concrete information, not rumors or stories, but facts." He then said that such information needed to be gathered and organized in a way that could be useful in interactions with the municipality, and for that "you need a well-structured organization, based in the villages, to funnel information up." Then he said that the best way to do this would be for the OSCE to work solely with the UPSM: "This is my offer, I welcome everyone else to support the UPSM and our work with the local government and that's all I have to say except to repeat: you have to deliver concrete facts from the field and if you do not deliver we can do no work."

This must have sounded familiar to those assembled. Nearly ten months prior, a similar diagnosis had come from the OSCE: returnees' problems lay in their lack of organizational skills, the form of the information they possessed, and how they communicated their problems. In response to this diagnosis, Adam, the Polish DO at the time, organized a seminar to train returnee representatives in "team work and citizen participation in public life." On a sunny July morning in 2002 in a hotel at the center of Sanski Most, about twenty returnee representatives attended, mostly from Sanski Most. A few members of the Sanski Most municipal government were also in attendance. At the beginning of the seminar, Adam told the assembled participants that they would be learning new skills and a new approach for how to "identify goals," "have successful dialogue with local authorities," and "work effectively with one another and with members of the international community." Attendees were broken up into group teams and given handouts listing all the different functional roles that there were in an organization (coordinator, idea person, implementer, etc.) and they were encouraged to identify their "emotional type" and a corresponding functional position within the team. Next they participated in a group exercise meant to teach them how to identify, prioritize, and analyze problems facing returnees. In an aside, Adam told me that "it is our experience that they just give stories and stories and problems and problems and we need to get them to prioritize . . . later we will get them to work on how to solve a problem."

It was during this exercise that some of the returnees began to speak out. One middle-aged returnee to Sanski Most said that they could not begin to talk about solving problems until returnees were given organizational infrastructure and financial support, something that the "international community" did not seem to understand. Others were skeptical about whether they could play any role in solving the problems facing them, like unemployment or health care. One young man was frustrated with the idea that "the government exists to serve its citizens," and would respond to returnee needs if they only acted in a proper way: "as NGOs, we can only ask for or demand things [*zahtjevati*], but we have no responsibility [*odgovornost*] . . . [the authorities] do not understand this. Who has the responsibility? Not we NGOs."

Another echoed this theme, stating, "legally, everything is fine. There is simply no will on the part of the authorities to do anything. What we need is influence [*uticaj*] from the internationals, for we have none." A prominent returnee representative from a village outside of Sanski Most dwelt on the issue of influence, saying "What we need are just a few politicians and political power and a number of these problems would be solved quickly. The OHR and OSCE would not need to be working on our problems if we had this political power." Yet another chimed in to ask, "Who exists in the government who is there to listen to us and do something about it, who is *paid* to do this?"

The meeting then dissolved into a general series of complaints about international donors and other institutions, to which Adam felt compelled to respond. He said that the OSCE could not solve these problems, but only play a mediating role between the returnees and the municipal governments. One returnee took issue with this, saying that the OSCE did have influence on the local government, but criticized the way in which it went about dealing with returnee problems. In particular he mentioned the practice of the OSCE taking individual cases and then asked why they should work in teams if the OSCE only reacts to individuals. To this barrage, Adam's voice rose:

> We are here to help you overcome your difficulties. Your problems are that you cannot identify priorities, you do not have the right information, and you are poorly prepared for meetings with the authorities. We know your dialogue with international organizations is unsuccessful. I am sorry to say but meetings often end up in individual cases or private interests. . . . I ask you, what have you done to address your problems to the local authorities? You have local councilors who are supposed to help you and get you answers from the mayor—are you taking advantage of these opportunities? You voted for them, they have to serve you. . . . Our role is to facilitate, but you are citizens of BiH state and [should] take full advantage of the legal institutions of this country.

Returning to the April meeting in the OSCE office, it was no surprise then that Markus faced similar critiques of his "offer." One returnee, responding to Markus' claim that they needed to develop a way to get "facts" from "the field," remarked that such a village-based "network" already existed in the form of thirty-three *mjesne zajednice*,[2] but that they got no financial support from the municipal government. How could they collect information without basic infrastructure like a computer? he asked. Another piped up saying that this is all fine but "We cannot always be at the beginning, as we have been for the last four years. This program of cooperation you talk about would be even better if we had members of the government here to hear about it." Another echoed this and complained that two Serb members of the municipal government were not present and did nothing to help Serbs in Sanski Most. She wondered whether they were wasting their time, and asked whether the international community would finally realize the gravity of the situation only when returnees gave up trying to make a life for themselves in Sanski Most and left for good.

The representative of the local chapter of the Serb Civil Forum took a different tack. He thanked Markus for the invitation and his willingness to help them solve problems. He then suggested that the OSCE was naïve: "I believe that you simply do not understand how government works, and who the key person is in that regard. Who is needed to solve these problems? The mayor." Moreover, he said, "The mayor actually has assistants for all important sectors of activity, including refugee return and property issues. That assistant is actually a Serb and in fact has all the authorization to take down our information and problems and answer our questions. But we have never had cooperation on this and in fact this Serb has told us that we should stop trying."

He continued that of the few Serbs in municipal government, one of them lived in Belgrade and had been to Sanski Most three times in three years. Another did not cooperate with people in her own party, and still another had lived in Banja

Luka for fifty years and was not even a returnee although he claimed to represent Serbs in Sanski Most. "Serb representatives make a game of our problems," he said. "Thus making all our initiatives go through the UPSM will not make things better because we will still be dealing with the same people on the other end. Nothing will really happen until we change those players."

At this point Miroslav Pantić (mentioned in the vignette that opened the book) weighed in, saying that we should be talking less about Serbs as returnees and more about Serbs as a constitutive people. At the moment, he said, when Bosniaks run everything in Sanski Most and Serbs are shut out, nothing will happen; the courts and police will not do anything because they are infested with corruption. He said that if the recently imposed constitutional amendments were implemented, Serbs would have 43 percent of the positions in the municipal government and that would solve *all* of their problems. He continued that "we will fight for our position in the Federation, for there can be no Bosnia without Serbs in the Federation. You can expect more problems because we will not stop fighting."

Then a few who were trying to get their land back from the Municipality weighed in, arguing that there was a double standard on the part of the international community. One argued, "The reputation of the OSCE in Sanski Most is very low among Serb refugees living in Prijedor [and waiting to return to Sanski Most] because no land has been returned, and yet Muslim returnees got their land back in Prijedor. You tell me to go to court, but why? The Muslims in Prijedor did not have to. The OSCE is of little value if its role is to listen to the municipal government more than to us." Another added, "We need your action on property, or you will be an accomplice to a terrible crime [i.e., Serb ethnic cleansing from Sanki Most]."

Markus concluded the meeting at that point by stating that they could take his offer or not, it was up to them. He said he had never guaranteed success when dealing with the municipality. After that they filed out, and he remarked to me that they were all too trapped in their problems and wondered whether they actually represented anyone else besides themselves. Everything was too personalized, he said, and thus their solution was also personalized: remove the person, and you remove the problem. It's always the same with them; nothing changes.

It turns out that he did manage to have a meeting or two with the head of UPSM before leaving Sanski Most, concentrating on the issue of employment. One afternoon in May, Markus told me what he would offer them. He began by again severely circumscribing what he felt the OSCE could do: it could do nothing about the constitutional amendments or Article 143. All he could do when it came to employment in public institutions was to try and get the municipality to commit to transparent fair hiring practices, which his office could then monitor for compliance. He showed me an elaborate set of procedures that he had drawn up in this regard.[3] Moreover, he said to me that fair hiring practices were the best long-term solution to the constant complaints about discrimination, because they would render visible the hidden processes that made discrimination and nepotism so easy. Still, based upon previous meetings, he was quite sure that the returnee representatives would not find his offer compelling. As it turned out, they did not.

This extended vignette offers examples of the clash of perspectives over what was to be done, and why and how the OSCE ought to act. Some suggested that Markus and Bernard were naïve to think anything could be accomplished without the mayor or municipal officials, while another noted that even the Serbs in municipal administration made no difference. Others used the moral metric of equality to suggest that he needed to do what other internationals had done elsewhere for Muslims. Still others used the OSCE's commitment to the goal of refugee return and a multiethnic Bosnia to motivate him, suggesting that these goals were in jeopardy and that recently returned Serbs might decide to leave for good—and he would be responsible. Finally, one returnee suggested Markus was failing in his responsibility to fight discrimination and the conditions that kept Serbs in a marginal position, and threatened social unrest if nothing was done to realize the constitutive status of Serbs in Sanski Most.

Later in our conversation, Markus reflected further on this general lack of enthusiasm for what he and the OSCE had to offer returnees, centering his reflections on returnee resistance to the organization's entextualization practices. He remarked that one of the hardest things for him to understand when he first arrived in Bosnia was why, when he held his "client hours" or other meetings to hear cases of human rights abuses, people would often only show up once and never return. Having witnessed more than a few such meetings, I knew that after hearing a given complaint (through his translator) Markus would begin by saying (through his translator) that the only option open to him was to investigate or "monitor" individual, "concrete cases." If the issue at hand was a claim of widespread and routine abuse made by a Serb returnee representative, this meant that the representative needed to find some person or persons to step forward to substantiate that claim. The same went for individual "clients." Substantiating the claim meant writing down all the information that Markus needed to track a case: the name of the client and their other personal information, such as resident address and contact information, and then the specific information of the case, including the names of the officials who may have been involved and the specific accusations at hand. With this information, Markus would then offer to make inquiries in the relevant municipal institutions as a kind of advocate of the "client" in order to learn more about the incident at issue and decide what to do next.

These meetings proceeded in a fairly repetitive way: returnees or their representatives would come to him with various complaints of abuse and discrimination, but often displayed an extreme reluctance to submit the kinds of information Markus required in the form he required, particularly once it became clear how he planned to proceed. When such information was not forthcoming, Markus found himself stating over and again that he needed "concrete cases"—"facts," not "rumors or stories"—and he routinely admonished returnee representatives that they had few facts or little information that he could use to deal with the municipality. For him, "stories" were unempirical, prone to exaggeration, and too close to their subjects. The unwillingness or inability to submit "concrete cases" in the form he required often led him to openly wonder whether his interlocutors were being honest with him or whether they were pursuing some personal agenda they would not reveal to him.

Returning to our conversation, he described the disappointment he saw in individuals when he offered them a course of action that did not match their expectations and hopes. Markus interpreted this according to his understanding of Bosnia as rampant with clientelism and the fetish of "personal connections," in addition to having a penchant for conspiracy theories. He said that people in Bosnia approached him like a big patron because they were used to dealing with powerful people to get things done and that decisions were made through personal connections with these powerful people, not through procedures or laws. Regarding the rule of law in Bosnia, he remarked that the only time Bosnia had anything approaching the rule of law was under the Austro-Hungarian Empire, "and that was centuries ago." It was this context that he drew upon when telling me about his visits with potential clients:

> When after listening to their problems I did not respond simply by saying "I will solve your problem," their face would fall. They would think, "The cow I brought you wasn't good enough, my smile was not nice enough, my story not sad enough for you to like me or take a personal interest in me . . . because if you took a personal interest in me to do something, you could, because you are OSCE." And they would not return, thinking they had failed to invoke personal interest for the kind of solution they thought I could do.

What are we to make of these breakdowns and failures—the failure to satisfy returnee concerns about employment with "transparency-oriented" solutions like fair hiring practices, the failure to document or respond to possible human rights abuses because potential clients shunned OSCE forms of aid, or the failure to respond to the possibility of systemic ethnic discrimination? Why the OSCE concern about the representivity of their interlocutors, or their focus on forms of information (the demands for "facts" and "concrete cases," not "stories" or "rumors") and organization (team work, different vocations for different organizational forms), as well as the behaviors guiding interaction ("problem-solving manners" and "goal-oriented tasks")?

To understand the OSCE responses to returnee demands and desires, we need to look more deeply into the role played by texts in how foreigners encountered Bosnian politics and society. The following discussion explores two notions of transparency in the work of the OSCE in Bosnia, both of which center on forms of mediation. The first focuses on text artifacts or documents, the second on bureaucratic rules and procedures. Both forms are ideologized as making possible the freedom of rational, objective, modern relations, whether of government or communication. Both are entailed in difference-making practices that authorized and valorized the OSCE's self-conception and its transformational mandate.

Ideologies of Transparency: The Promises of Written Texts

The focus on and problematization of the forms of knowledge in OSCE/Bosnian interactions—the demand for "concrete cases" to substantiate claims of abuse, the repeated call for "facts" and not "stories or rumors"—was tied to the primary means through which foreigners like Markus perceived Bosnian politics and society, managed the contradictions of intervention they faced, and realized the agentive capacities open to them to act in Bosnia—namely, through the creation, interpretation, and circulation of (English-language) documents. And it is here, in the semiotic ideology that informed the document-based practices which mediated the relationship between foreign actors and their Bosnian interlocutors, that the notion of transparency played such a critical legitimizing and authority-making role.

Textualism

The role that documents played for foreign intervention in Bosnia cannot be overstated, even if it is often underthematized (Riles 2006). As noted in chapter 4, documents and documentation can erase individual agency from decision making, depersonalize and abstract information from social interactions and individual biographies, and create social distance (Hull 2012). The power of documents in this regard lay in part in the belief that entextualizing information—putting it into text artifact form—separates knowledge from its socially mediated contexts and fixes it. Others have shown how this broad "textualist" ideology (Collins 1996), in which written texts are regarded as "linguistically transparent, with fixed, primarily denotational meanings, making them equally available to all" (Silverstein and Urban 1996, 6), underwrites the belief that text artifacts are thus context-independent for their meaning. This is a cultural view of language as principally a system for conveying semantic meaning. It orients one to the terms internal to the text artifact to decode its meaning—"the meaning of the text is in the text itself"—and is embodied in the notion that, as Olson notes, "written language is able to stand as an *unambiguous* or *autonomous* representation of meaning" (1977, 258, emphasis added).

The apparent ability of documents to separate knowledge from its social context goes a long way toward understanding their often unacknowledged role of managing uncertainty for OSCE staff. In contexts of cultural and linguistic difference like foreign intervention, the transparency, fixity, and autonomy of meaning contained in written texts acts to elide any overt concern with the conditions of their production and circulation, and this is particularly true of the transformative work of translation. Moreover, there is also an aesthetics to entextualized information, an impersonal and abstract quality taken by foreign actors like Markus to index its modernity, rationality, and universality.

The notion that the meaning of written texts is "universally available" was of course belied by the fact that in Bosnia all of the documents that circulated through "international" institutional circuits were rendered in the "international" language of English. This circulation excluded the vast majority of Bosnians who might raise questions about the commensurability of foreign text representations and Bosnian social life. Nevertheless, the ability of English-language entextualized information to circulate across Bosnia and through institutional circuits that traversed Vienna, Brussels, Geneva, New York, and other major European and global capitals endowed it with the aura of greater "universality" and thus more legitimacy than any document rendered in Bosnia's language(s), let alone information and knowledge that did not take written text form.[4]

These basic tenets of textualism—particularly the purported separation of knowledge from the social and cultural context that generated it—combined on a general level to implicitly reassure OSCE and other foreign officials in Bosnia that the documents and terms through which they apprehended Bosnian society and politics stood as adequate representations of the contexts of their intervention. As I will show below, making written texts the basis of communication and action in their interactions with their Bosnian interlocutors accounted to a large degree for the shape and limits of OSCE power in Bosnia.

Text Artifacts and OSCE Activity

There were, of course, organizational imperatives to the relationship OSCE staff had with documents. Like officials in any bureaucratic organization, most everyday practices of OSCE staff were mediated by written texts—their creation, circulation, and digestion. Indeed, as Smith notes, it is with and through such documents that organizations and their qualities are constituted: "the formality, designed, planned and organized character of formal organizations depends heavily upon documentary practices, which coordinate, order, provide continuity, monitor and organize relations between different segments and phases of organizational courses of action" (1984, 66). OSCE officials communicated and acted with them and through them and could not really act in a formal capacity without them. As I suggested above in the description of Markus's demand for "concrete cases" of complaints of abuse, entextualized or artifactualized information served as a stable referent; when rendered in English, it could constitute the grounds upon which officials like him felt confident in communicating across the distance constituted by linguistic (if not cultural) difference. If action is ethically acceptable only when one can be reasonably assured of the truth of the information at hand, written texts go a long way to satisfying those truth conditions necessary for foreign OSCE activity.

Such documents, then, were a key feature in the dominant form of agency claimed by the OSCE, namely, that of "monitoring" or surveillance. As I suggested above, this agentive capacity was in turn linked to their embodiment of neutrality and expert knowledge of democracy. Recall that Markus's mandate to serve the vulnerable returnee population by "monitoring" human rights violations and the rule of law required documenting claims in text artifact form (it was the artifact form that gave "concrete cases" of such abuse their "concreteness"). Entextualizing information allowed officials like Markus to make a given claim (or any information) more "transparent" to them.

Although the notion of monitoring might conjure up an image of simply observing preexisting practices and processes (or reconstructing them post facto), OSCE monitoring of human rights violations and the rule of law was in fact *transformative* work in at least two ways. The first transformed a given issue into the terms, language, and text form amenable to OSCE modes of understanding and action. The second was connected to OSCE democratization goals of increasing "transparency." Markus's solution regarding the problem of returnee employment and discrimination by municipal bureaucrats was to make the hiring process at the municipality more "transparent" by getting the municipality to commit to fair hiring practices, which would be a set of entextualized practices and procedures elaborated by Markus himself (working from a template provided by the OSCE).

He would then "monitor" future municipal hiring; that is, he would identify any gaps between his interpretation of these procedures and the practices of Bosnian institutions, and then police those gaps. In other words, this kind of "monitoring" was a way of establishing the authority of the OSCE by reshaping governmental processes and practices according to terms of its choosing, as well as by reorienting relations of power by making governmental practices contingent on OSCE approval.

This example also indicates that it is actually in the production and interpretation of documents that the kind of visibility valued by transparency-oriented practices was imagined to be achieved. Indeed, as Riles notes, transparency-oriented reforms designed to increase accountability are, in practical terms, usually "calls to documentation" (2006, 6), or as Stan puts it "the production of transparency is the production of knowledge" (2007, 258). I will return to this point below.

In sum, English-language entextualizations, underwritten by an ideology of transparent meaning that purports to separate information from its socially mediated and contingent context, did enormous work to manage the uncertainty that came with navigating a foreign context. They were key to the particular agentive capacities and modes of authority claimed by the OSCE. As we could see in the ethnographic vignette about Markus and his failure to advocate for the individual returnee clients in Sanski Most, anything *not* easily placed into English-language artifact form could be problematic for foreigners. It complicated the ability of OSCE actors to realize the agentive capacities open to them. Written texts were the key component that set in motion their monitoring mandate—lacking any Bosnian language skills, OSCE officials like Markus cannot do much without such documents.

Moreover, *non*-text-based forms of communication and circulation introduced the very uncertainty that written texts were supposed to manage: if the meaning of artifactualized information was ideologized as transparent, autonomous, and universally available, then unentextualized information pointed to the socially intersubjective nature of meaning, the ambiguity and ambivalence raised by practices of translation, and the fact of cultural difference, all of which—as we saw in the results of Miguel's conversation with Dubravka—foreign officials were poorly equipped to handle. Moreover, these officials operated within a political economy of knowledge highly conditioned by textualist ideology, one that related the reliability and truth of information to its ability to appear abstract, decontextualized, seamless, and "transparent," such that drawing attention to the ambiguities and contingencies in the production of knowledge—whether in text artifact form or not—could be used to devalue that knowledge (Rosga 2005).

I dwell on the relationship between written texts and foreign action in Bosnia not only because it illuminates how OSCE actors are socialized into the position that they do not need knowledge of Bosnian politics and society, as well as how they managed the correlated threat that the knowledge they did have may not have been an adequate representation thereof. It also reveals surveillance or "monitoring" as a critical if unacknowledged mode of foreign authority-making and transformation. More important for my concerns here, however, is the place of written texts—in particular their purported ability to separate knowledge from its social context—in how internationals drew lines of difference and stigmatized Bosnian behavior when contrasted to the way the OSCE did things.

Enlightenment, Modernity, and Europe

Writing, literacy, and the orientation toward written texts have a long history as signs of modernity, progress, civilization, and other post-Enlightenment self-definitions of Europe and Western superiority, as well as justification for Europe's colonial ascendance over preliterate, "savage" nations. Literacy, however, became an index of modernity and progress because of its purported ability to unlock human intellectual potential, as well as its ability to free knowledge and science (and politics) from the shackles of tradition. As Maurice Bloch (1998) argues in a critical engagement with the work of Jack Goody on literacy, there is a long history in post-Enlightenment thought that attributes political and personal domination to the social relations within which knowledge was embedded before writing and mass literacy. As Cody notes in his discussion of Bloch's essay,

> the politically liberating powers of separating knowledge from social bonds often attributed to literacy . . . can be found as a legacy of Enlightenment thought even in recent anthropological theorizations of the modernizing effects of literacy. Following this line of thought, "systems of communication are therefore to be judged in terms of their transparency," that is, in terms of their capacity to circumvent potentially oppressive forms of social mediation. (2007, 10)

Webb Keane's (2007) discussion of "the moral narrative of modernity" helps illustrate this last point further. While recognizing the problems with modernity as an analytic concept, he observes that the association of being "modern" with the emancipated subject has been powerful across a range of contexts. In his analysis of modernity and conversion to Christianity in colonial contexts, Keane notes that this emancipation is believed to come about when humans act upon their history (see also Taylor 1989). Keane's quotation of Kenelm Burridge on the kind of modern individual produced by Christian conversion resonates with the case here. Such an individual is defined by "the capacity to deliberately step outside custom, tradition, and given social roles, rights and obligations, scrutinize them, formulate a moral critique, and . . . envisage a new social order governed by new moralities" (1978, 13–14, quoted in Keane 2007, 52).

I argue that the foreign OSCE staff, as bearers, embodiments, and promoters of European modernity, came to interpret Bosnian society and politics—as well as their role in it—through this civilizing mission. Bosnian actions, behaviors, modes of communication, and beliefs about politics were seen as signs of the fetishism of "connections" to powerful officeholders or of irrationally paranoid fears of ethnic discrimination (felt but not seen) from which they needed to be freed to become truly modern, democratic, and "European." Certain forms of mediation—like documents, laws, or bureaucratic processes—were valorized precisely for their ability to abstract knowledge and emancipate individuals (and government) from their subjective and potentially oppressive social entanglements.

In other words, for OSCE officials there was a semiotic ideology—a set of beliefs about the use of language that ties linguistic forms to particular "types" of people—that associated those who used written text-based forms of knowledge and communication with the virtues of modernity—rationality, objectivity, and transparency. This was contrasted with those who do not use written text-based forms as embodying those negative qualities attributed to the preliterate—of being traditional, irrational, even paranoid, but above all, buried in the murkiness, subjectivity, and distortion of potentially problematic social relations. I would argue that this semiotic ideology helped to constitute the terms of the self/Other difference-making practices through which foreign officials like Markus cast his failure as the result of the backward or irrational nature of his interlocutors. In the example offered earlier of the routine breakdowns that happened in his interactions with returnees in his client hours, he interpreted his interlocutors' practices and behaviors—attempts to gain his favor, or the use of "stories" rather than "concrete" cases of abuse—as indexes of the "traditional," "corrupt," or dissimulating. In doing this he drew upon imagery associated with the figure of Europe's "not yet modern" and "traditional" subject, the peasant.

In this way, it appeared that the willingness of Bosnian returnees to submit their claims to foreign documentary practices becomes a metric for officials like Markus to judge the trustworthiness and truthfulness of those claims—as well as the modernity and rationality of those making them. Hence, in the interactions described earlier, the demand by Markus for "concrete" cases—not "rumors or stories"—was in part to test whether the complaints of returnees were the product of gossip or paranoid social thought (thus not worth taking seriously), or were cynical attempts to exploit the power of the OSCE for personal ends (and thus not worth taking seriously). The willingness and ability of Bosnians to give Markus information in the form he required also indexed for him the kinds of people they were—recall the remark about how they were trying to cultivate personal interest, a sign of clientelism, or the remark about the cow, a clear marking of the peasant, unmodern nature of his Bosnian interlocutors.

The moral nature of this modern/unmodern, self/Other distinction becomes clearer if we push this point further. OSCE training sessions like the one described earlier focused on disciplining individual and collective behavior, with the invitation to "identify your emotional type and corresponding institutional role" and the exhortation to work in a "problem-solving manner." They also focused attention on representational forms of organization, distinguishing NGOs from political parties and returnee organizations, as well as on the ordering of information: "facts" and not rumors needed to be prioritized and organized into a "clear agenda" with "goal-oriented tasks." Collectively, these were all calls to individual and collective self-transformation, with the argument that these "modern," procedure-oriented forms of behavior, of collective organization, and of information would reveal agentive capacities in the returnees that had thus far been (falsely or fetishistically) thought to reside in personal and intimate connections to powerful people in government. They might also have the effect of disenchantment, of dispelling the paranoid tendency to see ethnic discrimination as the unseen but nevertheless present force controlling their lives. If a sign of a modern, emancipated individual is the agentive capacity for self-reflection and self-transformation, then the failure of Bosnian returnees to respond to OSCE training, their continued insistence that the problems they faced lay with people, their complaints of systemic discrimination and their repeated calls upon the OSCE to intervene on their behalf all combined as continuing evidence of their lack of self-transformation—of their imprisonment in tradition and custom. Seen from this perspective, for OSCE officials to intervene in Bosnian society and politics as the returnees asked them to would be not only to step outside of their highly circumscribed set of mandated activities and violate their legitimacy as neutral "monitors," it would also be *immoral*, for it would make them complicit in supporting the cultural and social conditions that prevented Bosnians from becoming modern and free.

Thus encounters like those between returnees to Sanski Most and OSCE officials generated evidence confirming the need for what the OSCE was there to bring, namely, the forms of mediation that would increase transparency and dispel the conditions of subjective, unmodern, or rumor-based thinking and acting, and to create the conditions for rational decision-making and, by extension, to create free and rational subjects. At the same time, however, OSCE actions also confirmed notions that many Bosnians held about the relationship between power and knowledge. In order to appreciate this mutually productive, divergent (mis) understanding, we need to first look more closely at the transparency ideal that the OSCE promoted (rather than the one it relied upon), and the way that it was promoted.

Ideologies of Transparency: The Promises of Visibility

It is no surprise, then, given the OSCE's linking of visibility to democracy and accountability in its own activities (Coles 2007, 191–234), that it would cast its mode of surveillance—anchored in documentary practices and procedures—as an example to be replicated by the Bosnian public vis-à-vis its government.

Briefly, the relationship between accountability and transparency is that when the workings of government are made visible to a disembodied "public" (usually represented as omnipresent and ever-watching), citizens are given the sense that they have the power of surveillance over government. This is supposed to engender a sense of trust in government that is not based on intimate knowledge or social relations. This is the sort of trust that Giddens (1990) suggested was critical to modernity—the confidence in the functioning of institutions that cannot be directly monitored and controlled. More importantly, as Morris notes, "in the era of liberalization, transparency translates the idiom of accountancy into that of politics. It is somehow associated with an ethics of sincerity . . . [and is] thought to compel the performance of a certain honesty, and this honesty (or at least its performance), is thought to secure the possibility of smooth exchange relations in turn" (2004, 226). In other words, making the workings of government visible is supposed to induce self-policing and greater accountability on the part of government officials because exposure, disclosure, and other sorts of visibility make corrupt practices too risky to pursue.

As Bosnian government was problematized by the OSCE and Bosnians alike as nepotistic, corrupt, and unaccountable, and the Bosnian public was seen as powerless to do anything about it, the OSCE, like many "transparent government" reformers, saw its task in not only manufacturing an open institutional environment, but also creating the kinds of agents predisposed to monitor it. It did this through all sorts of training sessions as well as through offers to force government institutions to adopt transparency-oriented procedures like the fair hiring practices. In doing so, the OSCE provided for itself the power to monitor compliance with these new procedures and legal provisions. This placed the OSCE in a proxy position as a placeholder where an all-seeing Bosnian public would hopefully one day stand.

However, rather than seeing any regulation of governmental behavior to result from bureaucratic practices that produced visibility before an all-seeing public (as the transparency ideal would have it), the Bosnian returnees who appealed to the OSCE saw any such "self-policing" to be dependent upon the OSCE and thus an index of its authority. Thus procedures like fair hiring practices seemed for returnees to be an overly complicated way to solve a problem like unemployment—if OSCE actors had the authority and power to enforce compliance with practices they themselves developed, they had the power to get things done in a more direct manner. Moreover, as I suggested at the outset of this chapter, these returnees were already familiar with fairing hiring practices. The problem for them was not the practices, but their enforcement.

Indeed, this sort of power was well known in Bosnia, where in many contexts authority lay not in bureaucratic practices, nor truth in texts, but in social relations—in people and in their institutionally authorized positions of power. Operating under a different moral economy of knowledge control and circulation, this accounts for the reluctance of some returnees to submit to foreign text-making practices and for their tepid response to OSCE transparency-oriented solutions to problems like official discrimination or unemployment. Ironically, this divergence also accounts for why returnees solicited OSCE officials in ways that were interpreted by foreigners as evidence of the very problems that they were there to solve.

Bosnian Practices of Knowledge Control and Circulation

Most returnees I met were skeptical about the possibility of separating any bureaucratic practice of government, the meaning of knowledge, or access to information from the social relations in which they were embedded. They thus both critiqued the intimacies and interests of social relations and built many of their forms of trust upon them.

The conditions of everyday life under state socialism and one-party rule bred a well-developed wariness regarding the arbitrary and capricious exercise of bureaucratic or state power, and necessitated the cultivation of informal networks and the use of friends and connections to make life livable. Such strategies justified strong distinctions between the private and public, or the "us" of family and friends and the "them" of state officials and other political elites. Such distinctions operated according to different moral principles. As Gal and Kligman put it, "The cultural imperative to be honest and ethically responsible to those who counted as the private 'we' contrasted with distrust and a tolerance of duplicity and interpersonal manipulation in dealings with the public 'them'" (2000, 51). This meant, as Sampson argues, that "to reveal in the public sphere one's inner self, one's real thoughts, [was] not a sign of authenticity but of stupidity. The public sphere is a forum for demonstrating one's ability to misrepresent oneself" (1986, 56). Sampson goes onto argue that as the conditions which underpin these tactics endure over time, they become routinized, such that social connections are "not just a *utilitarian* 'last resort' when the formal system does not work. [Rather] they are *normative*, the proper way to do things, even when the bureaucracy *does* work. For it is via one's personal connections that one demonstrates to oneself and others one's social position" (1986, 60, emphasis in original).

In Bosnia, as elsewhere in highly bureaucratized societies, there was a well-developed understanding of the constant potential for unfairness and failure in interactions with bureaucrats and other agents of institutionalized government. Bosnians knew that bureaucrats can (and routinely do) use their positions to abdicate responsibility and accountability ("The law is the law—it is out of my hands," or "You don't have the correct documentation, so I cannot help you," or "I don't make the rules, I just have to follow them"), to discriminate against individuals or classes of people, or to pursue self-interested aims in the name of public service. In such contexts, one can never be quite sure that the reason for failure in interactions with bureaucrats lies in the letter of the law and official bureaucratic procedure, or is the result of something more personal, the ignorance of extralegal interactional codes, a hidden policy (of discrimination), or simple indifference. As Herzfeld (1993) makes clear, this potential for unfairness and "corruption" is intrinsic to the organization of bureaucratic practice itself, a stereotype across Western and non-Western contexts. Indeed, this potential for abuse in governmental power was identified by the great theorist of bureaucratic power, Max Weber, who as far back as the nineteenth century saw that "the logical outcome of bureaucratic rationality is secrecy, in direct conflict to democratic ideals of openness, as well as the antithesis of transparency" (Marcus and Powell 2003, 332).

In this context, often the most effective way to pursue any goals—particularly those that had to do with officials or other agents of government—was to do so informally, either through personal, intimate connections or by developing relations of obligation that were recognizably "private" and thus fell within the ethical rules of behavior associated with "us." Approaching a bureaucrat without a personal connection could be a very unstable and uncertain enterprise.

The end of socialist order in Bosnia did little to change the conditions that gave rise to the extreme wariness of officialdom and public exposure, or the reliance on personal networks and connections. If anything, the onset of war added new uncertainties to everyday life and only sharpened this division of the social world into "them" and "us."

For many returnees, then, personal, verbal, face-to-face interactions carried much more weight and offered much more protection than any textual, translated, or other similarly mediated interactions. Sampson argues that this was also the case for officials under socialism: "bureaucrats and even ministers learn which directives can be thrown into the drawer and which are to be taken seriously; those taken most seriously are those communicated orally" (1986, 53). This suggests that the relationship between visibility and the exercise of power posited by the OSCE is not a mischaracterization of Bosnian government: secrecy, the importance of face-to-face interactions, the reliance on private connections, and the deliberately verbal (and not textual) communication of information *were* ways through which power was exercised by those in positions of authority. But what went unrecognized by the OSCE officials was that these are also ways through which ordinary people protect themselves from the capriciousness of the powerful in an environment of continuing uncertainty. In Bosnia, when interacting with officials, most returnees saw their agency as consisting of preventing unwanted surveillance from accessing "the private" (thus controlling information about themselves and how it could be interpreted), of recourse to networks that may include such officials, of developing some sort of relationship with them, or of positing claims about abuse in general terms so that they did not have to "own" it.

Let us not forget that this is how Miguel chose to respond to Dubravka's accusations about one of the staff in his office. He did not create a documentary trail, did not write a letter to his boss detailing the allegations. That would have made him its author and in a sense responsible for it, as had been the case with his memo in which he charged—mistakenly—that there had been no official response to the grenade on the imam's balcony. He did not even make a phone call. Rather, he drove one and half hours roundtrip to Banja Luka to speak with his boss about it, face to face, behind closed doors—and even then he fretted that his boss would act in a way that would tie him to accusations about a coworker upon whom he depended, accusations that he really had no way of substantiating.

Just as Miguel's actions in this situation did not stop him from expounding the virtues and ideals of practices meant to make government visible, so too many of the returnees I spoke with did valorize the rule of law or see value in measures designed to "increase transparency" and accountability. This was particularly the case with those returnees who were left outside of the now largely monoethnic social networks that sprang up in the postwar period. Returnees were, however, skeptical about the ability of more rules—like those proposed by the OSCE—to subvert the ability of officials and bureaucrats to manipulate them for their own ends. Moreover, despite complaints to the contrary, most Bosnians and foreigners I met tolerated what would be called petty corruption as inevitable, as necessary for people to be able to pursue their own interests (Stan 2007, 266). Indeed, as Herzfeld put it, often "accusations of corruption . . . indicate the power of relations that the official ideology rejects and that social actors resent, but that neither can practically do without" (1993, 173).

Going Nowhere

This, in part, explains why returnee/foreigner interactions were so fraught. The foreign staff of the OSCE clearly fell into the public/"them" slot, and thus were seen as influential persons to be appealed to or as potential connections to be cultivated, but not necessarily as people to be trusted. Other factors militated against establishing the requirements for trust—the rapid change of foreign personnel meant that there was no time to establish a relationship, and the need for translation and the presence of an interpreter increased social distance and meant that communication could never be truly direct, interpersonal, or face to face. Most foreigners were shut out of Bosnian social networks because the culturally specific conditions necessary to establish trust were rarely established (or able to be established). Moreover, these conditions for establishing trust were likely to be interpreted by foreigners as evidence of the unmodern, fetishistic, or hidden practices of "personal connections" that they were there to transform—and this only exacerbated the uncertainty that returnees faced when interacting with the OSCE. Thus, many of the ordinary returnees coming to the OSCE for the first time felt uncomfortable with the kind of vulnerability and exposure that inhered in the "concrete cases" that the OSCE demanded in order to "monitor" their complaints. This was particularly true if there was the possibility that their claims of abuse and recourse to the OSCE could become known to powerful municipal authorities who were likely to be around long after the international officials had departed.

For those returnees and their representatives who regularly sought to animate OSCE interventions regarding the sometimes overlapping issues of ethnic discrimination and employment in the public sector, the tendency of the OSCE officials to diagnose returnee problems as located in their ignorance of organizational form, their self-interested manner of self-presentation, or the overly subjective, "rumor-based" information they communicated, appeared naïve at best and insulting at worst. It was naïve because it put responsibility on returnees for their problems, rather than recognizing that it was, as they saw it, a matter of being shut out of politically influential networks within the municipal government or of finding the offices of local government directed against them. It was insulting, because such a diagnosis was rendered in a language that suggested that they did not know how to behave in a modern, democratic, civilized, or "European" way.

Moreover, they found the highly circumscribed action offered by the OSCE—to investigate claims of abuse or institute and monitor "fair hiring practices"—to be an overly cumbersome way of confronting the problems they were dealing with. What they needed was international influence, not more bureaucratic procedures. Protests by the OSCE that they played only a mediating role, that they could only carry out "monitoring" activities of already existing law and procedures but otherwise had no other capacity to act—these appeared disingenuous for the returnees. It overlooked the fact that as members of the "international community," the OSCE had significant influence with local officials. Furthermore, returnees rightly saw "monitoring" as a kind of surveillance that entailed considerable power. However, the way that the OSCE sought to exercise its monitoring capacities—like the fair hiring practices—did not seem adequate to the nature of the problems returnees faced, and appeared designed more to reinforce the OSCE's authority than leverage it for returnees. Finally, some of the criticisms of OSCE officials like Markus, such as stigmatizing as unmodern returnees' tendency to identify the problems they faced with individuals in power rather than the systemic factors that allowed corruption to flourish, could appear hypocritical: by mid-2003, the OHR—fellow member of the "international community"—had removed over 100 Bosnian officials from their positions, a clear "personalization" of politics.

I began this chapter by asking how the OSCE could present fair hiring practices as something novel and transformative for Bosnia, given that there was already a commitment to fair hiring principles under the self-managing socialist regime. That is, how could they come to believe the notion that rationalized, technical procedures would transform a situation already saturated with such procedures? The simplest answer to the first question lies in the structuring conditions of foreign intervention that actively discouraged "internationals" from developing any specialized knowledge of Bosnian culture, language, or history. But I have shown that it was far more than that. Acknowledging the existence of fair hiring practices would have meant acknowledging the inadequacy of the self-defined role of internationals as the bearers of modernity's promises to a backward Balkan country. It would have threatened the critical self versus Other distinctions that legitimized their presence in Bosnia. It would also have taken away one of the key instruments with which they sought to carry out their mandate to monitor and transform the country, namely, the transparency-bearing, disenchanting, rationalizing procedures and entextualization practices that would help liberate the country and its people from the paranoia and problematic social relations that kept them from rationality, freedom, and "Europe." At times, foreigners came to experience the contradictions structuring their presence in Bosnia as an attack on the Enlightenment assumptions about fixed knowledge, transparent communication, and rational government that both helped them manage those contradictions and underwrote their agentive capacities. The transformative power foreigners invested in certain rationalizing, proceduralizing forms must have appeared as fetishistic to Bosnian returnees as the forms of sociality, paranoia, and irrational attachments that these forms were designed to disenchant.

Conclusion

One legacy of intervention encounters in postwar Bosnia and Herzegovina is the enduring place of the international community in the contemporary political discourse of ordinary Bosnians. Signs of this crop up in unexpected places. In May of 2016, I was sitting in the offices of a small cement and gravel company on the outskirts of Tuzla, a city in northeast Bosnia and Herzegovina. I was there as part of my research on postsocialist labor politics, asking questions about a hunger strike which workers at the company had only just recently called off. Through a haze of cigarette smoke which never really dissipated, a small group of workers told me about the difficulty they faced in restarting production, mostly due to debts the company had accrued in unpaid taxes. One of the group, a middle-aged worker and union representative named Senad, remarked that debt wasn't the real issue; much larger companies with much larger debts were allowed to continue to work, due to their connections with politicians. He said that the real issue was that the laws were applied unevenly and unfairly in Bosnia, something he imagined did not happen in Canada (where I work and live). He said that the problems they faced lay deep in the political system of postwar Bosnia, problems that seemed beyond their capacity to solve as individuals or as a small group of workers.

At this point Senad pivoted to complain about foreign organizations in the country, singling out the international community's current High Representative, Valentin Inzko, who, he said, got paid a big salary but did not do very much. He complained in particular about Inzko's equivocal position in relation to Bosnian politics: "Whenever you ask him about some [problem], he always responds that he is neither for this, nor for that. . . . He says, I am not responsible, you have a state, a government" to take care of such things.

And yet rather than reject Inzko, Senad instead said that he was "the only solution" to the political problems facing Bosnia and Herzegovina. He then made an observation whose logic I had heard many times before, that went something like this: when Bosnians and Herzegovinians go abroad, they are usually successful, because, as he put it, "we are smart and hardworking people." Therefore, if the problem did not lie with the capacities of individual people, then there must be something wrong with the political system and the political culture that nurtured it, something specific to Bosnia and Herzegovina: "here," he puzzled, "we are fools—when our politicians mistreat us, we accept it and become confused." He then arrived at his conclusion, "We need a good leader [like the High Representative] who will lead us . . . that is why I say we need a protectorate. You get everyone working again, then we'll see, maybe in fifteen or twenty years we'll have matured" enough for self-government.

The conversation then returned to the question of worker tactics and protest strategy. And yet the call for an international protectorate stuck with me. It was not the topics or framework of the discussion that were noteworthy—I was long used to the ways in which an encounter with an interested foreigner with the ability to communicate in B/C/S could animate a discussion of geopolitics and precise diagnoses for local problems and solutions. Often in such conversations I find myself called upon to stand in for the international community and asked to confirm my interlocutor's perspectives and diagnoses.

No, what made it noteworthy was the sheer staying power of the idea of an "international protectorate"—the demand for the suspension of ostensibly democratic institutional arrangements in favor of rule by unelected outsiders—as a part of the postwar political imagination in Bosnia and Herzegovina. What also stuck out were the complaints about the indecisiveness and ambivalence of powerful members of the international community. Such complaints—and appeals for international rule—were far more common during the high interventionist era that lasted for about a decade, from 1997 to 2006, and during which I carried out field research on intervention encounters. Indeed, in the first pages of this book we found Wolfgang Petritsch, High Representative at the turn of the century, rebuffing such calls for a protectorate on multiple occasions. Yet despite the radical scaling back of the international presence in the country, Senad's political diagnosis and prescription indexed the enduring legacy of international intervention twenty years after the Dayton Agreement was signed, including the continuing sense that developments in Bosnian politics and society—for better and for worse—depended upon the actions of powerful outsiders. It is not hard to see why, given the shifting geopolitical context in which Bosnia and Herzegovina finds itself today.

After all, some of the certainties which characterized international intervention in Bosnia and Herzegovina around the turn of the twenty-first century have become destabilized, such as the exportability of liberal democratic models of political organization or the inevitability and desirability of Bosnia's future membership in the European Union. EU accession processes remain stalled, and a wide range of foreign players have recently appeared, or amplified their presence. With very little in the way of financial input, Russia has made itself a patron of "fellow Orthodox" Serbs in the Republika Srpska, giving additional clout to the ever-present threat of secession. Turkey under Recep Tayyip Erdoğan has also found Bosnia and Herzegovina a convenient site to demonstrate a larger influence in the region. Development companies with links to foreign capital are building exclusive resorts amid Bosnia's natural beauty, creating vacation properties for clients from wealthy Gulf States who may not be able to afford Switzerland. Predatory foreign companies have designs on Bosnia's abundant waterways, seeking to build dams and extract cheap electricity; Chinese companies are building new coal-fired power stations that promise to worsen the country's already disastrous air pollution problems.

It could be argued that this situation is a failure of the international community's Europeanization strategy for withdrawal from Bosnia: due to the country's impending destination in the EU, responsibility for supervising the postwar peace was dubbed a European matter and slowly transferred from international to European institutions (even the High Representative gained the title EU Special Representative). Yet after the Greek economic crisis, Brexit, and the refugee crisis, there appears to be little enthusiasm in Brussels or elsewhere in Europe for adding a poor, fractious country to the EU. The rise of illiberal governments in Poland and Hungary has also raised questions about whether EU accession has the transformative effects on the political culture of new member states that so many expected. I have always felt that when it came to state-building in the Balkans, there was more at stake for foreign officials from the EU than their self-representation as benevolent, even aloof, civilizing missionaries would suggest. About six years ago I observed that "insofar as the multi-ethnic, multi-lingual, multi-cultural, and religiously diverse polities of the Balkans are seen increasingly to be a reflection of Europe's present and future, the Balkans might be thought of as a site of displaced anxiety about the viability of the European project itself" (Murphy et al. 2013, 14). Even then I could not have guessed at the changes that have occurred in the intervening period. Indeed, seventeen years on, Petritsch's confident assertion of the coming extinction of Bosnia's nationalist political parties—that such parties "don't exist in the rest of Europe any longer"—was not just wrong, but seems oddly anachronistic.

It is not my intention here to make causal arguments about the relationship between international intervention and the present condition of Bosnia and Herzegovina. As I stated in the Introduction, this book is written more for students and scholars of international intervention than for readers whose primary interest is in Bosnian politics and society. And even if recent geopolitical developments in the West make it more difficult to evoke (or invoke) a united "international community," international interventions continue to take place under the sign of humanitarianism, peacekeeping, peacebuilding, development and democratization. Many bear the hallmarks of the encounters I analyzed in this book, in part because many of the instabilities I identified are not unique to Bosnia.

Legitimacy and Performativity

In the Introduction, I argued that a focus on the question of legitimacy in intervention encounters was a useful method for identifying and accounting for the stakes, instabilities, and effects of international intervention. This is, in part, because questions about legitimacy were an everyday part of intervention encounters. They were so routinized for the High Representative that nearly every OHR press release and press conference was crafted in a way that anticipated such objections to the legitimacy of his perspectives and actions. Aid workers were on guard for situations that might call into question the legitimacy of their humanitarian status. Returnees routinely questioned OSCE officials' neutrality, and thus the legitimacy of their claim to be unbiased mediators in a context of ethnic difference. OSCE officials themselves questioned the legitimacy of a range of returnee claims, and the High Representative contested the legitimacy of the country's politicians as representatives of their constituents. Analysis of intervention encounters revealed not only these contestations of legitimacy, but also how these encounters were where the grounds and criteria for evaluating that legitimacy were created (as in the foundational moments of aid projects described in chapter 4), improvised (as in Petritsch's use of the recently created constitutional commissions to counter claims of discrimination and oppression by rebelling HDZ leaders), tested (as in whether the international championing and imposition of the constitutional amendments bestowed a new value on Serb or Bosniak returnee claims to municipal jobs as constitutive peoples), and rejected (as when OSCE officials questioned the claims made by returnees unwilling to submit their complaints about discrimination to foreign entextualization).

The stakes, instabilities, and effects revealed by attention to legitimacy were often related to the performative dimension of international intervention. In particular, they were related to the ability of foreigners and Bosnians alike to convincingly occupy particular subject positions or roles. For the representatives of international institutions, these were roles such as mediator, educator, or humanitarian. For the people of Bosnia and Herzegovina, these were roles such as "ethnic representative" or "vulnerable and needy returnee." I showed that performative requirements were bestowed upon those seeking to occupy such roles, and that determining whether any individual or collective enactment of a role was convincing depended upon the evaluation of a range of others. Closely related to the ability to convincingly occupy roles was the ability to persuade others of the legitimacy of one's perspective or interpretive framework. Thus many of the encounters I analyzed were made of attempts to define and interpret the performative requirements for those roles—and thus the relations, obligations and responsibilities that went with them.

The performative nature of legitimacy clearly had a bearing on the agency of those involved in intervention encounters, understood as the varied ability to wield means toward specifics ends. Successful enactments of roles were intersubjective because they depended upon the evaluation and recognition of others, and this gave those others power. For example, even when Jasmina succeeded in persuading returnees about the criteria for what it meant to be "humanitarian," fulfilling those criteria was also dependent upon returnees. This was the case because returnees were often the source of the information that allowed Jasmina to determine who among them was most needy; if that information was faulty, then her status as humanitarian could be threatened. In one case, when that threat was so great as to halt an aid project, it was the improvisation of a returnee representative—creating a special document that all potential beneficiaries signed attesting that her selection was indeed according to the most needy—that restored Jasmina's humanitarian credentials and allowed the project to proceed. In other words, the returnee representative staged a performance of returnee consent in order to provide evidence that the aid organization was fulfilling the criteria for being humanitarian.

One basic performative requirement to successfully occupy the role of foreign mediator was to demonstrate neutrality, and much of this book focuses upon the consequences of this for officials like the High Representative in Sarajevo or OSCE HROs in Sanski Most and Prijedor. Perhaps the most thorough description of the instabilities created by the performative requirements of neutrality was my analysis of the encounter between Miguel and Dubravka. So many aspects of Miguel's job depended upon his being able to demonstrate neutrality, and yet his ability to do so convincingly was contingent upon the actions of others (like local interpreters) and limited by his inability to access or navigate the local networks through which Bosnians made sense of politics and society. This limit was itself the result of performative requirements, because in some contexts being neutral also meant maintaining the hierarchical distinctions between "internationals" and the "locals" between whom they were in Bosnia to mediate. Enacting these distinctions often meant maintaining a social distance with Bosnians and a studied ignorance—or stigmatization—of the country's history, language, and culture.

At times it was the actions of fellow "internationals" that complicated the ability of OSCE officials to fulfill the requirements for neutrality: not acting toward Serbs in the same way that other foreigners had acted toward Muslims in similar circumstances could be pointed to as evidence of bias. This evidence could then be used to make demands upon OSCE officials, demands that they could contest, but could not dismiss.

The performative dimension of legitimacy could also be seen when different actors orchestrated events in order to provide evidence for themselves and for others that their claims to be "building democracy," "promoting local ownership," or "defending Serb self-determination" were true. At times, international attempts to orchestrate just such a performance became occasions for Bosnian politicians to do the same thing, but towards different ends. It is this dimension of legitimacy that also explains why publicity was so important for the High Representative. It allowed him to assert a monopoly over the authoritative discourses (like democracy and Europe) through which he justified his actions and perspectives and delegitimized those of his opponents. It further allowed him to contest the legitimacy of his opponents' actions by creating and circulating evidence that undermined their claims, and it allowed him to contest their attempts to delegitimize his actions by circulating a logic (of ambivalence) and temporal framework that suspended the contradictions of his position.

This amounts to a sustained argument that in order to understand how international intervention unfolds, we need to analyze the performative politics of categories, particularly those categories like "international" and "local" or "humanitarian" and "politics" through which interventions are legitimized and authorized. It is further evidence that top-down models of power are inadequate to account for the complexity and instability of the relations through which power is exercised, resisted, and otherwise constituted in intervention encounters. I have indicated how even the most coercive exercise of power—the imposition of laws, the removal and banning of officials from office, or armed seizure of a local bank—was always accompanied by efforts to legitimize such actions; and the reversal of some of those actions, such as removing the bans on individuals that prevented them from seeking public office, suggests limits on coercive power that are tied directly to the question of its legitimacy. And as already mentioned above, the

High Representative could not simply impose participation on Bosnian officials to demonstrate the "local ownership" over Bosnian government that would allow internationals to withdraw and declare "mission accomplished." Thus, although it may seem somewhat disingenuous when Petritsch's successor Paddy Ashdown stated, "If I pass a decree that is refused, my authority is gone like the morning dew" (quoted in Vulliamy 2005), my study has shown why there is considerable truth to his assertion.

Creativity and Innovation

Intervention encounters are not only where we learn about the power or instabilities of international intervention; they are also generative sites of invention and creativity. For example, chapter 2 documented the use of publicity as a site of improvisational cultural production as the High Representative attempted to redefine the meaning of *konstitutivnost naroda* in response to unexpected challenges (by the HDZ) and in pursuit of larger intervention goals. I showed the limits and unexpected outcomes of this process, such as the 2002 election results, the Sejdic-Finci ECHR decision in 2009, and how these amendments proliferated (1) new grounds to pursue postwar politics by pointing out that the way the amendments were implemented undermined democracy and security rather than advanced them, and (2) new encounters between returnees and international officials who had to figure out just how far to take the constitutive peoples principle.

My study also holds lessons for anyone studying international intervention in the midst or aftermath of ethnic or sectarian conflict. For example, I have shown how the commitment to neutrality by foreign officials in such contexts generates pragmatic evaluative frameworks like *the moral metric of equality*. When appealed to, such frameworks allow others to demand that foreign officials stay accountable to their self-legitimizing claims, and how such officials respond undoubtedly influences whether they are recognized as legitimate or not. As I have shown, these concerns have a direct influence on how the agents of intervention engage with their interlocutors. And these engagements, in turn, generate further evidence that confirm the accuracy of seeing the context of interventions through a sectarian lens—reproducing lines of conflict even as they try to overcome them.

Finally, in chapter 1 I described how the OHR used publicity to discursively stabilize a pragmatic ambivalence, a political innovation evolved in response to two means/ends contradictions of his position.[1] This allowed him, in part, to justify his perspective and actions while maintaining he was guided by democratic norms. Anthropologists have argued that one value of anthropological studies of democracy is that they reveal "alternative democracies," nonnormative ideas and practices that enrich and expand our understanding by challenging the supposed universality of Western cultural concepts and political philosophies (Nugent 2002; Paley 2002). My analysis revealed practices of democracy that are less nonnormative and more what I would call the result of "normative stress," that is, the attempt to hold to and promote Western democratic norms under circumstances that make it nearly impossible. Under such normative stress, the High Representative evolved the logic of ambivalence, and analysis of OHR actions and their representation revealed a recombinant approach to democratization, in which democracy was disaggregated into a set of related but distinct logics, values, and principles, any one of which could be used in intervention encounters to justify actions that would seem to violate others. Once disaggregated in this way, however, Bosnian politicians could also take a recombinant approach to democracy, arguing that "the will of the people" exercised through elections justified restrictions on the press or ignoring court rulings.

The larger point is that intervention encounters have something to teach us about the possibilities of democratic practice per se, not just some sort of "alternative," "Balkan," or "local" version of democracy, a conceptualization which often measures practices against some universal (Western) ideal type. As Tsing has argued (2005, 8), ideas like democracy that claim universal applicability only become "effective in particular historical conjunctures that give them content and force." It is through the "friction" of engagement that such "universals become practically effective." Recognizing this does not mean that we must accept the forms that such real existing democracy takes. Indeed, an encounters-based approach to democracy does not preclude the possibility of critique, including critique that might appeal to abstract universalist norms. It does mean, however, that for any critique to become "practically effective," it would require a new engagement. One such critical engagement is illustrated by the experiments in radical democratic participation and representation called "plenums," which emerged in the wake of mass uprisings in many Bosnian cities in 2014 (Arsenijević 2014; Kurtović 2015).

Humanitarianization, Entextualization, Recontextualization

In this book I have conceptualized three processes that should be useful in exploring and analyzing intervention encounters beyond Bosnia and Herzegovina. As long as the category "humanitarian" is defined by what it is not (such as "political"), we should expect to find aid workers engaged in the social and cultural work of making that distinction relevant in locally meaningful ways. But *humanitarianization*—establishing and maintaining a humanitarian field of action—takes a wide variety of forms; there are ways of humanitarianizing a social field of action other than relying upon the humanitarian versus politics distinction. For example, the humanitarian status of doctors or lawyers might hinge upon maintaining a distinction between professional and unprofessional (Malkki 2015), or any number of a host of nesting distinctions (Brada 2016). Humanitarianizing military action might be based upon a wholly different kind of social and cultural work. And within the humanitarian-politics distinction, one might imagine discourses other than ethnic division or *politika* filling the placeholder for politics when defining what counts as humanitarian. Yet as I mentioned earlier, any of these instances will undoubtedly introduce a set of performative requirements, be subjected to the evaluation of a diverse set of actors, and thus include a set of potential instabilities that need to be managed—instabilities that have the potential to shape the outcome of specific encounters as well as aid projects as a whole.

There are few signs that intervention agents have ceased pursuing their projects largely ignorant of the history, language, and culture of target societies (Mac Ginty and Richmond 2013, 778; Sabaratnam 2017). Thus we can expect they will continue to encounter their target societies and act upon them through the artifacts of *entextualization* practices—reports, translations of local media, templates of administrative reform, and so on. Under such circumstances, figuring out what information is entextualizable or not, and why, can be used to identify limits to intervention by noting what it excludes.[2] It can also reveal the modernist ideologies (like those about transparency) that make social distance from local populations and ignorance of their language, culture, and history a virtue, and explain the (mis)understanding and mutual dissatisfactions that emerge from intervention encounters. Analyzing how information is transformed when it is entextualized will also reveal how social settings become problematized—defined as subject to particular kinds of problems that imply particular kinds of solutions. But entextualization practices (and their ideological implications) need to be studied in interactions, because we cannot assume their effects. For example, such engagements may provide evidence to intervention agents of the limited utility of entextualization practices in making sense of or governing their interventions, and thus provide an opening to study how they respond to such limits. Alternatively, the experience of intervention encounters may provide evidence that such entextualization practices are necessary and legitimate.

To illustrate the value of *recontextualization* requires a more extended discussion. In chapter 2 I offered an in-depth analysis of a core instability that shaped the setting and the effects of international intervention: the fact that foreigners like Petritsch often have to pursue their goals using cultural forms and historical materials—and according to a timeline—not of their choosing.[3] I also described a method for investigating what happens when foreigners try to take such a form or material out of one context and make it serve a new purpose, or recontextualize it, in another. A few key questions include: What meanings or associations did this form or material have in its former context? Which of those does it bring to the new context, for whom, and under what conditions? What new meanings does it take on as a result of being recontextualized, for whom, and under what conditions? And how does it change the context into which it has now been put to use?

I should add that recontextualization processes can be studied at varying scales of interaction; much depends upon how you define and delineate what the relevant "context" is. In chapter 2 I analyzed the political meaning of a principle (*konstitutivnost naroda*) in relation to sociohistorical contexts (Yugoslav state socialism, Serb separatist state-building, Dayton-era democratization) by looking at its use in particular mass-mediated settings: Partisan propaganda, Communist Party–sanctioned history, state-socialist constitutions; parliamentary arguments about the question of Bosnian independence, the definition of sovereignty used to justify state-making violence, constitutional court cases about collective rights, battles over the legitimacy of the Dayton political order and the international role supervising it, and critical assessments of Bosnia's democratization, and Europeanization. But one could also study recontextualization processes in face-to-face interactions between just two people, or in the more circumscribed setting of a specific village-based campaign. Let me offer two examples from outside of Bosnia that illustrate the different scales at which recontextualization happens.

The first is how the *loya jirga* (often translated as "grand assembly") was used in Afghanistan after the US-led invasion overthrew the Taliban in 2001. The international community was looking for a "culturally authentic" vehicle to legitimize the post-Taliban political process and the loya jirga seemed ideal as a "traditional" form of political representation. A loya jirga was an adaptation of a *jirga* or "assembly," often used by Pashto-speaking people in village communities as a form of consensus-building and dispute resolution. The loya jirga was originally brought into being by powerful leaders as part of moves to centralize state authority by producing consent on issues of "national importance," such as choosing a head of state, adopting a new constitution, or settling a dispute of national relevance. It was adapted and recontextualized throughout the twentieth century to serve the interests of state centralizers, modernizers, Marxists, and even Islamists (Buchholz 2007; Hanifi 2004; Noelle-Karimi 2002).

At the end of 2001, a series of international agreements made in Bonn, Germany, aimed at the eventual reestablishment of the State of Afghanistan called for a loya jirga in 2002 to elect a transitional government, and foresaw a second such assembly to adopt a new constitution by the end of 2003. After that, theoretically, there would no longer be the need for the loya jirga because the kind of broad-based legitimacy it offered would be achieved through democratic elections and the representative institutions created by the new constitution. From the beginning, however, the use of the jirga was criticized from within Afghanistan and from without on the grounds that its legitimacy was manufactured and that it was not representative nor democratic. Scholars cautioned against relating the legitimacy of the loya jirga to its cultural authenticity, with some noting that it was an "invented tradition" useful precisely because of its symbolic status and adaptability (Buchholz 2007). Others argued that it was nothing more than "a consent-producing machinery constructed out of colonial misrepresentations unrelated to the Paxtuns, Afghan tribes, or tribalism, and independent of the wishes and aspirations of the people of Afghanistan" (Hanifi 2004). Thus while the loya jirga had a lot to offer as a vehicle for foreign-backed state-building, it was also a form that proved to be somewhat unstable and unpredictable in its functioning and effects. Analyzing how the loya jirga was recontextualized to fit this new, post-Taliban context (thus also helping to shape that context) offers a way to understand how and why international state-building unfolded as it did. While I do not carry out such an analysis here, I can point to some of the contours of the process.

International involvement in its use began by overseeing the election (and selection) of 1,450 delegates to the 2002 loya jirga in a process designed to be widely representative, both geographically and socially; for instance, it included women for the first time. Foreign involvement also extended into advocating for their preferred candidate to lead the transitional administration. The loya jirga form, however, bore the traces of its former contexts in ways that threatened to complicate its use by the international community to see its preferred candidate win. For example, a large faction of delegates called for the nomination of the former king of Afghanistan, Zahir Shah, to be head of state. This had a certain logic, as Shah himself had reigned as head of state in Afghanistan for forty years before going into exile in 1973; when he was head of state he himself had called at least four such loya jirgas (one of which was to approve the 1964 constitution). The loya jirga form thus may have born traces of its association with him as head of state, certainly more so than any other potential candidate. Moreover, some said that he alone was independent enough to confront the so-called warlords who exerted significant power in the wake of the Taliban's fall, but that he could do this only if acclaimed by the loya jirga.

His nomination was a serious enough threat to the US-backed candidate Hamid Karzai that the jirga was delayed by one day as Shah came under significant pressure by US and UN representatives to withdraw his candidacy, which he eventually did (the first person publicly to announce that Shah was not a candidate was US representative Zalmay Khalilzad). Instead the king was designated the "father of the nation," officially opened the 2002 loya jirga, and was later given a ceremonial supervisory role over the writing of the new constitution. In this and other examples, then, the 2002 loya jirga was marked by accusations of intimidation, and complaints were widespread of behind-the-scenes dealmaking involving international representatives and so-called warlords and militia leaders who had helped US and British forces oust the Taliban. And indeed, after Karzai's eventual election, when he named the officials in his Afghan transitional administration, militia-backed strong men were featured prominently. The loya jirga form thus came to be associated, in part, with the authority of Karzai and the continuing influence of warlords, all with the approval of the international community.

The loya jirga was adapted once again for the adoption of a new constitution in 2003, a process that included internationally backed consultation and delegate selection. The jirga itself was controversial and there was significant debate over whether the state should be organized along a parliamentary or presidential system (Karzai and the United States favored a presidential system with a strong executive, which is what was eventually adopted). Some members openly criticized the inclusion and domination of powerful militia leaders. Again, there were complaints about behind-the-scenes decision making by Karzai, militia and political party leaders, and international representatives. Nevertheless, the constitution was ratified by consensus, and Karzai was elected as president in the first elections after the constitution in 2004. The first National Assembly was elected in 2005. One might imagine that with a democratically elected president and a legislature of representatives elected from across Afghanistan, as well as an extensive court system to rule on questions of law, that there would no longer be a role for a loya jirga and the kind of mass consent it has been called upon to bestow.

This was most likely the view of many foreigners involved in Afghanistan, who had rewarded the 2002 and 2003 loya jirga with the approval and recognition of the international community. But this was not its last appearance. On multiple occasions Hamid Karzai raised the possibility of using the loya jirga form—sometimes as formally defined by the constitution, and sometimes as a "quasi" version—to legitimize his position outside of existing political institutions. Such moves were criticized for undermining the authority of constitutional bodies and the democratic credentials of the Afghan state; yet it proved difficult for foreign officials to reject the form since the international community had recontextualized it to legitimize its own state-building goals and as a result ended up creating associations between the loya jirga and Karzai as head of the Afghani state. Interestingly, given the broader analysis in chapter 1, some suggested that Karzai called a "consultative" loya jirga in 2013 because he faced a contradiction regarding a then upcoming bilateral security agreement with the United States that threatened his legitimacy. As Clark (2013) put it, the point of the jirga was "not to make an actual decision, but to give President Karzai the impression of having national political support for a military agreement which compromises Afghan sovereignty while, at the same time, allowing him to publically [*sic*] claim that it protects Afghan sovereignty." Such details offer an indication of the instabilities that a study of recontextualization can help illuminate in accounting for the ongoing unfolding of politics in intervention encounters.

While the examples of the *konstitutivnost naroda* principle and loya jirga form focus on large-scale processes of recontextualization, the framework can also be used to study processes under more intimate and socially proximate conditions. For example, it could be used to understand how foreigners in Afghanistan attempted to use the *jirga* (Pashto)/*shura* (Dari) as a vehicle to accomplish rural development aims as well as promote social transformation through the National Solidarity Program (NSP). The NSP was funded by the World Bank and a number of other Western countries and implemented by the newly formed Ministry of Rural Reconstruction and Development beginning in 2003. It aimed to reach 20,000 villages over four years, bestowing block grants of up to $60,000 per village committee. Like many such projects, it was designed to accomplish multiple goals: support rehabilitation or development activities; create links between rural communities and the newly formed central state government; promote capacity building in how to plan and manage development projects, and to do so in a way that reflected the needs and desires of the community. This last goal was to be accomplished through the formation of community development committees (CDCs) that would be directly elected by all the members of the village community through universal suffrage and according to principles of gender and social equality and inclusion. This program, and the CDC in particular, was imagined as a vehicle for social transformation and democracy building, explicitly challenging gender norms and local power structures (Boesen 2004).

Forming a CDC meant taking an existing cultural and historical form, the shura/jirga, and recontextualizing it as a vehicle for new aims in a new (statebuilding) context. Historically, a shura/jirga refers to a local council consisting of male representatives of all extended kin groups in a given community which is usually called when it is necessary to resolve community conflicts. Seen by foreigner donors as a local-level democratic institution, albeit one that reflected significant social hierarchies and inequalities, it was approached as a good vehicle to realize the goals of social transformation, particularly the inclusion of women in decision making.

A study of recontextualization processes would ask such questions as: What meanings or associations did the shura have in its pre-2003 context, and which of those associations did it bring to the new context of the NSP? What new meanings did it take on as a result of being recontextualized as a CDC or "new shura," and how did the "new shura" (as it was often called by participants) change the context into which it had now been put to use? Early studies of the NSP in practice point to the kinds of evidence you would need in order to answer these kinds of questions (Boesen 2004; Nixon 2008; Noelle-Karimi 2014). For example, studies detail that how members of the community responded to program itself, to the process of electing the CDC (or new shura), to the composition of the new shura, to the role of women, to the decision-making processes of the CDC once formed, and so on, depended upon a complex combination of factors. These included: preexisting experiences with development plans; the actions of those who occupied existing mediating roles between state institutions and local communities (positions like the *malik* or *qaliadar*, often translated as "headman"); preexisting community experiences with cooperation on projects for mutual or communitywide benefit (known sometimes as *ashar*); the reaction of religious authorities to the possibility of women as decision makers, or to allowing mixed-gender council membership (in some places separate women-only CDCs had to be formed); community perspectives on existing shura/jirga processes; whether people saw the inclusion of new social categories (youth, women) in decision-making roles as positive or as undermining the legitimacy of the council; and the influence of loyalties to kin lineage (*khaum*) and those relations constituted by coming from the same place (*votandar*). For those interested in understanding the legitimacy and the effects of the NSP projects and goals, it would seem necessary to track its recontextualization of the shura form on these complex and contingent grounds.

As we come to the end of the second decade of the twenty-first century, we may have entered a historical moment where there seems to be more skepticism than confidence in the Enlightenment promise of human progress toward peace and prosperity, and thus also in transnational action to save human lives and improve the human condition. This is in part because of the track record of international intervention since the end of the Cold War. It is also because of the staggering scale of dynamic processes associated with the Anthropocene, particularly climate change. Moreover, the current vision of global relations coming from traditional champions of the international community seems to be more about a "clash of civilizations" than an "end of history" in which we ought to celebrate the triumph of a universal model of human flourishing. But none of this diminishes the need for transnational interventions; indeed, one could argue we need them now more than ever. Of course, we probably need to reimagine and expand what counts as "intervention," as well as the conditions of encounters that constitute them. The effects of any intervention encounter, including their success or failure, will inevitably be forged in practical engagements across difference and inequality—but the relations thus formed need not be hierarchical, or reproduce inequality, or prevent us from building something in common.

Notes

INTRODUCTION

1. Officially the country is known as *Bosna i Hercegovina* (Bosnia and Herzegovina or Bosnia-Herzegovina in English), referring to the main two geographic regions comprising its territory; Bosnia occupies the central, north, and eastern parts of the country, and Herzegovina extends to the south and western parts of the country. In this book I use the shorthand "Bosnia" and BiH to refer to the country as a whole, as many of my interlocutors did. That said, I recognize that this is controversial for some, particularly those in Herzegovina who protest that this practice erases or otherwise diminishes their presence.

2. Around the time that the first multiparty elections in Bosnia and Herzegovina were being held in the early 1990s and the political and territorial form of Bosnia was uncertain, the term "Bosniak" (*Bošnjak*, distinct from "Bosnian" or *Bosanac*) was promoted by the Congress of Bosnian Muslim Intellectuals to designate the nonreligious ethnonational character of the Slavic-speaking Muslims of Bosnia. This was also done in part to counter those territorial-political claims to Bosnia made by Croats and Serbs that represented Muslims as islamicized Serbs or Croats. In this book I use the terms Bosniak (*Bošnjak*) and Bosnian Muslim (*Musliman*), along with their adjectival forms, interchangeably, as most of my interlocutors did. That said, when quoting or reporting speech, I render the terms as they were given. It should also be noted that while Serb, Croat, and Muslim/Bosniak are the largest present-day self-declared ethnonational identifications, there remain others that reflect settlement from the Ottoman period (Jew, Greek), Austro-Hungarian settlement policy (Czech, Italian, German, Ukrainian), and socialist Yugoslav labor migration (Slovene, Albanian, Hungarian, Macedonian). Also, as elsewhere in southeastern Europe, there is a sizable undocumented Romani population in Bosnia, many of whom are migrants from Kosovo, having fled during the 1999 war there.

3. Before the war, the language spoken in Bosnia and Herzegovina was called Serbo-Croatian or Croato-Serbian and rendered in both the Latin and Cyrillic scripts. As part of the nation- and state-building processes that accompanied the break-up of Yugoslavia, people now claim to be speakers of languages that match ethnonational and/or territorial categories like Serbian, Croatian, Montenegrin, and Bosnian. Bosnian/Croatian/Serbian (or B/C/S) is the widely used "politically correct" shorthand for the language(s) spoken in Bosnia.

4. The Peace Implementation Council is the international body that is responsible for overseeing the implementation of the General Framework Agreement, also known as the Dayton Agreement, which ended the war in BiH and ushered in its postwar order.

5. I use pseudonyms throughout this book except for public figures who appear in the news media.

6. Since I am an anthropologist, encounters lie at the center of my research practice and knowledge production—forming both the object of analysis (the interactions between and among people and things) and ethnographic method (how I learn through my encounters with people and things).

7. Ideas about performance and performativity tend to draw upon or combine the metaphorical language of the theater as advanced by Erving Goffman's *The Presentation of Self*

in Everyday Life (1959) or a more language-oriented understanding inspired by Austin (1962) and further worked out by Derrida (1972) and Butler (1990). See Jeffrey (2013, 20–32) for a good overview of the development of these ideas.

8. Most scholarship on international intervention is written for audiences in the countries of the self-proclaimed international community—current and future policymakers, practitioners, academics and other influential elites. Most of these studies are also motivated by efforts to advocate, improve, prevent, stop, discredit, or otherwise influence current or anticipated international action. The problem-solving paradigm is defined by its technocratic, legalist, and positivist approach. It is framed in dialogue with government policy interests, and focuses on the creation of international norms, on testing theoretical models, distilling "lessons learned" and "best practices" and on how and why intervention projects succeed or fail (Autesserre 2014; Carment, Prest, and Samy 2010; Dobbins et al. 2007; Holohan 2005; Knaus 2011; Pickering 2007; Skendaj 2014; Woodward 2017). The more critical strand is more concerned with showing how such interventions serve as new forms of transnational hegemony and (neo)imperialism. These critics regularly point to contradictions that reveal these relations of inequality and domination, often by arguing that actions aimed at doing good have the opposite effect. These authors and their readers are often less interested in the messy complexities of intervention encounters than in identifying mechanisms of rule, in the moral clarity of critique and, perhaps, in the pleasure of unmasking power (Ali 2000; Chandler 1999, 2006; Chomsky 2002; Feher 2000; Gregory 2004; Knaus and Martin 2003; Turner and Kühn 2016). Of course, this distinction is not absolute, and there are many scholars who sit somewhere in between.

9. One exception is Bliesemann de Guevara 2012.

10. Moore's study offers a specific example regarding the second European Union administrator of the divided Herzegovinian city of Mostar, Ricardo Perez Casado. Apparently his lack of familiarity with Bosnia and Herzegovina was viewed as positive in Brussels because he wouldn't be "burdened by the past" (2013: 134). I thank an anonymous reviewer for bringing this to my attention.

11. Other lines of difference include ethnicity, class, gender, and generation.

12. Prominent examples include Autesserre 2010, 2014; Heathershaw 2009, 2012; Holohan 2005; Jeffrey 2013; Moore 2013; Pickering 2007; Sabaratnam 2017; and Skendaj 2014.

INTERLUDE

1. For example, Kaufman (2002) shows that the wars in the Balkans were a critical backdrop to the decision taken by the United States and others to approve the enlargement of NATO. Bosnia was also the site of NATO's first international peacekeeping mission. Before Bosnia, NATO had never carried out a ground-force operation or an operation "out of area." It has since been active in this capacity in Kosovo, Macedonia, and Afghanistan, in a support capacity to other peacekeeping missions in Darfur and Iraq, as well as humanitarian missions in Pakistan and the United States. In Bosnia and Herzegovina the actions of NATO's International Force (IFOR) and Stabilization Force (SFOR) were novel experiments that constantly broke new ground, from arresting indicted war criminals to occupying parliament buildings during a political crisis, raiding domestic military barracks, reconstructing infrastructure, providing security to returning refugees, policing borders, and disarming civilian populations.

2. It has been reported that Robert Kaplan's *Balkan Ghosts* (1993), notorious for its representation of the Balkans as a site of irrational and intractable blood feuds, played a decisive role in persuading US president Clinton not to intervene in the early years of Bosnia and Herzegovina's war.

3. See Cowan 2007 for a longer history of such requirements in the Balkans, and Howland and White 2009 for a wider discussion of the recognition doctrine that has guided the admittance of new states into the UN.

4. The 1991 census held the proportions of the population to be 31 percent Serb, 17 percent Croat, and 44 percent Muslim. In Bosnia there were also small numbers of self-identifying Jews, Roms, Vlachs, Albanians, and those who chose, until 1991, to call themselves Yugoslavs. Yugoslav censuses distinguished up to thirty-four nationality categories, as well as several other types including those who declared a regional identity and those who did not declare a nationality at all (Friedman 1996, 91n4).

5. The Dayton Agreement also initiated a process that led to the creation of the district of Brčko, a condominium of the Federation and Republika Srpska. After some time under international supervision, it became a full self-governing administrative unit of the state.

6. Increasing an ethnic minority population through return was seen as likely to shift election results in a way unfavorable to nationalist parties of the ethnic majority. Moreover, "obstructing return"—and thus the implementation of a key element of the Dayton Agreement—became the most used pretext proffered by the OHR for removing officials from positions of power.

7. Refugee return also offered the international community a vehicle through which to promote further elements of the new international order. The privatization of socially owned housing, the promotion of transparency reforms in budgeting practices and municipal services, the privatization of those state firms still in operation, extensive electoral engineering and constitutional change were all promoted "in the name of return." This included a massive property repossession project, hundreds of millions of dollars' worth of housing reconstruction, and the creation of new positions of political representation in order to make the return of refugees "sustainable."

8. Much of the existing literature on refugee return in Bosnia has been interested in measuring the relative success of return, asking why refugees choose or choose not to return and what the factors for success might be. Empirical research on return in Bosnia by anthropologists and others has been more expansive, focusing on the ability of international efforts to reconstruct communities and achieve interethnic reconciliation and postwar justice (Dahlman and Tuathail 2005a, 2005b; Heimerl 2005; Sivac-Bryant 2016; Toal and Dahlman 2011; Tuathail and Dahlman 2004); on how concepts of "home" have become reorganized (Jansen 2006, 2007, 2008); as well as on the creation of new moral categories within and between ethnically defined populations (Kolind 2004, 2007; Stefansson 2003, 2004, 2007).

1. THE LIMITS OF FOREIGN AUTHORITY

1. All of the quoted material from anyone representing the OHR was taken, in English, from the OHR website (including those that appeared in Bosnian news media, such as in *Reporter*, *Dani*, or *Nezavisne Novine*). It was a regular practice of the OHR press office to supply both English and local-language versions of any form of publicity that featured a member of the OHR—an indication of the multiple audiences for OHR press output. All other quoted material from Bosnian into English is my own translation.

2. Compare Feldman 2008 who discusses the authorizing strategies developed by the UN administration of Gaza to hold the question of legitimacy "in abeyance."

3. Positing a state of exception to nation-state forms of territorialized sovereignty has led some to see international intervention as a form of (neo)imperialism (Chandler 2006; Duffield 2007; Gregory 2004). Giorgio Agamben (2005) has been influential in this regard. Drawing on the writing of Carl Schmitt, he argues that to declare a state of exception to the usual (constitutional, lawful) order of things is to stand outside of that order and

may be the ultimate sign of sovereign power itself. I am less interested here in inquiring into the sovereign status of the OHR or Bosnia and Herzegovina than I am in exploring what we might call a situation of "normative stress," when someone (like Petritsch) tried to maintain a norm (like that of sovereign statehood) under circumstances that seem to make that impossible.

4. It is part of my argument that the political logic of ambivalence was the product of the contradictory position of the OHR. Thus, although I focus mostly on events when Wolfgang Petritsch was High Representative, I occasionally include examples of OHR publicity from when others occupied that position, like British politician Paddy Ashdown.

5. In part, it is because of the public sphere's role as a privileged site for conjuring the mass abstractions of normative democratic theory and national self-determination, such as "the people," "the general interest," and "public opinion" (Anderson 1991; Fraser 2007; Habermas 1989), that it came to be a dominant space where the stagecraft of statecraft played out.

6. In a study that can be read fruitfully alongside this chapter, Graan (2016) offers an advanced theorization of the communicative dimensions of governmentality through an analysis of foreign publicity in postconflict Macedonia. While he recognizes the limits of foreign publicity as a form of governmentality, his analysis emphasizes instead the pervasive and often subtle effects that this form of public diplomacy had on Macedonian politics, even if it might have failed in specific instances.

7. The PIC comprises fifty-five countries and agencies that come together periodically at the ministerial level to define the goals of implementation for the coming period. A steering board of the PIC was also established to work under the chairmanship of the High Representative as the executive arm of the PIC. The steering board members are Canada, France, Germany, Italy, Russian, Japan, the United Kingdom, the United States, the presidency of the EU, the European Commission, and the Organization of the Islamic Conference, represented by Turkey. The steering board of the PIC nominates the High Representative. The United Nations Security Council then endorses the nomination. The OHR has the status of a diplomatic mission to Bosnia and Herzegovina, and is made up of diplomats seconded by the governments of the PIC countries, international experts hired directly, and national staff from Bosnia and Herzegovina.

8. For example, press releases went from around fifty in 1996 to 275 in 2001; press conferences increased from just a handful in the early years to sixty-two in 2002; interviews given or articles published went from fourteen in 1996 to seventy-four in 2001; and speeches from thirteen in 1996 to fifty in 2002.

9. Although space prevents me from detailing it here, there is a parallel story about forceful foreign intervention into the field of broadcast and print media licensing and regulation, ownership, and programming, and investment in and control over infrastructure. Much of this story has been told in Ahmetašević 2012; Kurspahic 2003; and Price 2002.

10. This period saw the expanded use of public information campaigns, including posters and billboards, paid advertising, and the foreign sponsorship of television and radio programming. For example, see Coles 2007 for an analysis of the OSCE's media campaign surrounding elections.

11. Take, for example, the response of one Canadian member of OHR's foreign staff when asked whether he was aware of the reaction of a Bosnian politician to an OHR decision: "No, I didn't have a chance to look at the media reports" (Leroux-Martin 2014, 26).

12. The preamble to the constitution that was included as Annex 4 of the Dayton Peace Agreement held that Bosnia and Herzegovina was determined by "Bosniacs, Croats, and Serbs as constituent peoples (along with Others)." The full text of the Dayton Agreement can be found at http://peacemaker.un.org/sites/peacemaker.un.org/files/BA_951121

_DaytonAgreement.pdf. The full text of the partial decision of the Constitutional Court of Bosnia and Herzegovina can be found in English at http://www.ustavnisud.ba/dokumenti/_en/u-5-98-12209.pdf.

13. https://web.archive.org/web/20100712083422/http://www.cpa-iraq.org/# and https://peacekeeping.un.org/en/mission/past/etimor/UntaetN.htm.

14. In yet another example, Kim Coles (2009) uses the term to describe how the experience of democracy promotion in one place, like Bosnia, can circulate to become an example used elsewhere in the world. She identifies how transnational institutions design new democratization projects by picking and choosing in a recombinant manner examples and elements from among previous projects.

15. Keeping open the question of the state has had other consequences. As Stef Jansen persuasively argued (2015), by keeping political discourse focused on arguments about unsettled state*hood*, Bosnian politicians have routinely been able to postpone action on the more quotidian concerns of ordinary Bosnians, which tend to focus on questions of state*craft*: "what the state does, claims to do, and should do" (12), such as support the health and wellbeing of the population.

2. THE USES OF HISTORY

1. Andjelić (2003) relates the story of a paramilitary operation that was staged in June and July of 1972 by Croatian nationalist émigrés in western Bosnia, which was largely inhabited by Bosnian Croats. He describes how a group of Bosnian-born Croats came secretly into the country to conduct terrorist actions against the communist regime, but they found no support among the local population. To counter this attack, the regime mobilized units of the Territorial Defense, which consisted of ordinary local people, as well as police units and the military police. All members of the paramilitary group were eventually killed in combat, or captured, tried, and executed. There were thirteen casualties on the side of the Bosnian forces: ten members of the Territorial Defense, one policeman, and two military policemen. Nine were Croats, three were Muslims, and one was a Serb. Andjelić argues that this was a case in which the nationalities policy of the regime worked, taking the fact that the majority of the defenders of the system were of the same ethnic group as the attackers as a significant example of the popular success of the policy of "brotherhood and unity" (2003, 40–41). Indeed, as a Croat returnee to Prijedor commented to me during fieldwork, while the key was not a perfect system, it was good insofar that "it gave people nothing to complain about" as far as discrimination was concerned.

2. Indeed, Andjelić argues that cosmopolitanism was one of the main characteristics among the various leaders of Bosnia's Communist Party, and that they were always the first to criticize the appearance of nationalism in the name of the group to which they belonged. Even in institutions like the universities where the national key formed the framework for informal bargaining regarding teaching positions and academic posts, the "moral-political suitability" of individuals, their membership in the party, and commitment to socialist ideology were of primary importance for access to any position within the faculties or administration (Weber 2007, 88–91).

3. The electoral law was written in a way that favored those parties that won the majority vote by apportioning them more seats than those who got fewer votes. For this reason, even though nonnationalist parties in some places garnered up to 20 percent of the vote, they were not awarded seats in the republican assembly in those proportions. Also, the fact that a staggering 25 percent of votes were disqualified remains an understudied and possibly significant reason behind the final election results.

4. The preamble to the Dayton State Constitution held that Bosnia and Herzegovina was determined by "Bosniacs, Croats, and Serbs as constituent peoples (along with Others)."

5. The court reasoned that the current functional basis of the Republika Srpska "as a nationally exclusive power" would prevent "the realization of the fundamental rights of all expelled persons to return to their homes of origin in order to restore the national structure of the population which had been disturbed by war and ethnic cleansing" (Constitutional Court of Bosnia and Herzegovina 2000, 12). The court concluded that

> after the Dayton Agreement came into force, there was and is systematic, long-lasting, purposeful discriminatory practice of the public authorities of RS in order to prevent so-called "minority" returns either through direct participation in violent incidents or by abstaining from the obligation to protect people against harassment, intimidation or violent attacks solely on the ground of ethnic origin, let alone the failure "to create the necessary political, economic and social conditions conducive to the voluntary return and harmonious reintegration" which follows from the right of all refugees and displaced persons freely to return to their homes of origin according to Article II.5 of the Constitution of BiH. (25)

6. In an opinion dated March 12, 2001, the Venice Commission zeroed in on the issue of refugee return and, importantly, foresaw a role for the High Representative when it argued that the authorities of the Republika Srpska would have to take clear and firm action to end the pattern of discriminatory behavior and "create the necessary conditions for the reintegration of the refugees and the High Representative will have to take the necessary steps if they fail to do so." In its recognition of a tension regarding possible ways to remedy the problems outlined in the court's decision, it foreshadowed later critiques that would emerge about the role of ethnic difference in the Dayton order. On the one hand, it doubted whether a "pure citizens approach is adequate" in Bosnia, recognizing that in the Republika Srpska there is "a Constitution based on an ethnically neutral approach and at the same time generalized discrimination." On the other hand, it identified a problem in setting up institutions on the basis of "artificial ethnic quotas rather than the democratic will" and the potential of other mechanisms, such as a veto over legislation that was considered contrary to the "vital national interests" of a particular group, in blocking decision making.

7. Parallels to the never-formed Council for Questions of the Establishment of Equality of the Nations and Nationalities of Bosnia and Herzegovina that was at the heart of the parliamentary impasse on the eve of the Bosnian war were never commented upon.

8. In a concession to the negotiations at Mrakovica and Sarajevo, this way of gauging proportional representation was considered temporary and was to last until Annex 7, guaranteeing the right of refugee return, was declared fulfilled.

9. They are similar to but distinct from another common process, which is to bring concepts, categories, and institutional arrangements from elsewhere and attempt to indigenize them in the target societies.

4. FROM HUMANITARIANISM TO HUMANITARIANIZATION

1. It may be that such an assertive or forceful claim on resources crossed a line for Jasmina and disrupted the image of refugees as passive subjects of need. In particular, this woman's reference to a politician and her suffering confronted aid staff with the fact that refugee return *was* part of a political project, however discomfiting that was to their humanitarian self-image, and that they too could be implicated as part of that project. As Malkki has noted, it is this contradiction—the expectation of refugees as passive, helpless needy subjects without history, and the reality of their active and morally charged self-presentation as victims of political misfortune—that can make refugees appear to be un-

trustworthy, "unreliable informants . . . dishonest, prone to exaggeration, even crafty and untrustworthy" (1996, 384).

2. In *The Human Condition* ([1958] 1998) Arendt distinguishes action from labor and work, the former being defined as activities that are necessary for bare living (the production of food, shelter) and which leave behind no lasting trace, and the latter as activity that has a defined end, leaves behind a lasting material product, and is directed at building and maintaining a world fit for human use. Action, by contrast, has an open-endedness to it, and its main product—power—is immaterial, but lasts as long as people continue to gather to act and speak together.

3. Power is distinguished from force (a natural phenomenon, not the product of human engagement), strength (a property of individuals, not groups), authority (based on hierarchy and not equality, as power is), and violence (based on coercion rather than consent) (Arendt 1972, 143–155). These can coexist or overlap in practice, but each corresponds to distinct phenomena that, for Arendt, become obscured if we do not differentiate between them.

4. The decision by powerful countries like the United States to define the conflict as a "humanitarian crisis" rather than war provided the space within which the United Nations took up a major role, and authorized a light military force (UNPROFOR) to protect the delivery of humanitarian aid to the war's victims. Dubbing Bosnia a "humanitarian crisis" also turned the United Nations High Commissioner for Refugees (UNHCR) from a relatively modest program that included the defense of refugee rights and the management of resettlement plans and refugee camps to one that ran aid convoys and relief airlifts like the one to Sarajevo, where it became the sole coordinator for NGOs accessing the various zones of the war. According to Rieff, the UNHCR estimated that at its most active, it was getting aid to more than 2.7 million people in Bosnia as well as 1.4 million in other parts of the former Yugoslavia, spending upward of a million dollars a day (2002, 136).

5. Given the various sources of funding and differing project timelines, it is difficult to come up with total figures. Still, to offer a snapshot of the amounts involved, the European Union dedicated over 36 million euros for housing reconstruction in Bosnia in 2000 alone, and in 2001 dedicated funds topped 50 million euros countrywide. Between 2000 and 2003 tens of millions of euros were dedicated to housing reconstruction and related infrastructure in Prijedor and Sanski Most. In addition to housing, many millions of euros more went to seeing that schools were rebuilt, electricity networks reconstructed and extended, sewage and water systems relaid and lengthened, roads built, and that agricultural income-generation projects donated seeds and livestock.

6. In these and other interactions, there appeared to be a belief that aid workers or their main Bosnian interlocutors had the ability to distribute resources as they saw fit—the trick was thus figuring out a way to motivate them. Although I never saw solicitations like this work, I did know of one foreign worker for a foreign aid organization who described using aid resources in ways not laid out in his organization's mandate: he rebuilt the destroyed family house belonging to staff of a local NGO as a kind of reward for their local humanitarian efforts; he also said that he made a deal with a local contractor who supplied the NGO's building materials to divert some of those materials to the family of a local girlfriend he had at the time. While I do not have many such examples, they could feed the expectation that resources were available if the right relationships could be forged.

7. Although need was the overriding and primary metric for who deserved housing reconstruction aid, a secondary consideration was whether potential beneficiaries displayed a "will to return." This was a response to the fact that earlier housing-reconstruction projects had built homes to which no one returned. They either lay unoccupied or were

sold to members of the area's ethnic majority—defeating the purpose of minority return. Thus aid workers' measurements of need extended to evaluating the "will to return" of potential beneficiaries. Had they registered in the municipality to which they planned on returning? Had they dedicated some personal resources to the rebuilding of their homes—for instance, laying the concrete foundation? Did they carry a foreign passport? Did they drive a car with foreign plates? Sometimes the evaluation of need and "will to return" were made using the same evidence. Finally, in addition to need and the "will to return," the international community prioritized large, multigenerational families in order to support a reproducing population; this was in response to an early common trend where only the very elderly returned to live in rebuilt houses, so that, as many told me, they could die on their native soil. In the eyes of international donors, such cases would only delay the effects of ethnic cleansing rather than reverse it.

5. ENTEXTUALIZATION AND THE MAKING OF INTERNATIONAL AUTHORITY

1. There are of course also other institutional imperatives that direct time and energy away from developing "local knowledge." Regarding foreign-policy-oriented institutions like the US State Department or the UN, Barnett argues that "expert" status has little to do with real knowledge and much more to do with bureaucratic position. While serving in the US mission to the UN in 1994 and assigned a portfolio that included Rwanda, he learned that "in-depth knowledge of the country was not necessary to carry out my daily activities . . . the knowledge that mattered most was not the particulars about Rwanda but rather the culture of the policy-making process in the U.S. government and the UN" (1997, 554). Indeed, he continues, "my status also derived from my possession of the 'facts' of the bureaucracy: who handled what issues, who had access to key decision makers, who my counterparts were in other missions to the UN and other departments in Washington, what had transpired in the Security Council, and what the precise language of past mandates was" (554–555).

2. A village-level institution of representative government, it was meant to place authority for dealing with village-level issues in the villagers themselves and provide the necessary resources to do so.

3. First he would require that job vacancies be published in a preagreed media outlet, that job requirements be specified, that the best candidate get the job, and that positive discrimination exist for Serbs in the case of two equally qualified candidates. In order to monitor the process, Markus would require the municipality to provide a monthly list of all people employed in the public sector. And perhaps later, he would push for multiethnic interview panels to oversee the hiring process.

4. Of course, these closed pathways of circulating information can also be seen as problematic by foreigners. As an American diplomat in Bosnia confided to Kim Coles about his previous posting with the US State Department, "Before, where I was stationed, I really understood [what was going on] because I got out there. Here, we don't have any idea. It's all recycled information or recirculated information. We're not really talking—just to other internationals" (Coles 2007, 28).

CONCLUSION

1. There are some interesting parallels here with Feldman's analysis (2008) of how government worked in Gaza under the British Mandate and the Egyptian administration, from arguments about the "exceptional" nature of services provided to the population, to how practices of "tactical government" kept questions about the legitimacy of government in the absence of a state or sovereignty "in abeyance."

2. Li (2007) notes a similar process for development projects in which their limits are often defined by the elements of a society that cannot be rendered technical.

3. This is similar to but distinct from another common process, which is to bring concepts, categories, and institutional arrangements from elsewhere and attempt to indigenize them in the target societies.

References

Acharya, Amitav. 2004. "How Ideas Spread: Whose Norms Matter? Norm Localization and Institutional Change in Asian Regionalism." *International Organization* 58 (Spring): 239–275.

Adler-Nissen, Rebecca, and Vincent Pouliot. 2014. "Power in Practice: Negotiating the International Intervention in Libya." *European Journal of International Relations* 20, no. 4: 889–911.

Agamben, Giorgio. 1998. *Homo Sacer: Sovereign Power and Bare Life*. Translated by Daniel Heller-Roazen. Stanford, CA: Stanford University Press.

——. 2005. *State of Exception*. Translated by Kevin Attell. Chicago: University of Chicago Press.

Agier, Michel. 2010. "Humanity as an Identity and Its Political Effects: A Note on Camps and Humanitarian Government." *Humanity* 1, no. 1: 29–46.

Ahmetašević, Nidžara. 2012. "Intervening in the Media Sector: Media Anarchy in Post-War Bosnia and Herzegovina." Uni Graz Working Paper 6 (December). Graz: Centre for Southeast European Studies.

Ali, Tariq, ed. 2000. *Masters of the Universe? NATO's Balkan Crusade*. New York: Verso.

Anderson, Benedict. 1991. *Imagined Communities: Reflections on the Origins and Spread of Nationalism*. New York: Verso.

Andjelić, Neven. 2003. *Bosnia-Herzegovina: The End of a Legacy*. Portland, OR: Frank Cass.

Andreas, Peter. 2008. *Blue Helmets and Black Markets: The Business of Survival in the Siege of Sarajevo*. Ithaca, NY: Cornell University Press.

Appadurai, Arjun. 1986. "Theory in Anthropology: Center and Periphery." *Comparative Studies in Society and History* 28, no. 2: 356–361.

Apthorpe, Raymond. 2011. "Coda. With Alice in Aidland: A Seriously Satirical Allegory." In *Adventures in Aidland: The Anthropology of Professionals in International Development*, edited by David Mosse, 199–219. New York: Berghahn.

Arendt, Hannah. (1951) 2004. *The Origins of Totalitarianism*. New York: Schocken.

——. (1954) 2006. *Between Past and Future: Eight Exercises in Political Thought*. New York: Penguin.

——. (1958) 1998. *The Human Condition*. 2nd ed. Chicago: University of Chicago Press.

——. 1972. *Crises of the Republic*. New York: Harcourt Brace Jovanovich.

Arsenijević, Damir. 2014. *Unbribable Bosnia and Herzegovina: The Fight for the Commons*. Baden-Baden: Nomos Verlag.

Austin, J. L. 1962. *How to Do Things with Words*. Cambridge, MA: Harvard University Press.

Autesserre, Severine. 2010. *The Trouble with the Congo: Local Violence and the Failure of International Peacebuilding*. Cambridge: Cambridge University Press.

——. 2014. *Peaceland: Conflict Resolution and the Everyday Politics of International Intervention*. Cambridge: Cambridge University Press.

Babić, Nikola, and Dušan Otašević. 1970. *ZAVNOBIH i Izgradnja Bosanskohercegovačke Državnosti*. [ZAVNOBIH and building Bosnian-Herzegovinian stateness]. Sarajevo: Muzej Revolucije BiH.

Barnett, Michael. 1997. "The UN Security Council, Indifference, and Genocide in Rwanda." *Cultural Anthropology* 12, no. 4: 551–578.

Barnett, Michael. 2011. *The Empire of Humanity: A History of Humanitarianism*. Ithaca, NY: Cornell University Press.

Bauman, Richard, and Charles L. Briggs. 1990. "Poetics and Performance as Critical Perspectives on Language and Social Life." *Annual Review of Anthropology* 19: 59–88.

——. 2003. *Voices of Modernity: Language Ideologies and the Politics of Inequality*. New York: Cambridge University Press.

Benthall, Jonathan. 2010. "Islamic Humanitarianism in Adversarial Context." In *Forces of Compassion: Humanitarianism between Ethics and Politics*, edited by Erica Bornstein and Peter Redfield, 99–122. Santa Fe, NM: SAR Press.

Bialasiewicz, Luisa, David Campbell, Stuart Elden, Stephen Graham, Alex Jeffrey, and Alison J. Williams. 2007. "Performing Security: The Imaginative Geographies of Current US Strategy." *Political Geography* 26, no. 4: 405–422.

Björkdahl, Annika, Kristine Höglund, Gearoid Millar, Jaïr van der Lijn, and Willemijn Verkoren, eds. 2016. *Peacebuilding and Friction: Global and Local Encounters in Post-Conflict Societies*. New York: Routledge.

Bliesemann de Guevara, Berit, ed. 2012. *Statebuilding and State-Formation: The Political Sociology of Intervention*. New York: Routledge.

Bloch, Maurice E. F. 1998. "Literacy and Enlightenment." In *How We Think They Think: Anthropological Approaches to Cognition, Memory, and Literacy*, 152–170. Boulder, CO: Westview.

Blommaert, Jan, and Jef Verschueren. 1996. "European Concepts of Nation-Building." In *The Politics of Difference: Ethnic Premises in a World of Power*, edited by Edwin N. Wilmsen and Patrick McAllister, 104–123. Chicago: University of Chicago Press.

——. 1998. "The Role of Language in European Nationalist Ideologies." In *Language Ideologies: Practice and Theory*, edited by Bambi Scheiffelin, Kathryn A. Woolard, and Paul V. Kroskrity, 189–210. New York: Oxford University Press.

Boesen, Inger W. 2004. "From Subjects to Citizens. Local Participation in the National Solidarity Programme." *AREU Working Paper Series*. Kabul: Afghan Research and Evaluation Unit, August.

Borneman, John. 2003. "Responsibility after Military Intervention: What Is Regime Change?" *PoLAR: Political and Legal Anthropology Review* 26, no. 1: 29–42.

Bourdieu, Pierre. 1991. *Language and Symbolic Power*. Cambridge, MA: Harvard University Press.

Brada, Betsy. 2016. "The Contingency of Humanitarianism: Moral Authority in an African HIV Clinic." *American Anthropologist* 118, no. 4: 755–771.

Bringa, Tone. 1995. *Being Muslim the Bosnian Way: Identity and Community in a Central Bosnian Village*. Princeton, NJ: Princeton University Press.

Brković, Čarna. 2014. "Scaling Humanitarianism: Humanitarian Actions in a Bosnian Town." *Ethnos: Journal of Anthropology* 81, no. 1: 1–26.

Brown, Keith. 2003. *The Past in Question: Modern Macedonia and the Uncertainties of Nation*. Princeton, NJ: Princeton University Press.

Broz, Svetlana. 2005. *Good People in an Evil Time: Portraits of Complicity and Resistance in the Bosnian War*. Edited by Laurie Kain Hart. Translated by Ellen Elias-Bursać. New York: Other Press.

Brubaker, Rogers. 1996. *Nationalism Reframed*. Cambridge: Cambridge University Press.

——. 2002. "Ethnicity without Groups." *European Journal of Sociology / Archives Européenes de Sociologie* 43, no. 2: 163–189.

Buchholz, Benjamin. 2007. "Thoughts on Afghanistan's *Loya Jirga*: A Myth?" *ASIEN* 104 (July): 23–33.

Budding, Audrey Helfant. 2008. "Nation/People/Republic: Self-Determination in Socialist Yugoslavia." In *State Collapse in South-Eastern Europe: New Perspectives on Yugo-*

slavia's Disintegration, edited by Lenard J. Cohen and Jasna Dragović-Soso, 91–130. West Lafayette, IN: Purdue University Press.

Burg, Steven L., and Paul S. Shoup. 1999. *The War in Bosnia-Herzegovina: Ethnic Conflict and International Intervention*. Armonk, NY: M. W. Sharpe.

Butler, Judith. 1990. *Gender Trouble: Feminism and the Subversion of Identity*. London: Routledge.

Calhoun, Craig. 1997. *Nationalism*. Minneapolis: University of Minnesota Press.

Carment, David, Stewart Prest, and Yiagadeesen Samy 2010. *Security, Development and the Fragile State: Bridging the Gap between Theory and Policy*. New York: Routledge.

Chakrabarty, Dipesh. 2000. *Provincializing Europe: Postcolonial Thought and Historical Difference*. Princeton, NJ: Princeton University Press.

Chandler, David. 1999. *Bosnia: Faking Democracy after Dayton*. London: Pluto Press.

——. 2006. *Empire in Denial: The Politics of State-Building*. London: Pluto Press.

Charlesworth, Hilary, and Jean-Marc Coicaud, eds. 2010. *Fault Lines of International Legitimacy*. New York: Cambridge University Press.

Chomsky, Noam. 2002. *The New Military Humanism: Lessons from Kosovo*. Monroe, ME: Common Courage.

Clark, Ian. 2005. *Legitimacy in International Society*. Oxford: Oxford University Press.

Clark, Kate. 2013. "The Lion Roars Again: BSA, Loya Jirga, and a strong sense of déjà vu." *Afghanistan Analysts Network*. 21 October. https://www.afghanistan-analysts.org/the-lion-roars-again-bsa-loya-jirga-and-a-sense-of-deja-vu/.

Cody, Francis P. 2007. "Literacy as Enlightenment: Written Language, Activist Mediation, and the State in Rural Tamilnadu, India." PhD diss., University of Michigan.

Cohn, Bernard. 1996. *Colonialism and Its Forms of Knowledge: The British in India*. Princeton, NJ: Princeton University Press.

Coles, Kimberley. 2009. "Recombinant Democracy Promotion" (University of Indiana's Democracy Consortium, Bloomington, IN, March 5–6).

——. 2007. *Democratic Designs: International Intervention and Electoral Practices in Postwar Bosnia-Herzegovina*. Ann Arbor: University of Michigan Press.

Collins, James. 1996. "Socialization to Text: Structure and Contradiction in Schooled Literacy." In *Natural Histories of Discourse*, edited by Michael Silverstein and Greg Urban, 203–228. Chicago: University of Chicago Press.

Comaroff, Jean, and John L. Comaroff. 1991. *Of Revelation and Revolution: Christianity, Colonialism, and Consciousness in South Africa*. Chicago: University of Chicago Press.

Comaroff, John L., and Jean Comaroff. 1992. "Of Totemism and Ethnicity." In *Ethnography and the Historical Imagination*, edited by John L. Comaroff and Jean Comaroff, 49–67. Boulder, CO: Westview.

——. 1997. *Of Revelation and Revolution: The Dialectics of Modernity on a South African Frontier*. Chicago: University of Chicago Press.

Constitutional Court of Bosnia and Herzegovina. 2000. Partial Decision on Case U-5/98 DO. *Službeni glasnik BiH* 36/00. English version of decision: http://www.ustavnisud.ba/dokumenti/_en/u-5-98-12209.pdf.

Cooper, Frederick, and Jane Burbank. 2012. "The Empire Effect." *Public Culture* 24, no. 2: 239–247.

Cowan, Jane. 2007. "The Supervised State." *Identities: Global Studies in Power and History* 14: 545–578.

Ćurak, Nerzuk. 2000. "Bosna Se Vraća Sebi." [Bosnia returns to its senses]. *Dani* (Sarajevo), July 7, 16–19.

Dahlman, Carl, and Gearóid Ó Tuathail. 2005a. "A Broken Bosnia: The Localized Geopolitics of Displacement and Return in Two Bosnian Places." *Annals of the Association of American Geographers* 95, no. 3: 644–662.

——. 2005b. "The Legacy of Ethnic Cleansing: The International Community and the Returns Process in Post-Dayton Bosnia-Herzegovina." *Political Geography* 24: 569–599.

Dani. 2003. "Fokus: Nismo ih izabrali, a vladaju." ["We did not elect them, but they are governing"]. March 7.

——. 2006. "Srbi u Federaciji BiH: ravnopravni građani drugog reda." ["Serbs in the Federation of BiH: Equal Citizens of a Second Class"]. December 8.

Denitch, Bogdan Denis. 1976. *The Legitimation of a Revolution: The Yugoslav Case*. New Haven, CT: Yale University Press.

Derrida, Jacques. 1988. "Signature Event Context." In *Limited Inc*, translated by Samuel Weber and Jeffrey Mehlman, 1–23. Evanston, IL: Northwestern University Press.

de Waal, Alex. 1997. *Famine Crimes: Politics and the Disaster Relief Industry in Africa*. London: African Rights.

Dirks, Nicolas. 2001. *Castes of Mind: Colonialism and the Making of Modern India*. Princeton, NJ: Princeton University Press.

Dobbins, James, Seth G. Jones, Keith Crane, and Beth Cole DeGrasse. 2007. *The Beginner's Guide to Nation-Building*. Santa Monica, CA: RAND Corporation.

Dodds, Klaus. 1996. "The 1982 Falklands War and a Critical Geopolitical Eye: Steve Bell and the if . . . Cartoons." *Political Geography* 15, nos. 6–7: 571–592.

Dodds, Klaus, and Sean Carter. 2014. *International Politics and Film*. New York: Columbia University Press.

Donia, Robert J. 2002. "Bosnian Krajina in the History of Bosnia and Herzegovina." International Criminal Tribunal for the Former Yugoslavia (ICTY). Prosecutor v. Radoslav Brdjanin (IT-99–36), Exhibit P53, January 24.

Duara, Prasenjit. 1995. *Rescuing History from the Nation: Questioning Narratives of Modern China*. Chicago: University of Chicago Press.

Duffield, Mark. 2001. *Global Governance and the New Wars: The Merging of Development and Security*. London: Zed Books.

——. 2007. *Development, Security, and Unending War: Governing the World of Peoples*. Cambridge: Polity.

Dumont, Louis. 1986. *Essays on Individualism: Modern Ideology in Anthropological Perspective*. Chicago: University of Chicago Press.

Dunn, Elizabeth Cullen. 2012. "The Chaos of Humanitarian Aid: Adhocracy in the Republic of Georgia." *Humanity* 3, no. 1: 1–23.

——. 2014. "Humanitarianism, Displacement, and the Politics of Nothing in Postwar Georgia." *Slavic Review* 73, no. 2: 287–306.

Faier, Lieba, and Lisa Rofel. 2014. "Ethnographies of Encounter." *Annual Review of Anthropology* 43: 363–377.

Fassin, Didier. 2011. *Humanitarian Reason: A Moral History of the Present*. Berkeley: University of California Press.

Fassin, Didier, and Mariella Pandolfi, eds. 2010. *Contemporary States of Emergency: The Politics of Military and Humanitarian Interventions*. New York: Zone Books.

Feher, Michel. 2000. *Powerless by Design: The Age of the International Community*. Durham, NC: Duke University Press.

Feldman, Ilana. 2007. "Difficult Distinctions: Refugee Law, Humanitarian Practice, and Political Identification in Gaza." *Cultural Anthropology* 22, no. 1: 129–169.

——. 2008. *Governing Gaza: Bureaucracy, Authority, and the Work of Rule*. Durham, NC: Duke University Press.

Ferguson, James, and Akhil Gupta. 2002. "Spatializing States: Toward an Ethnography of Neoliberal Governmentality." *American Ethnologist* 29, no. 4: 981–1002.

Fine, John V. A. 1983. *The Early Medieval Balkans: A Critical Survey from the Sixth to the Late Twelfth Century*. Ann Arbor: University of Michigan Press.

——. 1987. *The Late Medieval Balkans: A Critical Survey from the Late Twelfth Century to the Ottoman Conquest*. Ann Arbor: University of Michigan Press.

Foucault, Michel. 2002. *The Essential Works of Foucault, 1954–1984. Vol. 3, Power*. Edited by James D. Faubion. Translated by Robert Hurley. London: Penguin.

Fraser, Nancy. 2007. "Transnationalizing the Public Sphere: On the Legitimacy and Efficacy of Public Opinion in a Post-Westphalian World." *Theory, Culture and Society* 24, no. 4: 7–30.

Friedman, Victor A. 1996. "Observing the Observers: Language, Ethnicity, and Power in the 1994 Macedonian Census and Beyond." In *Toward Comprehensive Peace in Southeast Europe*, edited by Barnett R. Rubin, 81–105. New York: Twentieth Century Fund Press.

Fukuyama, Francis. 1992. *The End of History and the Last Man*. Toronto: Maxwell Macmillan Canada.

Gagnon, V. P. 2004. *The Myth of Ethnic War: Serbia and Croatia in the 1990s*. Ithaca, NY: Cornell University Press.

Gal, Susan. 1998. "Multiplicity and Contention among Language Ideologies: A Commentary." In *Language Ideologies: Practice and Theory*, edited by Bambi B. Scheiffelin, Kathryn A. Woolard, and Paul V. Kroskrity, 317–332. New York: Oxford University Press.

——. 2003. "Movements of Feminism: The Circulation of Discourses about Women." In *Recognition Struggles and Social Movements: Contested Identities, Agency and Power*, edited by Barbara Hobson, 93–118. New York: Cambridge University Press.

Gal, Susan, and Gail Kligman. 2000. *The Politics of Gender after Socialism*. Princeton, NJ: Princeton University Press.

Giddens, Anthony. 1990. *The Consequences of Modernity*. Stanford, CA: Stanford University Press.

Gilbert, Andrew. 2012. "Legitimacy Matters: Managing the Democratization Paradox of Foreign State-Building in Bosnia-Herzegovina." *Südosteuropa* 60, no. 4: 483–496.

——. 2013. "War and the Politics of Historical Imagination in Bosnia-Herzegovina." In *Transcending Fratricide: Political Mythologies, Reconciliations, and the Uncertain Future in the former Yugoslavia*, edited by Srđ Pavlović and Marko Živković, 165–188. Baden-Baden: Nomos Verlag.

Goffman, Irving. 1959. *The Presentation of Self in Everyday Life*. Garden City, NY: Doubleday.

Graan, Andrew. 2010. "Watching the World Watch: News Media and the Everyday Politics of International Oversight in Post-Conflict Macedonia." PhD diss., Department of Anthropology, University of Chicago.

——. 2016. "Strategic Publicity: On International Intervention and the Performativity of Public Communication in Postconflict Macedonia." *HAU: Journal of Ethnographic Theory* 6, no. 3: 277–303.

Grahovac, Mladen. 2003. "Revija." *Nezavisne Novine*. April 19, 21.

Grandits, Hannes. 2007. "The Power of 'Armchair Politicians': Ethnic Loyalty and Political Factionalism among Herzegovinian Croats." In *The New Bosnian Mosaic: Identities, Memories and Moral Claims in a Post-War Society*, edited by Xavier Bougarel, Elissa Helms, and Ger Duijzings, 101–122. Burlington, VT: Ashgate.

Gregory, Derek. 2004. *The Colonial Present: Afghanistan, Palestine, Iraq*. Oxford: Wiley-Blackwell.

Habermas, Jürgen. 1989. *Structural Transformation of the Public Sphere: An Inquiry into a Category of Bourgeois Society*. Cambridge, MA: MIT Press.

Hadžović, E. 2007. "Ekskluzivni kanali za ekskluzivne narode" [Exclusive channels for exclusive peoples]. *Dani* (Sarajevo), August 3.

Handler, Richard. 1988. *Nationalism and the Politics of Culture in Quebec.* Madison: University of Wisconsin Press.

Hanifi, Jamil M. 2004. "Colonial Production of Hegemony through the 'Loya Jerga' in Afghanistan." *Iranian Studies* 37, no. 2: 295–322.

Hayden, Robert M. 1990. *Social Courts in Theory and Practice: Yugoslav Workers' Courts in Comparative Perspective.* Philadelphia: University of Pennsylvania Press.

——. 1999. *Blueprints for a House Divided: The Constitutional Logic of the Yugoslav Conflicts.* Ann Arbor: University of Michigan Press.

Heathershaw, John. 2009. *Post-Conflict Tajikistan: The Politics of Peacebuilding and the Emergence of Legitimate Order.* New York: Routledge.

——. 2012. "Neither Built nor Formed: The Transformation of Post-Conflict States under International Intervention." In *Statebuilding and State-Formation: The Political Sociology of Intervention*, edited by Berit Bliesemann de Guevara, 246–259. New York: Routledge.

Heimerl, Daniela. 2005. "The Return of Refugees and Internally Displaced Persons: From Coercion to Sustainability?" *International Peacekeeping* 12, no. 3: 377–390.

Helms, Elissa. 2007. "'Politics is a Whore': Women, Morality and Victimhood in Post-War Bosnia-Herzegovina." In *The New Bosnian Mosaic: Social Identities, Collective Memories, and Moral Hierarchies in a Post-War Society*, edited by Xavier Bougarel, Elissa Helms, and Ger Duijzings, 235–353. Aldershot: Ashgate.

——. 2010. "The Gender of Coffee: Women, Refugee Return, and Reconciliation Initiatives after the Bosnian War." *Focaal. European Journal of Anthropology* 57 (Summer): 17–32.

Henig, David. 2012. "'Knocking on My Neighbour's Door': On Metamorphoses of Sociality in Rural Bosnia." *Critique of Anthropology* 32, no. 1: 3–19.

Herzfeld, Michael. 1987. *Anthropology through the Looking-Glass: Critical Ethnography in the Margins of Europe.* Cambridge: Cambridge University Press.

——. 1993. *The Social Production of Indifference: Exploring the Symbolic Roots of Western Bureaucracy.* Chicago: University of Chicago Press.

——. 2005. *Cultural Intimacy: Social Poetics in the Nation-State.* 2nd ed. New York: Routledge.

Heydemann, Steven, and Reinoud Leenders. 2011. "Resilient Authoritarianism in the Middle East: Lessons from Syria and Iran and Implications for Democracy Promotion." *Knowledge Programme Civil Society in West Asia Policy Paper 2.* Amsterdam: AISSR.

Higate, Paul, and Marsha Henry. 2009. *Insecure Spaces: Peacekeeping, Power, and Performance in Haiti, Kosovo and Liberia.* London: Zed Books.

Hilhorst, Dorothea, and Bram J. Jansen. 2010. "Humanitarian Space as Arena: A Perspective on the Everyday Politics of Aid." *Development and Change* 41, no. 6: 1117–1139.

Hoare, Marko Attila. 1999. "Bosnian Serbs and Anti-Bosnian Serbs." *Bosnia Report.* 8. January–March. http://www.bosnia.org.uk/bosrep/report_format.cfm?articleid=2803&reportid=125.

Holbrooke, Richard C. 1998. *To End a War.* New York: Random House.

Holohan, Anne. 2005. *Networks of Democracy: Lessons from Kosovo for Afghanistan, Iraq, and Beyond.* Palo Alto, CA: Stanford University Press.

Howland, Douglas, and Luise White. 2009. "Introduction: Sovereignty and the Study of States." In *The State of Sovereignty: Territories, Laws, Populations*, edited by Douglas Howland and Luise White, 1–18. Bloomington: Indiana University Press.

Hromadžić, Azra. 2015. *Citizens of an Empty Nation: Youth and State-Making in Postwar Bosnia-Herzegovina.* Philadelphia: University of Pennsylvania Press.

Hukanović, Rezak. 1996. *The Tenth Circle of Hell. A Memoir of Life in the Death Camps of Bosnia.* New York: Basic Books.

Hull, Matthew. 2012. "Documents and Bureaucracy." *Annual Review of Anthropology* 41: 251–267.

Ignatieff, Michael. 2003. *Empire Lite: Nation-Building in Bosnia, Kosovo, Afghanistan.* London: Vintage.

Inda, Jonathan Xavier. 2005. "Analytics of the Modern: An Introduction." In *Anthropologies of Modernity: Foucault, Government, and Life Politics*, edited by Jonathan Xavier Inda, 1–22. Malden, MA: Blackwell.

International Crisis Group. 2002. *Implementing Equality: The "Constituent Peoples" Decision in Bosnia and Herzegovina.* Balkans Report 128. Sarajevo and Brussels: International Crisis Group.

Jansen, Stef. 2006. "The Privatization of Home and Hope: Return, Reforms, and the Foreign Intervention in Bosnia-Herzegovina." *Dialectical Anthropology* 30: 177–199.

——. 2007. "Troubled locations: Return, the life course, and transformations of 'home' in Bosnia-Herzegovina" *Focaal. European Journal of Anthropology* 49: 15–30.

——. 2008. ""Home" and return in the foreign intervention in Bosnia-Herzegovina: an anthropological critique" *In Deconstructing the reconstruction: human rights and rule of law in postwar Bosnia and Herzegovina*, edited by Dina Francesca Haynes, 31–53. Aldershot: Ashgate.

——. 2015. *Yearnings in the Meantime: "Normal Lives" and the State in a Sarajevo Apartment Complex.* New York: Berghahn.

Jeffrey, Alex. 2013. *The Improvised State: Sovereignty, Performance, and Agency in Dayton Bosnia.* Malden, MA: Wiley & Sons.

Jeffrey, Alex, Fiona McConnell, and Alice Wilson. 2015. "Understanding Legitimacy: Perspectives from Anomalous Geopolitical Spaces." *Geoforum* 66: 177–183.

Jelavich, Barbara. 1983. *History of the Balkans.* 2 vols. New York: Cambridge University Press.

Kapetanović, Hajro. 1972. *25. krajiških radnih brigade.* [The 25th Krajina Worker's Brigade]. Banja Luka: NIP "Glas."

Kaplan, Robert. 1993. *Balkan Ghosts. A Journey through History.* New York: St. Martin's Press.

Kappler, Stephanie. 2014. *Local Agency and Peacebuilding: EU and International Engagement in Bosnia-Herzegovina, Cyprus and South Africa.* London: Palgrave Macmillan.

Kaufman, 2002. *NATO and the Former Yugoslavia. Crisis, Conflict, and the Atlantic Alliance.* Lanham, MD: Rowman & Littlefield.

Keane, Webb. 2007. *Christian Moderns: Freedom and Fetish in the Mission Encounter.* Berkeley: University of California Press.

Kecmanović, Dušan. 2002. *Ethnic Times: Exploring Ethnonationalism in the Former Yugoslavia.* Westport, CT: Praeger.

Keil, Soeren, and Valery Perry, eds. 2015. *State-Building and Democratization in Bosnia and Herzegovina.* New York: Routledge.

Kelly, John D., and Martha Kaplan. 2001. *Represented Communities: Fiji and World Decolonization.* Chicago: University of Chicago Press.

——. 2009. "Legal Fictions after Empire." In *The State of Sovereignty: Territories, Laws, Populations*, edited by Douglas Howland and Luise White, 169–195. Bloomington: Indiana University Press.

Knaus, Gerald. 2011. "The Rise and Fall of Liberal Imperialism." In *Can Intervention Work?*, edited by Rory Stewart and Gerald Knaus, 91–192. New York: W. W. Norton.
Knaus, Gerald, and Felix Martin. 2003. "Travails of the European Raj." *Journal of Democracy* 14, no. 3: 60–74.
Kolind, Torsten. 2004. "Post-war Identifications: Counterdiscursive Practices in a Bosnian Town." PhD diss., Aarhus University.
——. 2007. "In Search of 'Decent People': Resistance to the Ethnicization of Everyday Life among the Muslims of Stolac." In *The New Bosnian Mosaic: Social Identities, Collective Memories, and Moral Hierarchies in a Post-War Society*, edited by Xavier Bougarel, Elissa Helms, and Ger Duijzings, 123–138. Burlington, VT: Ashgate.
Kumar, Radha. 1997. *Divide and Fall? Bosnia in the Annals of Partition*. New York: Verso.
Kurspahic, Kemal. 2003. *Prime Time Crime: Balkan Media in War and Peace*. Washington, DC: US Institute of Peace Press.
Kurtović, Larisa. 2015. "'Who Sows Hunger, Reaps Rage': On Protest, Indignation and Redistributive Justice in Post-Dayton Bosnia-Herzegovina." *Southeast European and Black Sea Studies* 15, no. 4: 639–659.
Lake, David A. 2016. *The Statebuilder's Dilemma: On the Limits of Foreign Intervention*. Ithaca, NY: Cornell University Press.
Leroux-Martin, Phillippe. 2014. *Diplomatic Counterinsurgency: Lessons from Bosnia and Herzegovina*. New York: Cambridge University Press.
Levitt, Peggy, and Sally Merry. 2009. "Vernacularization on the Ground: Local Uses of Global Women's Rights in Peru, China, India and the United States." *Global Networks* 9, no. 4: 441–461.
Li, Tania. 2007. *The Will to Improve: Governmentality, Development, and the Practice of Politics*. Durham, NC: Duke University Press.
Mac Ginty, Roger. 2010. "Hybrid Peace: The Interaction between Top-Down and Bottom-Up Peace." *Security Dialogue* 41, no. 4: 391–412.
——. 2011. *International Peacebuilding and Local Resistance*. London: Palgrave.
Mac Ginty, Roger, and Oliver P. Richmond. 2013. "The Local Turn in Peace Building: A Critical Agenda for Peace." *Third World Quarterly* 34, no. 5: 763–783.
Majstorović, Danijela. 2007. "Construction of Europeanization in the High Representative's Discourse in Bosnia and Herzegovina." *Discourse and Society* 18, no. 5: 627–651.
Malcolm, Noel. 1996. *Bosnia: A Short History*. New York: New York University Press.
Malkki, Liisa. 1992. "National Geographic: Rooting of Peoples and Territorialization of National Identity among Scholars and Refugees." *Cultural Anthropology* 7, no. 1: 24–44.
——. 1995. "Refugees and Exile: From 'Refugee Studies' to the National Order of Things." *Annual Review of Anthropology*. 24: 495–523.
——. 1996. "Speechless Emissaries: Refugees, Humanitarianism, and Dehistoricization." *Cultural Anthropology* 11, no. 3: 377–404.
——. 2015. *The Need to Help: The Domestic Arts of International Humanitarianism*. Durham, NC: Duke University Press.
Marcus, George E., and Michael G. Powell. 2003. "From Conspiracy Theories in the Incipient New World Order of the 1990s to the Regimes of Transparency Now." *Anthropological Quarterly* 76, no. 2: 323–334.
McKay, Ramah. 2012. "Afterlives: Humanitarian Histories and Critical Subjects in Mozambique." *Cultural Anthropology* 27, no. 2: 286–309.
McLeod, Laura. 2016. *Gender Politics and Security Discourse: Personal-Political Imaginations and Feminism in "Post-Conflict" Serbia*. New York: Routledge.

Metiljević, Asim. 2001. "Koga štiti OHR-ov ekspert Neussl?!" [Who is OHR expert Neussl protecting?!]. *Slobodna Bosna* July 21, 22–23.

Moore, Adam. 2013. *Peacebuilding in Practice: Local Experience in Two Bosnian Towns.* Ithaca, NY: Cornell University Press.

Morris, Rosalind. 2004. "Intimacy and Corruption in Thailand's Age of Transparency." In *Off Stage/On Display: Intimacy and Ethnography in the Age of Public Culture*, edited by Andrew Shryock, 225–243. Stanford, CA: Stanford University Press.

Mosse, David, ed. 2011. *Adventures in Aidland: The Anthropology of Professionals in International Development.* New York: Berghahn.

Mosse, David, and David Lewis, eds. 2006. *Development Brokers and Translators: The Ethnography of Aid and Agencies.* Bloomington, CT: Kumarian.

Mujkić, Asim. 2007. "We the Citizens of Ethnopolis." *Constellations* 14, no. 1: 112–128.

Murphy, Alexander, Alex Jeffrey, Andrew Gilbert, Adam Moore, Gerard Toal, and Carl T. Dahlman. 2013. "Reading Gerard Toal and Carl T. Dahlman's *Bosnia Remade: Ethnic Cleansing and Its Reversal.*" *Political Geography* 36: 12–20.

Nixon, Hamish. 2008. "Subnational State-Building in Afghanistan." *AREU Synthesis Paper Series.* Kabul: Afghan Research and Evaluation Unit.

Noelle-Karimi, Christine. 2002. "The *Loya Jirga*—An Effective Political Tool? A Historical Overview." In *Afghanistan: A Country without a State?*, edited by Christine Noelle-Karimi, Conrad Schetter, and Reinhard Schlagintweit, 37–50. Frankfurt and London: IKO.

——. 2014. "*Jirga*, *Shura*, and Community Development Councils: Village Institutions and State Interference." In *Local Politics in Afghanistan: A Century of Intervention in the Social Order*, edited by Conrad Schetter, 39–58. New York: Oxford University Press.

Nugent, David. 2002. "Alternative Democracies: The Evolution of the Public Sphere in 20th Century Peru." *PoLAR: Political and Legal Anthropology Review* 25, no. 1: 151–163.

Office of the High Representative (OHR). 1997. "PIC Bonn Conclusions." PIC Main Meeting Bonn. http://www.ohr.int/?p=54137.

——. 1999a. "High Representative and OSCE Head of Mission Announce the Removal from Office of Various Public Officials." Press release, November 29: http://www.ohr.int/?p=54655.

——. 1999b. "New Year's Letter by the High Representative to the Citizens of Bosnia and Herzegovina: 'Can Bosnia and Herzegovina and Europe Work as One?'" Press release, December 31: http://www.ohr.int/?p=54318.

——. 1999c. "Removal from Office of Nikola Poplasen." Press release, March 5: http://www.ohr.int/?p=55123.

——. 2000a. "Decision by the BiH Constitutional Court." Press release, July 4: http://www.ohr.int/?p=56755.

——. 2000b. "The High Representative Calls for Moderation in the Discussion of the Constitutional Court Decision." Press release, July 7: http://www.ohr.int/?p=56743.

——. 2000c. "The High Representative Discusses Protectorate in DANI." Press release, March 3: http://www.ohr.int/?p=57099.

——. 2000d. "High Representative's New Year's Message to the Citizens of Bosnia and Herzegovina." Press release, December 29: http://www.ohr.int/?p=56351.

——. 2000e. "An Open Letter to the Pensioners of BiH from the High Representative." Press release, December 5: http://www.ohr.int/?p=56431.

——. 2000f. "Speech by the High Representative, Wolfgang Petritsch[,] at the International Forfaiting Conference 'The Future of Bosnia and Herzegovina in an Integrative Europe.'" Speech, September 7: http://www.ohr.int/?p=57823.

——. 2000g. "Speech by the High Representative, Wolfgang Petritsch, to 'Circle 99.'" Speech, November 2: http://www.ohr.int/?p=57811.

——. 2001a. "Article by High Representative, Wolfgang Petritsch: 'A Chance for the Republika Srpska.'" Article, *Reporter* (Banja Luka), December 25: http://www.ohr.int/?p=52961.

——. 2001b. "Article by the High Representative, Wolfgang Petritsch 'Enough of Lies.'" *Reporter* (Banja Luka), November 12: http://www.ohr.int/?p=53345.

——. 2001c. "Decision Establishing Interim Procedures to Protect Vital Interests of Constituent Peoples and Others, Including Freedom from Discrimination." Decision, January 11: http://www.ohr.int/?p=67112.

——. 2001d. "Easter Message by High Representative Wolfgang Petritsch." Press release, April 13: https://web.archive.org/web/20150605225640/http://www.ohr.int/ohr-dept/presso/pressr/default.asp?content_id=4346.

——. 2001e. "HDZ again Rejects Offer for Dialogue." Press release, March 29: http://www.ohr.int/?p=53597.

——. 2001f. "High Representative Appoints Croat Members of the Federation Constitutional Commission." Press release, April 20: http://www.ohr.int/?p=56199.

——. 2001g. "High Representative Names Members of the Constitutional Commissions of the Entity Parliaments." Press release, February 7: http://www.ohr.int/?p=56271.

——. 2001h. "The High Representative's New Year's Message to the Citizens of Bosnia and Herzegovina." Press release, December 31: http://www.ohr.int/?p=52941.

——. 2001i. "High Representative's Press Conference on the Dismissal of HDZ Officials." Press conference, March 7: http://www.ohr.int/?p=57947.

——. 2001j. "Personal Message from the High Representative to the People of BiH." Press release, March 7: https://web.archive.org/web/20150605225508/http://www.ohr.int/ohr-dept/presso/pressr/default.asp?content_id=4246.

——. 2002a. "High Representative Removes Nikola Grabovac." Press release, June 14: http://www.ohr.int/?p=51085.

——. 2002b. "On the Eve of Final Talks, the High Representative Presses Bosnia and Herzegovina's Leaders for a Domestic Solution." Press release, March 24: http://www.ohr.int/?p=52117.

——. 2002c. "Press Conference of the High Representative, Wolfgang Petritsch, on the Completion of the Constitutional Reform Process in Bosnia and Herzegovina's Entities." Press conference, April 19: http://www.ohr.int/?p=51769.

——. 2003. "Parliament Failing Europe's Test." Press release, October 16: http://www.ohr.int/?p=47343.

Olson, David. 1977. "From Utterance to Text: The Bias of Language in Speech and Writing." *Harvard Education Review* 43: 257–281.

O'Reilly, Maria. 2018. *Gendered Agency in War and Peace: Gender Justice and Women's Activism in Post-Conflict Bosnia and Herzegovina*. London: Palgrave Macmillan.

Organization for Security and Co-operation in Europe (OSCE). 1990. "Charter of Paris for a New Europe." https://www.osce.org/mc/39516?download=true.

——. 1992. "Helsinki Document 1992: The Challenges of Change." https://www.osce.org/mc/39530?download=true.

Organization for Security and Co-operation in Europe (OSCE) MiBH. 2006. *1995–2005. Ten Years OSCE Mission to Bosnia and Herzegovina*. Sarajevo: OSCE Mission to Bosnia and Herzegovina.

Paley, Julia. 2002. "Toward an Anthropology of Democracy." *Annual Review of Anthropology* 31: 469–496.

Pandolfi, Mariella. 2008. "Laboratory of Intervention: The Humanitarian Governance of the Postcommunist Balkan Territories." In *Postcolonial Disorders*, edited by Mary-

Jo DelVecchio Good, Sandra Teresa Hyde, Sarah Pinto, and Byron J. Good, 157–186. Berkeley: University of California Press.

Paris, Roland, and Timothy D. Sisk. 2007. *Managing Contradictions: The Inherent Dilemmas of Postwar State-Building.* New York: International Peace Academy.

Pećanin, Senad, Ivan Lovrenović, Nerzuk Ćurak, and Mile Stojić. 2000. "Deset teza za Bosnu i Hercegovinu" [Ten theses for Bosnia and Herzegovina]. *Dani* (Sarajevo), January 28, 16–17.

Pickering, Paula. 2007. *Peacebuilding in the Balkans: The View from the Ground Floor.* Ithaca, NY: Cornell University Press.

Povinelli, Elizabeth. 2011. *Economies of Abandonment: Social Belonging and Endurances in Late Liberalism.* Durham, NC: Duke University Press.

Price, Monroe E. 2002. "Bosnia-Hercegovina and Post-Conflict Media Restructuring." In *Media Reform: Democratizing the Media, Democratizing the State*, edited by Monroe E. Price, Beata Rozumilowicz, and Stefaan G. Verhulst, 89–106. New York: Routledge.

Redfield, Peter. 2008. "Sacrifice, Triage, and Global Humanitarianism." In *Humanitarianism in Question: Power, Politics, Ethics*, edited by Michael Barnett and Thomas G. Weiss, 196–241. Ithaca, NY: Cornell University Press.

——. 2010. "The Impossible Problem of Neutrality." In *Forces of Compassion: Humanitarianism between Ethics and Politics*, edited by Erica Bornstein and Peter Redfield, 53–70. Santa Fe, NM: SAR Press.

Richmond, Oliver. 2012. "A Pedagogy of Peacebuilding: Infrapolitics, Resistance, and Liberation." *International Political Sociology* 6, no. 2: 115–131.

Rieff, David. 2002. *A Bed for the Night: Humanitarianism in Crisis.* New York: Simon and Schuster.

Riles, Annelise. 2006. Introduction. In *Documents: Artifacts of Modern Knowledge*, edited by Annelise Riles, 1–38. Ann Arbor: University of Michigan Press.

Robbins, Joel. 2013. "Beyond the Suffering Slot: Toward an Anthropology of the Good." *Journal of the Royal Anthropological Institute* 19, no. 3: 447–462.

Robins, Steven. 2009. "Humanitarian Aid beyond 'Bare Survival': Social Movement Responses to Xenophobic Violence in South Africa." *American Ethnologist* 36, no. 4: 637–650.

Robison, Bridget. 2004. "Putting Bosnia in Its Place: Critical Geopolitics and the Representation of Bosnia in the British Print Media." *Geopolitics* 9, no. 2: 378–401.

Rose, Nikolas, and Peter Miller. 1992. "Political Power beyond the State: Problematics of Government." *British Journal of Sociology* 43, no. 2: 173–205.

Rosga, AnnJanette. 2005. "The Traffic in Children: The Funding of Translation and the Translation of Funding." *PoLAR: Political and Legal Anthropology Review* 28, no. 2: 258–281.

Sabaratnam, Meera. 2017. *Decolonising Intervention: International Statebuilding in Mozambique.* New York: Rowman and Littlefield International.

Sampson, Steven. 1986. "The Informal Sector in Eastern Europe." *Telos* 66: 44–66.

Sanders, Todd, and Harry West. 2003. "Power Revealed and Concealed in the New World Order." In *Transparency and Conspiracy: Ethnographies of Suspicion in the New World Order*, edited by Todd Sanders and Harry West, 1–37. Durham, NC: Duke University Press.

Sending, Ole Jacob. 2015. *The Politics of Expertise: Competing for Authority in Global Governance.* Ann Arbor: University of Michigan Press.

Shoup, Paul. 1968. *Communism and the Yugoslav National Question.* New York: Columbia University Press.

Silverstein, Michael, and Greg Urban. 1996. "The Natural History of Discourse." In *Natural Histories of Discourse*, edited by Michael Silverstein and Greg Urban, 1–17. Chicago: University of Chicago Press.

Sivac-Bryant, Sebina. 2016. *Re-Making Kozarac: Agency, Reconciliation, and Contested Return in Post-War Bosnia*. London: Palgrave Macmillan.

Skendaj, Elton. 2014. *Creating Kosovo: International Oversight and the Making of Ethical Institutions*. Ithaca, NY: Cornell University Press.

Smith, Dorothy. 1984. "Textually Mediated Social Organization." *International Social Science Journal* 36, no. 1: 59–75.

Sorabji, Cornelia. 2008. "Bosnian Neighbourhoods Revisited: Tolerance, Commitment and *komšiluk* in Sarajevo." In *On the Margins of Religion*, edited by Frances Pine and Joao Pina-Cabral, 97–112. Oxford: Berghahn.

Službeni Glasnik Srpskog Naroda u Bosni i Hercegovini [Official gazette of the Serb Nation in Bosnia and Herzegovina] (Sarajevo). 1992. Year 1, no. 3, March 16.

Stan, Sabina. 2007. "Transparency: Seeing, Counting and Experiencing the System." *Anthropologica* 49: 257–273.

Stefansson, Anders H. 2003. "Under My Own Sky? The Cultural Dynamics of Refugee Return and (Re)Integration in Post-War Sarajevo." PhD diss., Institut for Anthropology, Copenhagen University.

——. 2004. "Refugee Returns to Sarajevo and Their Challenge to Contemporary Narrative of Mobility." In *Coming Home? Refugees, Migrants, and Those who Stayed Behind*, edited by Lynellyn Long and Ellen Oxfeld, 170–186. Philadelphia: University of Pennsylvania Press.

——. 2007. "Urban Exile: Locals, Newcomers and the Cultural Transformation of Sarajevo." In *The New Bosnian Mosaic: Identities, Memories and Moral Claims in a Post-War Society*, edited by Xavier Bougarel, Elissa Helms, and Ger Duijzings, 59–78. Burlington, VT: Ashgate.

Stewart, Rory. 2011. "The Plane to Kabul." In *Can Intervention Work?*, edited by Rory Stewart and Gerald Knaus, 1–90. New York: W. W. Norton.

Stewart, Rory, and Gerald Knaus. 2011. *Can Intervention Work?* New York: W. W. Norton.

Stoler, Ann. 2002. *Carnal Knowledge and Imperial Power*. Berkeley: University of California Press.

Taylor, Charles. 1989. *Sources of the Self: The Making of Modern Identity*. Cambridge, MA: Harvard University Press.

Terry, Fiona. 2002. *Condemned to Repeat? The Paradox of Humanitarian Action*. Ithaca, NY: Cornell University Press.

Thorpe, Nick. 2005. "Bosnia's Horrific War Memories." *BBC News*, January 29. http://news.bbc.co.uk/2/hi/programmes/from_our_own_correspondent/4216475.stm.

Ticktin, Miriam. 2006. "Where Ethics and Politics Meet: The Violence of Humanitarianism in France." *American Ethnologist* 33, no. 1: 33–49.

——. 2014. "Transnational Humanitarianism." *Annual Review of Anthropology* 43: 273–289.

Toal, Gerard. 2013. "'Republika Srpska Will Have a Referendum': The Rhetorical Politics of Milorad Dodik." *Nationalities Papers* 41, no. 1: 166–204.

Toal, Gerard [Gearóid Ó Tuathail], and Carl T. Dahlman. 2011. *Bosnia Remade: Ethnic Cleansing and Its Reversal*. New York: Oxford University Press.

Tsing, Anna. 2005. *Friction: An Ethnography of Global Connections*. Princeton, NJ: Princeton University Press.

Tuathail, Gearóid Ó [Gerard Toal], and Carl Dahlman. 2004. "The Effort to Reverse Ethnic Cleansing in Bosnia-Herzegovina: The Limits of Returns." *Eurasian Geography and Economics* 45, no. 6: 439–464.

Turner, Mandy, and Florian P. Kühn. 2014. *The Politics of International Intervention: The Tyranny of Peace*. New York: Routledge.

Venice Commission (European Commission for Democracy through Law). 2001. "Opinion on the Implications of Partial Decision III of the Constitutional Court of Bosnia and Herzegovina in Case U 5/98 on the Issue of the 'Constituent Peoples'." Council of Europe, Venice Commission, March 12. http://www.venice.coe.int/webforms/documents/CDL-INF(2001)006-e.asp.

Vulliamy, Ed. 2005. "Farewell, Sarajevo." *The Guardian*, November 2. https://www.theguardian.com/world/2005/nov/02/warcrimes.politics.

Weber, Bodo. 2007. *The Crisis of the Universities in Bosnia and Herzegovina and the Prospects of Junior Scholars*. Sarajevo: Friedrich Ebert Foundation of Bosnia and Herzegovina.

Wilmsen, Edwin N. 1996. "Introduction: Premises of Power in Ethnic Politics." In *The Politics of Difference: Ethnic Premises in a World of Power*, edited by Edwin N. Wilmsen and Patrick McAllister, 104–123. Chicago: University of Chicago Press.

Woodward, Susan L. 1995. *Balkan Tragedy: Chaos and Dissolution after the Cold War*. Washington, DC: Brookings Institution.

——. 2017. *The Ideology of Failed States: Why Intervention Fails*. New York: Cambridge University Press.

Zaum, Dominik. 2012. "Exit and International Administrations." In *Exit Strategies and State Building*, edited by Richard Caplan, 137–158. New York: Oxford University Press.

——. 2013. *Legitimating International Institutions*. New York: Routledge.

Živak, Vedrana. 2001. "Mujo ne može biti predsjednik RS, a Radoje Federacije." [Mujo cannot be the president of the RS, neither can Radoje in the Federation]. *Nezavisne Novine*, August 23.

Index

Notes: Page numbers in *italics* refer to illustrative matter.

www.ingramcontent.com/pod-product-compliance
Lightning Source LLC
LaVergne TN
LVHW091516200926
848483LV00005B/427/J